JOURNEY OF HOPE

Don,
THANKS FOR YOUR
SUPPORT. I HOPE YOU
ENJOY THE JOURNEY.
PEACE,
Bill Peeke
4-20-04

JOURNEY OF HOPE

. . .From Violence To Healing

Bill Pelke

Foreword By Sister Helen Prejean
Author Of *Dead Man Walking*

ISBN : Hardcover 1-4134-1992-5
Softcover 1-4134-1991-7

This book was printed in the United States of America.

To order additional copies of this book, contact:
Xlibris Corporation
1-888-795-4274
www.Xlibris.com
Orders@Xlibris.com
19104

CONTENTS

DEDICATED TO:

MY LORD AND SAVIOUR
JESUS CHRIST

AND TO:

RUTH ELIZABETH PELKE
"NANA"

Acknowledgements

There are three special people who have been very important to me in this Journey, Cuzzin' Judi Weyhe, SueZann Bosler and Marietta Jaeger-Lane. All three of these wonderful ladies have provided a constant support, friendship, encouragement and strength. All three are murder victim family members who have come to the point of forgiveness for the person who killed their loved one, and that is what this *Journey* is all about.

I thank George White and Sam Reese Sheppard, along with SueZann and Marietta for helping me incorporate *Journey of Hope . . . from Violence to Healing* into a non-profit organization. Their powerful stories made a great foundation for the *Journey*.

I thank my three children, Christina, Robert and Rebekah, and my grandchildren, Blake, Kyle, Cory, Jake, Katie, Hailey, Angela and Bubby for their love. My *Journey* has taken me far away from them too often. I apologize that I have not spent more time with you.

I thank my mom and dad for raising me in a home filled with love and for pointing the way to God. They taught me that as Christians, we should hate the sin, but love the sinner. I thank my sister Dottie and her family for their love. I also thank my Aunt Ruthie and other members of the family that have prayed for me and been supportive of my journey.

I give special thanks to my friend Wayne Crawley, who has been with me all the way on this journey. Thanks to my good friend Dennis Eaton, also Dave Thomas, Cool Chuck Brady, Richard Smith, Steve and Madelyn Kayafas, Larry Click, Tom Sullivan and Big Mike Hennings and other coworkers from Bethlehem Steel who encouraged me in my journey.

Abe Bonowitz, Rick Halperin and Magdaleno Rose-Avila will always have a special place in my heart. Their leadership in the grassroots activist movement has been tremendously inspiring.

I thank *Amnesty International* and the fantastic people I met through them like Mike Radelet, Sue Gunawardena-Vaughn, Eileen Welch, Kristin Houlé and many others. The *National Coalition to Abolish the Death Penalty* introduced me to wonderful people like Leigh Dingerson, Steve Hawkins, Jonathan Gradess, David Elliott, Jotaka Eaddy, David Kaczynski, Leona Martin, Brooke Matschek, Brenda Lewis, Adjoa Aiyetoro, Sapna Mirchandani and again, many more.

I thank *Murder Victims Families for Reconciliation* and all that they have done to help the *Journey* and me. People like Renny Cushing, Kate Lowenstein, Liz Coleman, Susannah Sheffer, Pat Bane and Marie Deans have made *MVFR* a powerful organization for abolition of the death penalty. The membership of *MVFR* inspires us all.

Organizations like *Citizens United for Alternatives to the Death Penalty, Hands Off Cain, St. Egidio, Equal Justice, Citizen United for the rehabilitation of Errants,* The *Moratorium Campaign, Equal Justice, American Civil Liberty Union,* The *Bruderhof, People of Faith Against the Death Penalty, Death Penalty Information Center* and others are comprised of wonderful people that have been a pleasure to work with.

Alaskans Against the Death Penalty gave me a home when I moved to Alaska, and it gave me to opportunity to work with great people like Rich and Nancy Curtner, Hugh and Lanie Fleischer, Mary Grisco, Jim McComas, Averil Lerman, Susan Orlansky, Angela Liston, Dale Kelly, George Gee, Debra Seaton, and many others.

Barb Hood and Dirk Sisson are two special people have been a tremendous help and encouragement since I moved to Alaska.

Barb has been fantastic with her advice on this manuscript and I am very thankful for the time she spent helping me.

Thank you to those who have hosted and organized *Journeys* like Dave Atwood, Ed and Mary Ruth Weir, Mike Penzato, Troy Reimer, Lorry Post, Claudia King, Tom Block, Jeff Stack, Jana Schroeder, Bob and Rachel Gross, Toni Moore, Maureen Kelly, Sara Sharpe, Henry Heller, Jeff Garis, Marisa Gwaltney, Laura Van Voorhis, Steve Dear, Andie Wigodsky and others.

Thank you especially to fellow *Journey* travelers like Sally Peck, Mike Kennedy, Ruth Andrews, Rachel King, Barbara Lewis, Anne Coleman, Sue Norton, Aba Gayle, Sadie Bankston, Shirley Dicks, Robin and Trevor Dicks, Claudia Whitman, Ron Callen, Randall Dale Adams, Jill Fratta Adams, Stephanie Coward, Jane Davis, Bud Welch, Ken and Lois Robison, Charlie King and Karen Brandow, Jennifer Bishop Jenkins, Jeanne Bishop, Melodee Smith, Ron Carlson, Karl Shelley, Sandra Pressey, Paula Efflie, Pajama Lady, November West, Karen Sebung, Dick Dieter, Ken McGill, Jane Henderson, Tim Stanton and so many others.

A special thanks to *Journey* board members and staff past and present not already mentioned: Joan Betz, Stephanie Gibson, Steve Earle, Brian Roberts, Brian Halderman, Ari Kohen, Juan Melendez, Sonia Jacobs, Leigh Eason, Phyllis Pautrat and Amy Smith.

Thank you to Jane Henderson, Diana Rust-Tierney, Josh Noble, Anne Hamilton, Charlie Sullivan, Ginnie and Conrad Ahrens, Buffy Weill-Greenberg, Sheldon Himelfarb, Carolyn Gray, Gary and Sue Gauger, Bill Babbitt, Jane Bowman, Johann Christoph Arnold, Steve Wiser, Paul Buttons, Gil Barth, Randy and Leanna Walker, Judy Pelke, Ken and Taniya Michiaels, Joan Brett, Randy Tatel, Cathy Johnson, Sally Harris, Sandy Avila, Doug Lindsay, Karen Hooper, Micki Dickoff, Christi Smith, and Leah.

A special thank you to my friends overseas for your continued support of the Journey: Carlo Santoro, Mario Marrazitti, Marianne Sormani, and Gea Knol.

In memory of the late Mary Hutchinson, Bill Shain, Grant Verbeck, Ruth Morris, Lois Williamson and Muneer Deeb. You are missed.

Vern Boerman, my high school English teacher at *Illiana Christian High School* in Lansing, Illinois over 35 years ago worked many, many hours so that this message of forgiveness could be spread. Thank you so very much.

Of course I must thank Sister Helen Prejean. You are my inspiration.

I can't possibly mention all the people who have helped and encouraged me in my *Journey* and this manuscript, but I do thank all of you who have helped make this work possible.

Last, but definitely not least I want to thank and acknowledge Kathy Harris, my partner. Kathy has been a tremendous help with the *Journey* organization, a huge help with this manuscript, and to me personally. Kathy is a great abolitionist in her own right. Thank you Kathy for all you have done, and especially for loving me.

Foreword
By Sister Helen Prejean
Author Of *Dead Man Walking*

This is an adventure story like *Swiss Family Robinson* or *Huckleberry Finn* or *Moby Dick*, only it's an adventure of soul and spirit; it's an adventure of faith. In these pages Bill Pelke takes us through some pretty amazing terrain: the vicious murder by four teenage girls of his grandmother, Ruth Pelke, the struggle and divisions in a family trying to cope with such a tragedy, a story, woven alongside Bill's personal search for intimate and sustaining love with Judy (finding and losing and re-finding and losing), and at the epicenter of it all—Bill's spiritual journey, which leads him to forgive 15-year-old Paula Cooper, the only one of the young girls who received a death sentence for Ruth Pelke's murder. As Bill recounts, this seminal act of forgiveness of Paula Cooper precipitates the transformation of virtually every other relationship in his life and his life-mission, which brings him to Rome and into the hearts of the Italian people, who gather two million signatures asking for Paula Cooper's life to be spared from the death sentence. Just the international dimensions make this an amazing story.

I met Bill Pelke when he joined us on the road for two weeks in May of 1990 as we marched in religious pilgrimage from death row in Florida to the Martin Luther King Center in Atlanta, Georgia. I have to say that Bill Pelke is one of the most sincere and transparent and generous people I have ever met. There is not an ounce of guile in this man, and I understood at once his passion to devote his life energies to the abolition of the death penalty as a way of honoring his grandmother. I understood because I've been brought into that white-hot fire of passion against the death penalty myself, although I have not had anyone murdered in my family. I could see from the beginning of our long trek on the road that Bill was stable and trustworthy and could handle media interviews, so as we made our way down the road and media requested to speak to a member of a murder victim's family, I turned many of them over to Bill Pelke.

I find the fresh writing in this book interesting. Bill's never written a book before, and he just sort of belts all these stories out, weaving together outward events and inward reflection in a way that amazes me. I love his homespun language: the "forgetter's key" hidden in a special place outside his grandmother's house and the description of a prosecutor as a "banty-hen rooster." Sometimes his understated way of describing things stuns me, which, I suspect, only a sincere, first-time writer like Bill can pull off: "I can tell you first hand that Florida in August is very hot," (about Vietnam) "heading off to war was a strange feeling," (his feelings after his grandmother's death) "I had been involved in what I call anguishing prayer.'

So, reader, prepare yourself for a freshly told and amazing soul adventure. Some of life's deepest conflicts are in this story: life or death, compassion or vengeance, love or hate. We all know in some way or other the soul struggles that Bill Pelke is talking about in these pages, and his transparent account calls us all to be better persons and to earnestly pray that we might get caught up in such a full-soul mission and purpose that gets Bill Pelke out of bed every morning and fills him with missionary zeal. Not all will identify with the religious zeal that fires Bill Pelke, but we all know passion when we meet it, and we can all pray to be consumed by such a lofty passion that frees us from ego and self-serving. This is a refreshing adventure story. Fasten you seat belt. You're in for quite a ride.

Chapter 1

The Bad News

"Bill, I've got some bad news about Nana."

It was Frank, my brother-in-law, on the phone. I had just gotten off of work from Bethlehem Steel, and had gone to Judy's house. Judy, my girlfriend, lived next door to me. When I heard Frank's voice, I was surprised that he would call me at her house. When he said it's "bad news about Nana," I immediately assumed she had died. Nana was my grandmother, the oldest person in our family. It stood to reason that the bad news would be her death. But I was not prepared for the rest of the news that followed.

Frank said my father had just asked him to relay the news to me. My father had found her body when he stopped by her house for a visit. There was evidence of a robbery, Frank said, but he was not sure if Nana's death was a direct result of the home invasion or not. Frank said my father was going home to Crown Point, Indiana, and that members of the family would be gathering there in the evening. I told Frank, "I'll be there."

I immediately called my three kids, Chris, Bob and Becky, and told them that Nana had died, that Grandpa had found her body, and that her death may have been due to a home invasion.

A short time later, when I turned on the local TV news, reality began to sink in. The lead story was about Nana. The reporter stated that Ruth Pelke, a seventy-eight-year-old Bible teacher from Gary, Indiana, had been stabbed to death in her home in an apparent robbery.

I could see Nana's house in the background as the story unfolded. I saw four men carrying a gurney out of her front door, onto the porch and down the steps. Nana's body was covered with a blanket. I could see my father standing alongside the house talking to a policeman. The report stated that the stepson, Robert Pelke, had found her body and that he had refused to be interviewed by the media. I suddenly wanted to be with my dad, give him a hug, and tell him I loved him.

I called Bethlehem Steel and talked to Bob Brown, one of my foremen. I told him of Nana's death and said I would be off of work till further notice. I left immediately and began the forty-five-minute drive to my mom and dad's house in Crown Point.

As I drove, I began to think about Nana. The news reporter had called her a Bible teacher. Although that was true, being a Bible teacher was not what I thought of when I thought of Nana. I thought about Nana, the grandmother. To me, she was half of the very important team "Nana and Granddad." Granddad was what we called my grandfather, Oscar. When he had died a few years earlier, it was hard for me to adjust and picture Nana without him. It seemed like they were always together. She had been a wonderful wife to Granddad. She had also been a wonderful grandmother.

Nana had married Granddad in 1944. It was about three years after his first wife, Dorothy, had died from leukemia. Granddad and Dorothy had three children. I knew them as Aunt Fran, my dad (Bob) and Aunt Ruthie. My dad and Aunt Fran were both married and had already started their own families when Granddad married Nana. Aunt Ruthie was the only one still living at home and the only one to live with both Nana and Granddad. Nana had spent most of her life working on her parents' farm in the countryside of Peru, Indiana. Her limited social life was wrapped around church activities. She was thirty-eight years old when she married Granddad, and had never been married before.

Nana was the only grandmother I knew. Altogether Nana had nine grandchildren and fifteen great-grandchildren. One of the things that always stood out to me about Nana was how she loved us as her grandchildren and our kids as her great-grandchildren. We were very special to her, and I always felt it was because she had no children of her own.

Nana and Granddad

Nana had attended the Church of the Brethren in Peru, but after her marriage to Granddad, they attended Central Baptist Church in downtown Gary. In the late fifties, Nana and Granddad joined the new Glen Park Baptist Church, only a few blocks from where they lived. My family moved to Indiana when I was in the third grade. My dad, my mom (Lola) and my sister (Dottie) also joined the Glen Park Baptist Church. From the ages of eight to thirty, I saw Nana almost every week and sometimes four or five times a week. I thought of Nana as a very religious person, very involved in the activities of her church.

Nana and Granddad were there the night in 1965 when I graduated from *Illiana Christian High School* in Lansing, Illinois. They were there the night in 1977 when I graduated with honors from *Hyles-Anderson College* in Crown Point, Indiana. Nana and Granddad were very happy for me, sure that I would be going into full-time Christian work. However, shortly after graduation,

I dropped completely out of church. I kept working at the steel mill.

When I had been involved with the church, Nana was always there. Sunday mornings, Nana would teach a Sunday school class and then stay for the morning worship service. On Sunday evenings, she would be at church for Bible Training Union and then stay for the evening worship service. Every Wednesday, she would be there for prayer meeting. Then she stayed for choir practice, until she developed some heart problems. Occasionally, Nana would leave the prayer meeting early and go downstairs where the youth groups were meeting. She would tell Bible stories to both the *AWANA* Boys and the *Pioneer Girls* clubs.

Nana and Granddad were also involved in the church's visitation program. They visited both new members and those who were sick and shut in. They did this Thursdays and Saturdays. Nana was also involved in the woman's missionary circle and worked on quilts for missionaries who would visit our church when they were on home on furlough. Anytime a missionary would come to our area, they would stay at Nana's because she lived so close to the church. When the church doors were open, Nana was there.

But five years before Nana's death, Glen Park Baptist Church had closed its doors when the neighborhood started "going bad." The members started a new church fifteen miles farther south in Crown Point, Indiana, and called it South Park Baptist.

Nana was also involved with an organization outside of the church called *Child Evangelism*. She conducted *Five-Day Clubs* where she shared her faith with children in a non-church, neighborhood atmosphere. My brother-in-law Frank was also involved in the *Child Evangelism* program with Nana. *Five-Day Clubs* usually happened in the summer and generally took place at the home of a person with children. These children would invite their friends and Nana would tell Bible stories. Nana told her stories by a method called the flannel-graph board. The flannel-graph board was a thin board about three feet long and about two and a half feet high, covered with a flannel material; it rested on an easel.

Nana would place cutout pictures of Bible characters on the board. These pictures had material on the back of them and they would stick on the storyboard.

I remember Nana telling these flannel-graph Bible stories to me when I was a child. My favorite was "Joseph and His Coat of Many Colors." She put Joseph's picture on the board. Then Nana told us how his father loved him so much that he had a special robe of many colors made for him. She would take the colorful robe and put it on Joseph. She then put on the board a group of men in long plain robes, Joseph's brothers. Nana told how they were extremely jealous and very angry with their brother Joseph. Finally, they sold him to some slave traders passing through the area. This ended their father's favoritism, they thought.

Nana told many other Bible stories. My other childhood favorites were "Three Men in the Fiery Furnace," "David and Goliath," "Daniel in the Lion's Den," and "Jonah and the Whale." When I got older and had children of my own I was able to watch Nana tell those same flannel-graph stories to them. They made *Kool-Aid* and cookies to give their friends who came to hear Nana tell Bible stories.

"Why would anyone kill such a nice, sweet woman?" I asked myself, as I drove toward my dad's house. "Oh, my poor family, how terrible this will be for them. Oh, my poor father."

Chapter 2

My Father's Story

My dad found Nana's body. As soon as I arrived at his house, he began to tell us what had happened.

My dad said that he had called Nana's that afternoon to inquire about some measurements, so he could do some repair work. She didn't answer the telephone, so he decided to drive to her house. She didn't answer the door when he rang the bell and knocked. He bent over to look through the mail drop slot. When he saw clutter on the floor, he knew something was wrong because he knew Nana would not have left the house a mess. When he checked the garage, he saw the car was gone. He walked to the back of the house to get "the forgetter's key."

Once inside, he found Nana's body on the dining room floor. She was dead. He went to the telephone but the cord had been ripped out of the wall. He ran out the front door and tried to get help from the neighbors. He frantically knocked on several doors. Nobody answered. Then he saw a lady park her car and get out. He ran up to her and said he needed to call the police because his mother had just been killed.

I had never before heard my dad refer to Nana as his mother. Since she was his stepmother, he always referred to her as Ruth or Nana. Perhaps he told the lady it was his mother just to simplify things. The police came and before long, the media showed up.

My dad refused to do any interviews with the media because he felt that they would sensationalize what had taken place. He felt it was his job to protect our family. My dad wanted to shield my mom, his two sisters and my sister from what he had seen.

That is why he didn't even say initially that Nana had been killed as a result of the home invasion. He wanted to break the news gently to the family. We had no idea who had committed the crime, but I figured that it was probably some twenty-five-year-old Gary heroin addict looking for money for a "fix." I assumed he had broken into Nana's house, was confronted by her, and then killed her.

My father had wanted to repair Nana's house to meet the Gary city code so she could sell it. The city of Gary had gone through a lot of changes in the last ten years and our family felt it would be safer for her to move. In fact, her house had been burglarized a number of times in recent years.

My dad told us about how he and Mom had visited Nana on Monday evening, the last evening before her death. They had talked about her moving to a safer place. When Granddad was still alive, Nana had talked about moving. But since his death two years earlier, Nana seemed resigned to live in her home of over forty years for the rest of her life. Her memories were there, she said. Dad reported to us that she had told them on that last evening that she would live *here* until she lived *there*. As she finished, her finger was pointing toward heaven. "And," as my father said later, "the next time I saw her, she was *there*!"

When I left my parents' house that evening, I felt my dad would be all right, but I was worried about Mom and my two aunts. As I drove home that night, I prayed for God's grace and lots of it. I hadn't prayed much in the past seven years, but now God had my attention.

Already I was beginning a bit of what my friend George White calls "survivor's guilt." Nana was killed on May 14 1985. It was the day of my son Bob's fifteenth birthday. Since Bob's mother, Mary, and I had divorced the previous year, I was no longer the one responsible for birthday parties—where they would be held, when, or who would be invited. I suddenly felt, "If I hadn't been divorced, Nana would have been invited to his birthday party. If Nana had come to the party, she would still be alive!" That thought bothered me for a long time.

I was not looking forward to tomorrow. Dad was going to be at Nana's "for some cleanup" and my cousin Dorothy Ann was going to help him. I told him I would stop by, too.

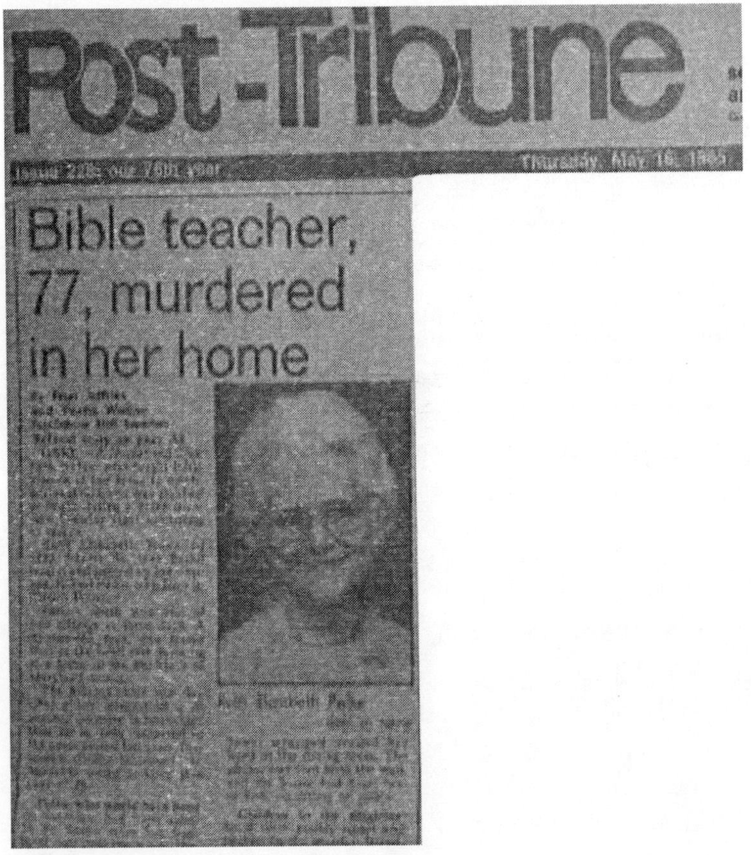

Post-Tribune

Bible teacher, 77, murdered in her home

Gary ***Post Tribune*** May 16, 1985

When the local paper, the Gary ***Post Tribune***, came out the next morning, Nana's death was the front page headline: **Bible**

Teacher, 77, Murdered in Her Home. There was a picture of Nana that my mother had given to the paper. It showed her beautiful smile. There was also a picture of her house. The article had some facts that I didn't yet know. It stated that Nana had been stabbed multiple times and had a laceration to her head that could have been caused by being struck by a heavy object.

Several of Nana's neighbors were interviewed; they were shocked at the manner of her death as they told the reporter what a good lady Nana was.

According to the newspaper:

> Children in the neighborhood were visibly upset and shaken by the murder. Standing near the Pelke home Wednesday afternoon, some cried, while others shook their heads in disbelief that someone would murder the 'meek and mild' Bible study teacher. They talked about the summer Bible classes she held for them.
>
> The classes were nice according to fourteen-year-old Eric Jackson, who lived in the neighborhood. He said, "She served cookies and stuff and told us to come back. She gave us verses to learn and if we remembered them she would give us a box of candy."
>
> Thirteen-year-old Desmond Smith said, "I couldn't believe it. She was so nice to everybody." Desmond said he didn't believe the killer could be from the neighborhood. "It couldn't be anybody from around here. She was too nice to people around here."
>
> Another neighbor, Neil Hayes talked about Mrs. Pelke taking kids to the Glen Park Church before it moved to Crown Point. "She wasn't prejudiced," said Hayes, who is black.

My mother was also quoted as saying, "We tried to get her to move but she wouldn't. We were afraid for her life."

After reading the article, I began the twenty-minute drive to Nana's house to meet my dad.

As I drove to Nana's I began to think about Mother's Day. Two days before Nana's death was Mother's Day. I had worked the day shift. After that, Judy and I drove to my mom's church for the evening service. I had known that my mom and dad were having lunch with Nana, so I thought Nana would visit their church that night. As it turned out, Nana had visited my parents' church that morning and had gone to her own church that evening. On that Sunday, I had Mother's Day corsages for both Nana and my mother. My mom said that she would be going to Nana's house the next night, and offered to bring Nana's corsage for me.

When I got to Nana's house, my dad was there and so was my cousin Dorothy Ann. They were both on their hands and knees washing blood off the walls and floor. The sight made me sick . . . a terrible sight! Family members should never have to do that when a loved one has been killed, but my dad and Dorothy Ann did.

How much more could my dad take? I continued to pray for him and the rest of the family. At the time of her death, all three of Nana's stepchildren and all nine grandchildren had professed their faith and love in Jesus. Now, her life had come to this, with her blood splattered all over the wall. I had to leave the dining area where dad and Dorothy Ann were busy. I couldn't have done what they were doing.

I went into the kitchen. The kitchen was not the mess the living and dining rooms had been. After I looked around, I opened the refrigerator. On the top shelf was the corsage I had gotten Nana. It was a bit of comfort that Nana had gotten it and knew I had been thinking of her. It was no comfort that she would never wear it.

Nana's neighborhood had changed dramatically in the last twenty years. When I graduated from high school in 1965, Glen Park was still one of the finer sections of Gary. In the many years she had lived there, Nana had made some good neighborhood friends. They all tried to take care of each other. Now they felt bad that they had not been able to prevent her death. But that is Gary—Gary, Indiana, "The murder capital of the United States" for several years in a row. Most of the deaths were drug related, and I was sure this one was, too.

Chapter 3

Young Murderers

On Friday morning, I went to get a haircut for the wake and the funeral. One of the beauticians read me the headline from that morning's Gary ***Post-Tribune***. It read: **4 Held in Home-Invasion Killing**. The article went on to say that four girls from *Lew Wallace High School* had been arrested for the stabbing death of Ruth Elizabeth Pelke. Police said the girls—one 14, two 15, and one 16—gained the woman's confidence by saying they wanted to join her Bible class. At first, the police search centered on one of the fifteen-year-olds who had been seen riding in the stolen car, which still hadn't been found.

The next day, the ***Post-Tribune*** was even more revealing. Jack Crawford, the Lake County prosecutor, said the state would seek the death penalty against one of the girls, a sixteen-year-old named Karen Corder. The newspaper reported:

> Crawford said that as far as he knew this was the first time in Lake County history four juvenile females had been charged with planning and carrying out a murder. He also said it might be the first time the death penalty was being sought against a female juvenile. All girls were identified as freshman students at Lew Wallace High School. Besides Corder, Crawford identified April Beverly, age fifteen; Paula Cooper, age fifteen; and Denise

Thomas age fourteen. Corder was being held in the Lake County jail and the other three were being held at the Lake County Detention Center.

According to Crawford, "The home invasion and killing netted $10 and Pelke's old car." Lake County Coroner Daniel D. Thomas said, "Pelke was stabbed 33 times." Investigators said, "After Pelke was stabbed, the butcher knife was left in her body for between 20 and 45 minutes while the house was being ransacked."

"While in her home, evidence indicates that Miss Cooper grabbed Mrs. Pelke, struck her with a flower vase, and stabbed her repeatedly," Crawford said. "Cooper told Miss Corder to 'hold the knife' in Mrs. Pelke's chest while the other young women ransacked the house. Mrs. Pelke was still alive at this time." Crawford also added that Pelke apparently struggled to remove the knife from her body during this time.

Crawford said, "The girls allegedly planned the robbery and killing during a lunch break at school Tuesday, and again about 1:00 P.M. at Beverly's home, less than a block from where Pelke lived for forty-four years. Paula Cooper obtained a large butcher knife from April's house".

Crawford said, "The girls wanted money, and Beverly, who had heard of Pelke's Bible classes, suggested the idea of robbing her. She believed Pelke had a substantial amount of money in the house."

The girls gained entrance to Pelke's home by pretending to be interested in the Bible study courses. When Pelke turned her back to go to her desk for information about Bible classes, she was attacked. Gary Police Chief Virgil Motley said, "The girls put a towel over Pelke's face and tried to smother her. They also didn't want to see her face."

Authorities stated that after leaving the home,

> Corders and Thomas were dropped off near Wallace High School and Beverly and Cooper went joy riding in the car and gave a lift to several schoolmates.
>
> "Several students called and told us they saw the girls in the car," Motley said. They apparently picked up Beverly's brother, Tony.

They went to a *McDonald's* restaurant in Hammond where police found the bloodstained knife that had killed Nana. The three then went on to Illinois where they slept in the car Tuesday night and then ran out of gas on Wednesday. Investigators recovered the car on Friday and had it towed.

The ***Chicago Sun-Times*** reported that Sergeant William Burns said the girls had been smoking marijuana and drinking wine before the slaying. Burns said, "Pelke, who lived alone, was an elderly woman who loved children."

News of Nana's death traveled nationwide quickly, mostly due to Chicago's super station ***WGN-TV***. Our family began getting calls from around the country from friends who knew Nana. The outpouring of sympathy and love was tremendous.

I continued to pray for my dad and the rest of the family as funeral plans went forward. I was so proud of my dad. In spite of what he had been through in the preceding days, he greeted guests at the funeral home and took care of the arrangements. He could not have handled himself better. One thing struck me in particular about the wake and funeral—the presence of God's grace. In spite of the unthinkable thing that had happened, there was no doubt that God's grace was present at the funeral home and with our family.

Rev. Marvin Troyer and several others spoke at Nana's funeral. Pastor Troyer had married Mary and me shortly after I got out of the Army after Viet Nam. I had not seen him since my divorce. He had been Nana and Granddad's pastor for many years, although he presently was at a different church.

After conversation with my sister Dottie, we decided that the grandsons should be the pallbearers. We told her it would be a great honor.

Hundreds of people attended the wake and funeral. TV cameras followed the procession to the cemetery. I was glad they were covering it because I wanted everyone to know about Nana, who she was and the kind of person she was.

My cousin, Judi Weyhe, led us in several songs at the graveside. God gave Judi the talent of a beautiful voice. The words to one of the songs she sang were, "In the sweet bye and bye, we shall meet on that beautiful shore."

We all left and went our separate ways.

Chapter 4

A Dismal Picture

The story of the four young suspects began to unfold. It was a dismal tale. A month after Nana was killed, the ***Chicago Tribune*** headlined: **4 Unlikely Suspects in Savage Slaying.** That picture of Nana's beautiful smiling face accompanied the article by Wes Smith and John O'Brien on June 17, 1985

> Four teenage girls gathered at lunchtime a few weeks ago to share in some Stroh's beer, a bottle of Wild Irish Rose wine, a little marijuana and a plan to rob the elderly woman across the alley, investigators say.
>
> The girls hadn't known each other long, but April Beverly, Denise Thomas, Karen Corder and Paula Cooper faced uncertain futures because of teenage pregnancy, problems in school or trouble with the law.
>
> Now they share another burden. Each is charged in the May 14 slaying and robbery of 78-year-old Ruth Pelke of Gary.
>
> Pelke, who once taught Bible classes to Beverly, and was a friend of her family, was stabbed 33 times and beaten with a vase. One of her alleged attackers has said she pushed a butcher knife through the woman's chest and out her back "to see how it would feel," investigators said.

Only $10 was taken from her home. It paid for orange soda, snack cakes and meals at a fast-food restaurant, investigators said. The victim's 1977 Plymouth also was taken for a joy ride, they said.

Murder is not uncommon in Gary. There were 66 murders there last year and 18 in the first four months of this year. But the killing of Pelke has disturbed the community, officials said. The most unsettling thing is not the brutality of her slaying but the suspects: four teenage girls . . .

But more than a simple mugging is involved in Pelke's slaying, and even those who deal daily with violent crime and violent juvenile crime are unable to explain how four teenage girls could be suspected in such a cold-blooded slaying.

"Sometimes I quit trying to find answers, but when you see kids raised with no father or no mother, or parents who can't read and write, the kids seem predestined to have problems," said Keith Medved, a Lake County public defender for juveniles.

"It's not a defense for killing anybody, but if from Day 1 you have that type of life, it seems the cards are stacked against you," he said. "My client [April Beverly] is 15 and seven months pregnant. That tells you something. It doesn't ensure a very rosy future."

Beverly, Thomas and Cooper are being held on juvenile murder charges, but prosecutors will try to move their cases into adult court this month. Corder, 16, has been charged as an adult and may face the death penalty if convicted. Prosecutors said they might seek the death penalty for one or all of the others.

"People are angry with what happened to Ruth Pelke," Crawford said . . .

Pelke, who friends said, "knew no color lines," taught Bible classes to neighborhood children and fixed meals for Beverly's family after her mother died.

She had lived in the Glen Park neighborhood for 44 years and watched it change from an area of affluent whites to a racially mixed community frequently preyed upon by burglars and thieves. Her home has been burglarized five times in recent years. But the day before she was slain, the widow told her stepson, Robert, that she did not want to leave her neat home.

"When I leave here, it will be to go there," she told her stepson, gesturing up. "I have good neighbors; they watch out for me."

Police said one of those neighbors, Beverly, allegedly led three friends to Pelke's house under the guise of inquiring about Bible classes. Investigators said Beverly stood watch as Pelke was stabbed to death.

Until her mother died of a stroke four years ago, Beverly was a "normal girl," said her sister Sandra, 24. The youngest of 11 children, Beverly tagged after Sandra. "She wanted to be like me; I graduated from college," Sandra said.

But the death of her mother sent Beverly into her teenage years without a parent to keep her straight, Sandra said.

"Our father only dropped around when he felt like it. I feel if he had taken better care of the kids, April would not be where she is," she said . . .

Like Beverly, Karen "Pookie" Corder has no mother. Her mother died when the girl was 11, leaving her with her father. A family friend, who asked not to be identified, said she did what she could to steer Corder straight.

But Corder had a son when she was 13 and still in junior high school.

"If you don't have a mother's guidance, then you don't touch all the bases," said the woman, who served as Corder's unofficial "godmother."

Classmates said Corder frequently stayed out past midnight at a local skating rink with her young son.

Gary Detective William Kennedy, who works in security at *Lew Wallace High School* where Corder, Cooper and Thomas were students, said the short, stocky Corder often seemed jealous of the more popular, more attractive girls in the school . . .

The godmother was present when Corder gave a videotaped statement to detectives about the Pelke slaying.

"Listening to that was like '*Helter Skelter*' or the Manson family," the friend said. "I don't know what frame of mind she could have been in. She is not an evil child. In general, she is a sweet child. I don't know what made her go that way. Karen was a follower, not a leader."

Investigators and classmates said the most dominant personality among the four girls is that of Paula Cooper, 15, who investigators called a "chronic runaway." Classmates at Lew Wallace called her a bully.

Cooper had only recently moved back into her family's home in the Marshalltown area on the eastern edge of Gary after running away from or being ordered out of at least three youth homes. She was put in the homes after complaining that her father abused her. He has denied that.

Cooper was kicked out of the Mayflower Home for neglected girls in Hammond in December for skipping school. Officials there said she would sign out each day and "go to school and walk out the back door to spend the day with friends," said Judy Lewis, director of the Mayflower Home.

Investigators said they believe Cooper led the attack on Pelke and is responsible for most of the stab wounds. She also is responsible for the quick arrests of the four, they said, by leaving a white denim jacket in the woman's home. It contained a receipt with Cooper's name on it for birth-control pills.

Police officers weren't sure who the "Paula Cooper" named on the receipt was until her mother, Gloria, called to report her missing just hours after Pelke was found. Mrs. Cooper said she had last seen her daughter leaving for school May 14. She had written her an excuse to get out of class early to have her birth-control prescription filled.

Unlike the other girls, Denise Thomas, 14, had strong parental guidance, though her mother and stepfather are separated. Classmates and investigators agree she does not fit the profiles of the others. Prosecutors also said she probably had a lesser role in the slaying.

"Denise is a quiet person, a very timid girl. But in the last couple months her grades dropped and she has been talking to the wrong kind," said Irene Taylor, 40, who has been separated from her second husband, Lester Taylor, for a year and a half. Taylor, who lives in Hammond, shares support for their six children, Mrs. Taylor said.

"Denise has a totally concerned family," Mrs. Taylor said, "my husband whips them when they need it. It is not like some families where the father disowns them and never looks back. This girl is from a good family. Until they put her in jail, she had never even spent the night away from home."

Mrs. Taylor said that until her daughter was arrested, she did not know Denise had been skipping classes three or four times a week.

CHAPTER 5

Nana Eulogized

The press eulogized Nana. The Gary ***Post-Tribune*** again printed the beautiful picture of Nana, and a picture of her Glen Park home. The headline: **A Woman's Faith in Religion Stays Strong to the End.** It began with a written prayer found in Nana's Bible, and dated October 1982, less than three years before her death:

I would not have you grieve for me today
Nor weep beside my vacant chair.
Could you but know my daily portion here
You would not, could not, wish me there.

She had been "Nana" to her nine grandchildren and fifteen great-grandchildren.

Ruth Pelke was an evangelist, a religious witness, a Bible schoolteacher and a friend. She knitted booties and hats for new babies in the parish and held Bible school classes in her back yard. Even at seventy-eight, she drove her friends to church.

"She made no pretense of having money," her stepson, Robert, said. "She didn't flash it around." Instead, she gave most of it to missionaries.

He said that instead of getting her television set and dryer fixed, she gave her money to the church.

Before Pelke was killed on May 14, she "saved" many children. Saving someone means helping them to accept religion. Her goal was to show children "the same Jesus she knew," her stepson said. One of the children was April Beverly, a suspect in her death. Another was one of Beverly's brothers.

From their Crown Point home, Robert Pelke and his wife, Lola, talked about his stepmother, a woman he'd known all his life.

"She was just a common good woman, trying to do her best," her stepson said.

She worked in a factory near Wabash during World War II until she married Oscar Pelke. She moved to Gary's Glen Park neighborhood in 1944.

Robert Pelke said he wants his stepmother remembered as a common woman who "lived to follow the Scriptures."

"She wasn't working her way into heaven," Lola said. "Rather she had already accepted that she would go (to heaven) before she started working for the church."

"The Lord says, 'Serve me in private and I'll reward you publicly,'" Robert Pelke said. His stepmother believed that.

Ruth Pelke kept records on children she had taught. On their attendance sheet is their date of birth and the day they were saved. Some of her students are now in their early thirties. In a book at least two years old is April Beverly's name.

The Pelkes are not seeking revenge. Justice, they said, is in the hands of the prosecuting attorney.

"When we see Jesus, then he'll give us the answers. If he wants us to know, he'll tell us," he said.

Media coverage of the "Pelke" case continued because it was unique: the death penalty was being sought for teenage girls. Victor Streib, a law professor at *Cleveland State University*, stated it was not unusual for fourteen and fifteen-year-olds to be tried as adults, but added, "To face the death penalty is what makes this case extraordinary."

"Indiana is the only state that says ten-year-olds can be tried as adults," said Streib. "Only fourteen other states issue the death penalty to people who commit a murder before they are eighteen. And these states have minimum ages of 14, 15, 16, or 17. At what ages does a child know?" Streib asked. "A three-year-old has no idea what he's doing; a thirty-year-old does. Adolescents, however, may not understand the idea of death . . . Yeah, they can mean to stab, mean to kill, but do they really know what it means?"

Prof. Streib earned his law degree from *Indiana University* and was a member of the Indiana Law board. He noted that Indiana has executed only three people under eighteen, all three seventeen-year-old boys, the latest in 1920.

Streib went on to note that in all of U.S. history, only nine girls have been executed.

> "The first was a twelve-year-old Indian girl who was executed for murdering a six-year-old white girl. The other eight were black girls; most of them slaves accused of murdering white children. The latest juvenile girl in this country to be executed was in 1912. Her name was Virginia Christian, a seventeen-year-old, mentally deficient black girl from Virginia. She was executed for killing her white female employer," Streib said.
>
> "Throughout history, blacks have received the death penalty more often than whites. All four girls in the Pelke case were black. Still," he said, "it would be extraordinary if the girls got the death penalty. Juries tend to be more sympathetic toward them (girls)."

> "Of the thirty-three people on death row in this country who were seventeen or younger at the time of the crime, only two are girls," he said. "Obviously, you can't let a murderer free," Streib said. "Prosecutors often file death penalty charges because they want to start bargaining from a strong position."
>
> The Lake County Prosecutor's Office declined to make a comment on Streib's statements because the cases are pending.

An editorial in the Gary ***Post-Tribune*** followed with an editorial about the deterrent value of the death penalty. It granted that the deterrent value of such a punishment in this case is questionable, because it assumes that people like these four girls read about courts, that they are logical, and that they weigh the consequences of acts against the possible gain—logical assumptions probably wasted on young people like these.

"When a person like Ruth Elizabeth Pelke dies," said the editor, "there is bound to be sorrow in the community. When such a person is the victim of a violent attack, the sorrow is accompanied by anger. Both are rational reactions to an irrational deed."

Chapter 6

The Legal Process Begins

Four months after the murder—in September of 1985—the trial of Denise Thomas began. However, a mistrial was called after the prosecution's chief investigator admitted he had met and talked with three jurors in the case. Her trial was reset for November.

At her subsequent trial, on November 7, 1985, Denise Thomas was convicted of taking part in the robbery-murder of Nana. She denied an active part in the killing. She was accused of hitting Nana over the head with a vase, but denied it.

"When Paula was stabbing her, I think she was saying the Lord's Prayer. I was just standing there quiet," Denise said.

"Cooper stuck the knife in the lady and asked me to hold it, I said no, so she asked Karen," Thomas said. "Corder did hold the knife in Pelke and asked her where her money was." Thomas also testified that Corder said, "This bitch won't die!" and then watched as Corder took a towel and tried to smother the lady. Denise also testified that Cooper and Beverly threatened to kill her if she went to the police.

The next month Denise Thomas was sentenced to thirty-five years in prison. Public defender Richard Wolter's voice quivered and he was teary-eyed as he asked Lake Superior Court Judge James E. Kimbrough for mercy. Deputy Prosecutor, James McNew spoke with a restrained, cold fury as he pointed at Thomas and said, "What about tears from Ruth E. Pelke? I've never seen such a vicious crime."

"In my twenty-seven years in law, I've never seen a case fraught with such strong emotions," Judge Kimbrough said. He was referring to an incident after the guilty verdict was announced November 7, when prosecutor's office employees were heard laughing nearby.

In explaining why members of his office staff laughed after the guilty verdict was announced, Lake County Prosecutor Jack Crawford said, "The conviction was a reason for happiness." He also said it would help in the prosecution of the other three girls because the state was still seeking the death penalty for them.

A few months later, it was announced that the second defendant, April Beverly, was expected to plead guilty to a robbery charge with the request for the death penalty being dropped. That left Karen Corder and Paula Cooper as the only two still facing the possibility of the death penalty.

The death penalty for juveniles continued to be a big issue in the media. The ***CBS*** program ***60 Minutes*** did a story in March that asked the question, "Are these teens too young to die?" The program was about the remaining two defendants, Karen Corder and Paula Cooper. My dad was asked if he wanted to be interviewed for the program. He refused.

Chapter 7

Karen Corder on Trial

The trial of the third defendant, Karen Corder, was set for March 26, 1986. To the surprise of many, Karen pled guilty to murder after being urged to do so by public defender David Olson. Olson felt it was the only way to save her life. When Olson sat in on the trial of Denise Thomas, he saw how the jury reacted to the evidence.

According to the ***Post Tribune:***

> Olson stated, "I was worried that a jury, angered by the evidence in Pelke's killing, would return a quick recommendation for death against Karen Corder."
>
> "Her crime was gruesome," Olson added. "There would be no thought of compromise; the jury would concentrate on the crime. We figured that by presenting the evidence directly to Judge Kimbrough [without a jury] there would be less of an emotional reaction."

Olson went on to say that he believed Kimbrough would then spare Karen's life. May 29 was set for the sentencing hearing.

At the May sentencing hearing, Karen Corder's plea was, "Judge, please let me live."

> In an emotion-choked voice, she told Judge Kimbrough, "I'm real sorry for what I done to Mrs. Pelke

> and her family. I pray for them and ask the Lord to have the family forgive me for what I done. I know it was a terrible thing to do. I have a son who is four years old, and that's one of the reasons why I want to live. I also want to prove to society I'm not as bad a person as they think I am."

At this sentencing hearing, Deputy Prosecutor James W. McNew sought the death penalty. He presented the evidence of the twelve-inch butcher knife used to kill Nana. The evidence showed the stabbing was so violent that the carpet and padding beneath the body was cut and the floorboards chipped by the knife thrusts.

My dad told Judge Kimbrough he doubted the sincerity of Corder's sorrow. From the witness stand he said, "I believe the court shouldn't consider any sentence less than the maximum allowed by state laws for this crime."

> Karen Corder's lawyers argued that Corder should be spared because of her youth. Public defender Olson said she was under the domination of the fourth defendant, Paula Cooper, the alleged leader of the four, and was also under the influence of marijuana and alcohol at the time of the crime. "Is this the only solution we have, to execute our children?" he asked.
>
> But prosecutor McNew countered with, "What horror Mrs. Pelke felt, to be pinned to her own dining room floor! The act was so reprehensible that the state is seeking the death penalty."
>
> In her confession, Karen Corder stated, "She [Paula Cooper] stabbed her in the back and then kept on stabbing her, and I was telling her to stop. The lady said, 'You aren't going to kill me?' Paula left the knife in her and after that she told me to hold the knife. I held the knife for around ten to fifteen minutes and about two or three minutes later, the lady was dead . . ."

Detective William Kennedy, Jr. questioned Corder during her confession. He asked, "Did you stab the lady after you took hold of the knife?" Corder answered, "No, I just pushed it in a little bit to see if it would go down further and then I moved it from side to side."

Judge Kimbrough said he would give his decision in twenty-four hours. He did. He elected to give Karen Corder the maximum prison term, sixty years, and spare her the electric chair. He cited Karen's age, lack of other criminal convictions, and the influence of the remaining defendant, Paula Cooper, as mitigating circumstances that led him to reject the death penalty in favor of the maximum prison term.

Leaving the courtroom, Karen Corder, now seventeen, declined comment. So did my father.

Public defender David Olson said, "From day one, we thought the best we could do would be to save Karen's life."

Lake County Prosecutor Jack Crawford said, "I'm disappointed, but we accept the court's decision. Now we will continue to vigorously pursue the death penalty for Paula Cooper.

CHAPTER 8

Paula Cooper

Legal focus and public attention now shifted to the final defendant, Paula Cooper. Her bench trial would be before Judge Kimbrough. ***Post Tribune*** reporter Barbara Thomas did a profile of Paula Cooper, and reported that:

> Cooper told attorney, Kevin Relphorde, that at one time the abuse from her father was so bad that her mother decided to kill herself. Rhonda, Cooper's older sister, wanted to die, too. Paula, who was eleven then, decided that if her mom and sister were dead, she wanted to die also.

Paula said that her mother told the girls they would all go to see Jesus and wanted the girls to fall asleep in the car. Once they were asleep in the closed garage, her mother started the car. Her mother then changed her mind and took the girls out of the car. Paula woke up when she heard her mother coughing in the front yard.

Although Paula's father was thrown out of the house a few years ago, he came back, and she claimed the abuse got even worse. When she ran away, the juvenile court returned her home against her wishes.

The next time in court, Paula was sent to live with an aunt in Michigan City, Indiana. But four months before Nana's murder, she returned home. In her lengthy profile, Barbara Thomas said:

> Cooper told attorney Relphorde that her father beat her and her sister with everything from his fists to electrical cords. Once, after running away, she was picked up by the police. On the way home from the police station, her father stopped the car, took her outside and beat her.
>
> When they got home, Cooper jumped out of the car and ran down the street yelling. Neighbors called the police and she was taken to a foster home.
>
> Paula Cooper and her sister Rhonda eventually developed a system. They would run away at night and return in the morning after their father left for work. They either slept in the back yard or in the back seat of their father's car. In the mornings, their mother would let them in the house to shower, eat breakfast, and change clothes.
>
> One day Paula refused to open her eyes, talk, or get out of bed. Her parents took her to the Tri-City Comprehensive Community Center in East Chicago where she spent four days under observation. She told Attorney Relphorde that she did it to get out of the house.
>
> Cooper's mother, Gloria, no longer lives with her husband . . . sister Rhonda is the only family member to offer continual support.
>
> Paula Cooper has gained weight since the murder, her attorney said. She told him she is being treated well in jail, saying, "It's better than outside."

At the bench trial before Judge Kimbrough, Paula Cooper elected to plead guilty to inflicting the majority of the stab wounds that killed Nana. She pleaded guilty to murder and felony murder. Cooper had agreed to the plea without asking prosecutors to give up their request for the death penalty. "It was a surprise," said prosecutor's office spokeswoman Diane Donovan.

After Karen Corder's trial, my dad had said that the way Judge Kimbrough had worded Corder's sentence, he would have to sentence Paula Cooper to death.

Paula Cooper's sentencing hearing was scheduled for July 11, 1986.

Chapter 9

Paula Cooper's Sentencing Hearing

Before the Paula Cooper sentencing, I had not been to any of the trials or sentencing hearings of any of the girls. My father, however, had testified at both the mistrial and official trial of Denise Thomas, and at Karen Corder's sentencing hearing. And now he was now going to testify at Paula Cooper's hearing.

This would be the fourth time for him to look at the gruesome pictures taken the day of the crime. He would testify to what he had seen and verify that the pictures were in fact from the crime scene.

I don't know if it was because my dad had said he felt the judge would sentence Paula Cooper to death or what, but I felt that I needed to go to the sentencing hearing. I took the day off work and made plans to attend court with my girlfriend Judy.

A lot of things had recently been said about Paula Cooper in the news. First, there was the question of remorse. Rumor had it that there had been some sort of conflict with a female guard and in anger Cooper had responded that she would kill the guard's grandmother too.

Other rumors flew. There had been a scandal at the prison where Cooper was incarcerated, and several male guards were reported to have had sex with Cooper. At least three people were suspended, or lost their jobs. Reputedly, Cooper had sex with the guards in hope of getting pregnant. Supposedly, she believed that if she were pregnant, she would avoid the death penalty.

We walked into the courtroom and took a seat. I was unaware that there are sides for prosecution and defense. We had inadvertently sat on the defendant's side. As I looked around the courtroom, I saw my mom and dad, my sister and Frank and their daughter Kim, Aunt Fran and Uncle Mel and several other people I knew. A reporter from ***ABC*** news approached to ask if I would make a statement on camera outside the courtroom after the decision was given. I said that I would.

Cameras were not allowed in the courtroom. The TV media from Chicago were setting up outside. I had not seen any of the four girls, except on TV or their pictures in the paper. The first time I saw Paula Cooper was when she entered the courtroom. She was handcuffed, led by a prison matron. She was smiling and laughing as she came into the room. The prison matron had probably said something to her that was funny, trying to loosen her up for the day's events. I was offended. I thought, "You killed Nana, and yet you are smiling!" and then I said to myself, "You won't be smiling when this day is over."

At the time, I didn't have real strong feelings about the death penalty. In high school, we had debates about the death penalty, but I don't even remember which side of the issue I took. I know the response of the majority of people from my college and church when the death penalty was reinstated in 1976 was positive.

I felt that whatever the law called for was fine with me. If the law said the death penalty was okay, then okay; if the law said that the death penalty was wrong, then that was okay, too. I can't say I particularly wanted Paula Cooper to die, but I was in favor of the prosecution seeking the death penalty for her.

I knew that people around the country were being sentenced to death for various crimes of murder, and some were even being executed. I felt if they didn't give the death sentence to Cooper, then they were telling my family and me that Nana was not an important enough person for her killing to warrant a death sentence. I knew if Cooper were sentenced to death, it would mean additional news coverage and more people would know who Nana was. Nana was a special person and I wanted everyone in the world to know it. So it was all right with me to sentence Cooper to death.

Lake County Prosecutor Jack Crawford had worked with my dad and his two sisters. My father was the spokesperson for the family with the prosecutor's office. They had a good relationship and my dad was satisfied with the work his office was doing. My father let Crawford know the family supported his decision to go for the death sentence.

We all rose as Lake County Superior Court Judge James Kimbrough entered the court. The power of life and death was in his hands.

There were three reasons why I didn't think Judge Kimbrough would actually sentence Paula Cooper to death. First of all, I knew he was personally opposed to the death penalty. The second reason was Cooper was only fifteen years old at the time of the crime. The third reason was that Judge Kimbrough was black, the defense attorney was black, and Cooper was black. It seemed to make some sense that he might have mercy in her case.

Deputy prosecutor James W. McNew began to call his witnesses. Once again, as he had in the other trials, my father took the stand. At McNew's leading, my father testified as to what he had seen on May 15, 1985. Once again he identified pictures from the crime scene. McNew asked my father what he thought the penalty for Cooper should be. He answered that she should be punished to the full extent of the law.

Public Defender Kevin Relphorde evidently didn't feel my dad really wanted the death penalty, since my dad didn't actually say so when McNew questioned him. Relphorde asked my dad what he meant by "the full extent of the law." My dad answered that he meant the death penalty.

Immediately, Relphorde asked my dad if Nana was a forgiving person. I could see where Relphorde was going, but my dad wasn't going there. He answered, "Yes, Ruth did believe in forgiveness, but she wasn't a dummy. She would not have turned her back a second time." Relphorde mentioned something about the Bible. My dad had written a letter to the judge listing about thirty Bible references that mention death as a punishment. He said the Bible called for the death penalty. From my Bible knowledge I knew the scriptures were from the Old Testament.

My father stated that it would be a travesty of justice if the death penalty were not given. He then took his seat in the gallery.

Assistant prosecutor McNew called Frances Irons, a former correction's officer, to testify. She stated that Paula Cooper had once told her, "Yeah, I stabbed an old lady. I'd stab the bitch again. I'd stab your [expletive] grandmother."

The prosecution called four more witnesses to testify.

Court had started a little after ten and sometime around twelve, after the prosecution rested their case, they stopped for a lunch break. I went to downtown and bought a pair of shoes for the TV interview. In the afternoon session, the defense began to call their witnesses.

Rhonda Cooper, Paula's sister, was the first witness called. Rhonda talked about the abusiveness of their father, Herman. She told how he regularly beat them with an electrical cord and once beat and raped their mother, Gloria, in their presence. (I thought it quite strange that neither Gloria nor Herman Cooper was in court to see if their daughter would live or die.) Rhonda blamed her dad for Paula turning out the way she did. She begged the judge to have mercy and give Paula a chance; she pleaded that Paula not be given the death sentence.

Prosecutor McNew asked Rhonda why she had not responded violently to the abuse like her sister had. Rhonda had no answer.

Then Ronald Williams, Cooper's uncle, testified on her behalf. He told the judge that Gloria Cooper, Paula's mother, was "crazy, a very sick person." He testified that she tried to kill herself and the two girls once during a domestic dispute. He said, "They sat in a running car in a closed garage until they passed out from carbon monoxide poisoning, but were rescued by Gary firefighters." He said he loved Paula and begged for her to have a chance at life. He said he would be willing to take her into his home and raise her.

Then a social worker testified to the type of life that Cooper had lived. She described abuse, runaway attempts, the home situation and other aspects of Cooper's life that produced a very troubled teen.

Finally, Frank Brogno took the witness stand. His testifying for Paula was a shock, because he had also been an expert witness for Corder. At Corder's hearing, he testified that Corder had been under the influence of a dominating personality, namely Paula Cooper. The prosecution now questioned if it was proper for him to testify for both Karen Corder and Paula Cooper. The judge ruled it was okay.

When questioned by public defender Relphorde, Brogno stated that Paula had certain psychological problems. He said that Paula was driven to antisocial behavior because "her home life was chaotic and severely lacking in loving and security." But prosecutor McNew made it very difficult for Brogno. Brogno had made many statements in the Karen Corder trial suggesting the evil influence of her friend Paula Cooper; now it seemed these statements were coming back to haunt him as he tried to help Paula Cooper.

Prosecutor McNew reminded me of a banty-hen rooster, the way he moved around and looked at people when he was trying to make a point. I almost felt sorry for Paula Cooper in a way because I didn't feel her attorney was doing a very good job for her. I wondered why an attorney would allow his client to plead guilty yet not get a guarantee of a life sentence in return.

Paula Cooper was then given a chance to speak. She stood up and said, "I am very sorry for what I did. All I can ask you is not to take my life. I'm not a gang member or leader. I never denied what I did. Everybody put the blame on me. The other three girls didn't tell the whole story." She noted that they took full part in the crime, but weren't condemned to death.

Paula then turned to the courtroom and to my family and said, "I didn't kill your mother on purpose. I hope you can find compassion in your heart to forgive me. How will you feel when I'm in my grave? Will that bring her back?" Paula then looked at prosecutor McNew and claimed that his wanting her to be killed by the state was just as bad as what she had done.

As her testimony ended, and the judge was about to give his decision, there was a loud disturbance in the courtroom. An old man began crying and wailing loudly, "They are going to kill my baby! They are going to kill my baby!" The judge ordered the bailiff to escort the man from the courtroom because it was disrupting the proceedings. I watched as the old man walked by me; I saw the tears rolling down his cheeks. It was Paula Cooper's grandfather.

Chapter 10

Judge Kimbrough Speaks

Then Judge Kimbrough began. He said:

> *The Court, in this case, finds that the State has proved beyond a reasonable doubt that on May 14th, 1985, Paula Cooper did intentionally kill Ruth Pelke while committing a robbery . . . The Court finds that Paula Cooper inflicted thirty-three stab wounds in the body of Ruth Pelke . . .*
>
> *In mitigation, the Court finds that the defendant has no history of a prior criminal record. As to the other mitigation circumstances, I believe that there are none, and if they were considered, they would be considered, I suppose in a negative sense, in that one of them provides for, "The defendant acted under the substantial domination of another." All the evidence in this case and in the related cases has indicated that Paula Cooper was not acting under anyone's domination. But, the evidence tends to indicate that she was a dominant personality in the commission of this crime.*
>
> *There is no evidence in this case—although it may have been mentioned in some other proceedings—that there was alcohol and /or marijuana. There is no proof of that in this case.*

There is some, and has been some evidence today, that the defendant, Cooper, was suffering from some personality disorder and that she was or displayed some anti-social personality traits. I do not believe that they rise to the level of the mitigating circumstance.

The Court cannot find any other mitigating circumstance, other than the defendant's age, and the lack of any history of criminal convictions or criminal conduct.

That is what the law requires the Court to do before sentence is pronounced. And that is all there is. I have done all that the law requires.

When death penalty cases are considered and when judges speak from the bench to justify their positions, they are making a political utterance, in my judgment. I will take this opportunity to make my politics known on the subject.

In 1985, unfortunately, there was assigned to this courtroom a series of cases involving young men from Gary, Indiana, all of whom, except one or two of the eleven, were under the age of twenty-one—they were teenagers.

Almost immediately on the heels of these cases came the murder of Ruth Pelke; and four young women were charged with that murder. The State sought to seek the death penalty against all at that point.

This case has received an unusual amount of publicity. There is worldwide interest in the outcome of these proceedings today and the Court is certainly aware of that interest.

When I graduated from DePaul University Law School in 1959, I am certain that I felt as strongly as anyone in this room about my position on the death penalty. And that was, I was totally against it. And I was not in the minority of the population of this country. I was one that made up approximately 68 percent of the population at that time who said that no, no, no; the death penalty is not proper.

That was almost thirty years ago; and times have changed. And maybe children, kids, young people like Paula Cooper have contributed to that change because of their violent activities. But now, the overwhelming majority of the population in this country says the death penalty is a proper penalty.

I attempted, in this case, to do for Paula Cooper what I did in the Karen Corder case, and that was write out some details and lengthy findings. I frankly could not. I will incorporate my findings specifically in this case in writing later for purposes of any further proceedings.

But I guess, for the first time, the real serious question that I have been faced with in all of these cases finally had to be addressed. I believe that the argument that I just listened to probably put it in focus better than all of the turmoil I have been through in the last several months.

Mr. McNew speaks eloquently. The position of the majority of the population in this country, they want justice. Justice to them means death. On the other hand, there is a substantial part of the population, the minority now, who think that the death penalty is not a fair or just punishment. And between those poles are all kinds of shades of difference.

If Paula Cooper was twenty-six years of age and committed the acts that she pled guilty to, I don't believe this courtroom would have more than three people in it. I don't think there would be any interest in it. I don't think the decision of any judge would be difficult, because Paula Cooper committed a crime, which clearly falls within the provisions of the law. She was, and I agree with Dr. Brogno, and it may be because I have a child, she [Paula Cooper] was a child.

The fundamental question is, is this an appropriate penalty for someone of a minority age? I don't know if it is proper. I don't know what the right political answer to that question is.

I ran for the State Representative office in 1966. I suppose if I had been successful, I would have been a party to those who made this law. I would have been a part of that decision-making process.

We all in this courtroom would have been better off if they had set out some specific provisions for minors. But they did not. The law is pervasive. It covers all.

I don't believe that I am ever going to be quite the same after these four cases. They have had a very profound effect on me. They have made me come to grips with the question of whether or not a judge can hold personal beliefs, which are inconsistent at all with the laws we are sworn to uphold.

And for those of you, who have no appreciation of it, it is not a simple question. It is not a simple question for me.

I would say to Mr. Pelke, I have read your letter. And I have heard you speak on two prior occasions. And I suppose I am at odds with almost everyone who has spoken on some point.

I do not believe that the failure to impose the death penalty today would be unbiblical. I believe that there are passages in the Bible that say a person who takes a life shall die by man's hand. I believe that there are other passages (but I don't profess to be an expert in religion) in the Bible, which are merciful, and do not demand and mandate an eye for an eye. It is not a travesty of justice if, in any case, if a Court does not impose the death penalty, because the statute provides for alternatives. It is a viable alternative. It's reasonable. It is there in the law.

The Court's duty is to find what the appropriate law is in this case. And I believe that the overwhelming responsibility of any judge is to impose that sentence which does not necessarily satisfy him or any party or any segment of the community, but that which is justified by the facts and circumstances of the case. I hope that my decision does that. It has been arrived at after much, much thought about the subject.

I will tell you, very frankly now, on the record, that I do not believe in the death penalty. I have examined myself closely on that point. And there are many laws that I don't believe in, that I think are poorly drawn and need to be reworked.

This is one. It needs some clarification on whether or not children ought to be subject to the death penalty. It needs clarification . . . Maybe in twenty years, after we have had our fill of executions, we will swing the pendulum back the other way and think they are unconstitutional.

Maybe.

Stand up, Paula.

All of the evidence in this case, including your statement, indicates that you stabbed Ruth Pelke thirty-three times.

I am concerned about your background. I am concerned that you were born into a household where your father abused you; and your mother either participated or allowed it to happen. And those seem to be explanations or some indication of why you may be the type of personality that you are. They are not excuses, however.

You committed the act. And you must pay the penalty. The law requires me to find that the mitigating circumstances outweigh the aggravating circumstances in this case. They do not. They do not.

Count # 1 is the knowing and intentional killing of

another human being. I believe the facts of this case would cause that count to be merged into count # 2, that is, the killing of Ruth Pelke while attempting or committing a robbery.

The law requires me, and I do now, impose the death penalty. The law also provides for an automatic review. I am going to direct you, and order you, Mr. Relphorde, to prepare a Motion to Correct Errors, so that the Indiana Supreme Court can review this matter.

Paula Cooper will be committed and ordered transferred to the Indiana Women's Prison pending further order of this Court. That is the judgment of the Court.

His gavel sounded loud and clear.

It was over. There was a hush in the court. Paula Cooper was led off to death row. Tears were rolling down her cheeks.

When I walked out of the courtroom, the cameras were there. I was asked for my comment. I was still sort of stunned because I didn't really think she would be sentenced to death. My response was "I felt like the judge did what he had to do." Then I sort of choked up and I finished with "but it won't bring my grandmother back."

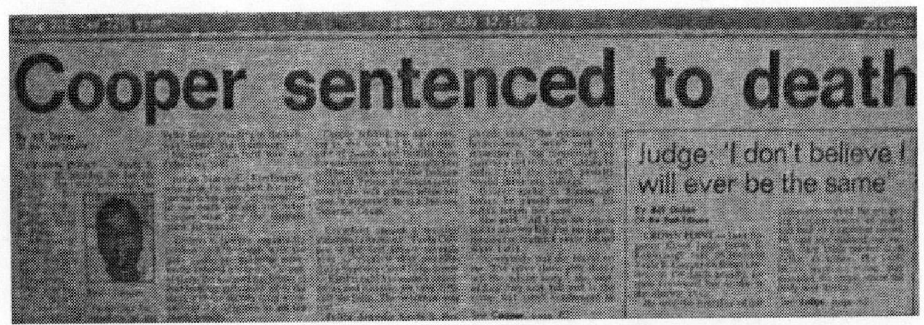

Cooper sentenced to death

Judge: 'I don't believe I will ever be the same'

Gary ***Post Tribune*** July 12, 1986

CHAPTER 11

Public Reaction Begins

The local newspapers began running another deluge of articles about Nana's death and Paula Cooper's death sentence. A lot of people and organizations gave their opinions of the death penalty.

For example, local Gary Police Chief Virgil Motley said, "I really don't know if it will do any good. I'm hoping that it will be a deterrent to some of the youngsters out there with weapons. In this case I would imagine they were all equally guilty. The only thing I have in my mind is who can look at all the facts and say, this one should die and the rest should live." Motley said he supported the death penalty, but questioned the fairness of singling Cooper out for execution.

An elderly woman, who wanted to remain anonymous, told the ***Post-Tribune,*** "The Bible says, 'Thou shall not kill.' I don't want to judge people so I won't comment further, but that is what God and the Bible said."

Paul Panther, a federal probation officer who personally opposes the death penalty, said, "Public support for executions reflects a recurring cycle of sentiment favorable to the death penalty. I think we're in a cycle of having and not having a death penalty . . . Statistics on murder haven't changed that much, and there are no numbers showing that murders are reduced in states where there is a death penalty."

Valery Jordan, age 27, said, "It (the death sentence) won't prove anything. It won't bring that murdered woman back. It won't scare anyone. The death penalty was an easy way out. Cooper won't get a chance to pay the price. She won't be locked up in a cell. She won't be scared or think about what she did. She can't pass the word on to others: 'Don't do it because this is what happened to me.'"

Rev. Paul Arnold, President of the Interfaith Clergy Council of Gary, and pastor of Grace United Methodist Church was an opponent of the death penalty. He disagreed with the emphasis put on punishment in the criminal justice system. "The question we're raising is whether the punishment system works. Our society tends to punish people, rather than emphasize working with them to change their attitude to help them be worthwhile members of society. Rather than a punishment system, I'd like to see a system that works to help people change."

Denise Lynch, 29, said, "Age should not make a difference here, but still I am not sure I am in favor of a death penalty. A lot of juveniles use age as a defense against the death penalty. The same should apply to juveniles as well as adults."

Vicki Jordon, 24 said, "She should have been given life. She grew up in an environment that was bad on her. It made her think the way she did. I think they wanted this to be history. If she were twenty-six would anyone have cared? She cannot be held responsible for her actions. It was her parents' fault. She was brought up that way."

Judge Kimbrough soon denied a request by Kevin Relphorde, Cooper's public defender, to overturn the death sentence on grounds the Indiana death penalty law was unconstitutional and that Kimbrough made legal mistakes in imposing the sentence. Kimbrough agreed with prosecutors that no mistakes were made and the death penalty is constitutional and proper in this case.

As area interest grew, Indiana State representative Earline Rogers instructed legislative staffers to begin work on a bill to raise the minimum age for the death penalty in the state from ten to sixteen. Rogers acknowledged that the action would not be able to save Paula Cooper and that her greatest regret is that she didn't act sooner. "I have been in office for five years. I wish I had proposed this legislation last year in time to save Paula Cooper. I also think that her case will make getting the legislation passed more difficult. We can't help Paula Cooper, but we can help other juveniles."

"It bothers me that she was sentenced near the twenty-year anniversary of Richard Speck. It's unfair that he killed all those women and yet he'll sit in a jail cell in Illinois the rest of his life and Paula Cooper, because she's in Indiana, may die. Until there is some across-the-board fairness, no one should pay the ultimate penalty, especially not a child."

"Most people were shocked that she got the death penalty in the first place," Rogers added. "But this is a very conservative state. I don't know which way they are going to go. Even though we won't be voting on Paula Cooper's life or death, she will be on everyone's mind . . . The fact that Indiana has the lowest age in the country for the death penalty, ten, is not a proud distinction."

CHAPTER 12

The Circle Widens

Soon the international community began showing concern in the Paula Cooper case. There is no death penalty in Europe. "Because we do not have the death penalty in Holland we do not know what it is to put someone to death," said Josephine Modderman of Amsterdam. Modderman was working on a story about Cooper for the national Dutch magazine ***Nieuwe Revu (New Review***). "To read the Paula Cooper thing to us is so unbelievable. We are not saying it is right or wrong, but it is very interesting to us that a young girl would be put to death," the Dutch writer said.

The Cooper case was adding fuel to the international debate on capital punishment. Media representatives from Australia, London, West Germany, Italy and other foreign locations had contacted the prosecutor's office, the defense attorney's office and the Gary ***Post-Tribune*** about Nana's murder. West German television did an interview with Paula that was seen by six million viewers.

Erich Follath, a correspondent for ***Stern*** magazine, Germany's largest weekly national magazine, wrote an article about the thirty-three juveniles on death row in America. "It's very interesting information to our readers. We don't have a death penalty and it's very different in the United States. Theoretically, in Indiana, a child as young as ten could be put to death. That is surprising to our readers. One of the problems is I don't want my readers to be sympathetic with the criminal. It is difficult to write because I don't believe in the death sentence at all. I don't think it helps deter crime."

Michael O'Regan, an Australian writer in Rupert Murdoch's ***News Limited of America***, said that recent executions of two Australians in Malaysia for drug running has renewed interest in the topic for his country, which has no death penalty. "To put a sixteen-year-old to death, and a girl as well, is shocking to people. It sounds barbaric to some of them actually."

Glamour magazine ran a survey of 1,600 of its young women readers and found that 70 percent favored the death penalty for minors who commit murder. "If they're old enough to commit the crime, then they're old enough to suffer the consequences," seemed a typical response. "I believe a lot of minors who commit crimes do so because they know they can get away with murder," wrote one; "I think that we make a mockery of the justice system by basing the punishment on a criminal's age."

> Victor Streib, the law professor at Cleveland State University-Marshall School of Law, who has been researching the issue, stated, "Paula Cooper represents the kind of case capital punishment foes have been looking for in hopes of getting the U.S. Supreme Court to forbid death sentences for juveniles. A lot of people are saying, *It's the Paula Cooper case.*"
>
> A dozen protesters from the Italian *Radical* Party demonstrated outside the U.S. Embassy in Rome against the death sentence given to Cooper. They carried signs reading: "For Whom the Bell Tolls" and "Death Penalty Equals Barbarity". They also gave a letter to U.S. officials for Ambassador Maxwell Rabb.
>
> Jack Crawford, Lake County Indiana Prosecutor, commented that Italy's *Radical* Party was not in a position to criticize the Cooper sentence: "The Italians do not understand that America has a tremendous problem with murders committed by young people." Crawford

> added, "I just don't think they're in a good position to judge our sentence guidelines when, to my knowledge, they don't have anywhere near the crime problem that we do here. Of all the things I have to worry about, the *Radica*l Party in Italy is the least of my concerns."
>
> Then seventy-eight members of the Italian Parliament signed a letter to Ambassador Rabb asking that the death sentence be dropped for Cooper, which, they added "moved us to horror." Their letter stated, "We judge that the values on which are constructed the democratic order of the West should give to the world a concrete and constant example in the face of the darkness of barbarism, arrogance and absolute power. The death penalty can't represent an acceptable practice on the moral level nor is it useful in the fight against violence and criminal behavior."

Judge Kimbrough said in response, "It doesn't surprise me because they don't have a death penalty at all . . . I had no idea this case would have the international significance that it has."

Chapter 13

The Local Folk Speak

Local reaction to the Paula Cooper decision continued unabated. For months it provided grist for the letters-to-the-editor column of the local Gary ***Post-Tribune.*** The responses ranged from thoughtful to perplexed to vitriolic.

Felicia Burleigh of Gary wrote:

> Two wrongs don't make a right.
>
> I don't condone what Paula Cooper did. She was as wrong as a person can be, but the death penalty?
>
> I've come to the conclusion of racial prejudice. It was meant to look good by using a black judge to do the dirty work, but isn't that the way it's been since slavery days?

Raymond J. Vince of East Chicago wrote:

> Down in my heart I honestly believe Kimbrough made the toughest decision of his life. However, he had a job to do. To make a decision concerning a life is no easy task indeed . . .

Laurie Wing of Merrillville wrote:

Some people would argue that everyone has choices. It is true. However, society also has choices. When society chooses to kill its children rather than to find out why they are so disturbed and do its utmost to correct that disturbed pattern, on an individual or a societal basis, we are all diminished through the actions that we advocate by lack of outcry.

In effect, though it will not bring back Ruth Pelke or change the pattern of poverty's abusive absurdities or insure that our children grow up wiser, gentler, less hungry and not beaten or raped, "we" are willing to see a child have the life burned out of him/her.

William A. Hill of Gary wrote:

In my opinion, Paula Cooper is a very sick product of a sicker society. Be forewarned that if something isn't done in our community and country soon to ameliorate this sickness that prevails, our future headlines may be filled daily with the news of "kids that kill."

Kevin L. McDonald of Merrillville wrote:

Anybody, regardless of race, demented enough to commit this type of crime should receive the death penalty.

J.W. Henderson of Chesterton wrote:

I am sick and tired of hearing about Paula Cooper. She committed the crime and should pay for it—like an adult. A 16-year-old knows the difference between right and wrong. She should have thought about murdering Ruth Pelke before she did it. If it didn't bother her to do it, what makes all of you so sure it bothers her now? White or black, 16 or 61, the sentence she received was fair . . . .

Edward Wells of Hobart wrote:

> .... Cleaning out all those now on death row would save a lot of money.
>
> .... A society that supports a concept of caging human beings for their crimes (and giving them all the comforts of home) and also supports bastardy through welfare is a sick society.
>
> .... Let's do it. Execute 'em all and be done with it once and for all.

Betty Fain of Portage wrote:

> If Cooper can kill this viciously at 16, just imagine what she could accomplish if she were allowed to grow up and improve her technique.

Odessa Scott from Rochester, New York, wrote:

> Even though there is no way humanly possible to give back life to Ruth Pelke, or to ease the pain of her family, friends or anyone else, I believe to take Paula's (or any young child's) life only adds pain to many more people. Any sane adult who hears about Paula's tragedy must feel some anxiety when they realize that their child or the child of a loved one could be electrocuted in this country.

Leticia Zimmer of Hobart was shocked by the sentence:

> I never believed he would do it. It is not ours or the judge's decision to put a young girl to death. It's God's right to choose when He wants us to leave this earth.
>
> No one condones what she did. It is unforgivable. But putting a young girl to death will not solve anything.

> I would rather see her in jail for all her life so she could pay for her crime in a just manner. God put us on this earth; let God take us away.
>
> No real good will come of this. In time everyone will forget, but Kimbrough will not. He will have to live with his decision.
>
> Pelke did not deserve to die, but Cooper put her to death. She started to pay for that the day she was caught. She cannot pay what she owes if she dies.

Elaine Bradley of Gary wrote:

> My God! If they would have had you in their lives, they would have never committed this act. What is needed is a national revival. We cannot save ourselves from ourselves; only God can do that.

Pelham V. Chatman of Gary wrote:

> If Ruth Pelke could speak, what would she say?
>
> This current controversy surrounding Paula Cooper is bothering the conscience of this nation. I believe it bothers Judge James Kimbrough, too.
>
> I abhor capital punishment, but no one is above the law, regardless of age, sex or station in life.

The ***Post-Tribune*** itself ran an editorial that questioned selective punishment, executing a minor, and the death penalty itself:

> . . . . Gloating over the fact that Cooper is the first female juvenile ever to receive the death penalty in this country will do little good. That isn't an accomplishment to be proud of; it should bring sadness. That some children have such little respect for life, such little reason for being, is an indictment this society must face . . . .

Meanwhile, ***USA TODAY*** released parts of a letter that was sent by Paula Cooper saying she's sorry for stabbing a seventy-eight-year-old Bible teacher thirty-three times last year. She also said, "This isn't fair to be in a hot prison locked up for twenty-three hours a day." ***USA TODAY*** commented:

> Cooper's case has drawn international attention because of her youth and she has been interviewed on *60 Minutes* and West German TV. A book is planned. "If you want information, fine, but how much will you pay me?" Cooper wrote. "I need financial support. I've done two TV programs and I wasn't offered a dime. Well, that's the end of that."

Chapter 14

My Personal Chaos

In spite of all that was being said and written about "The Cooper Case," I wasn't paying much attention. My personal life was a real mess: Judy and I broke up.

The break up was mutual, but I was really in love with Judy; and I wanted us to get back together again.

When it didn't work out, I became very depressed, and felt totally devastated. After about four weeks of being at the lowest ebb of my life, I began to pray. It was the only way I could find any peace.

I couldn't talk to my friends. They all simply said, give her up and find someone else. I didn't want to give her up. So I prayed, prayed, and prayed some more.

And then came November 2, 1986. It was about a year and a half after Nana's death.

That day, I was scheduled to work the three-to-eleven shift at Bethlehem Steel. When I got to work, I talked with Kevin Walker and Lavelle Stewart, the two other overhead crane operators I would be working with. Then I got my "line-up" for the evening: I was to take crane #509 down to the roughing mill area and wait for several mechanics. When I got my overhead crane to the designated area, I noticed the mechanics had not yet arrived. So I sat back in my crane seat and once again started to pray about my problem with Judy.

The only time I had done much praying during the previous ten years was when Nana had been killed, but these last few weeks I was almost praying without ceasing. I had been involved in what I called anguishing prayer.

I began praying by asking God why. Why? Why everything? Why this problem with Judy? I couldn't think straight. A few days earlier I had become so unglued that I was banging my head against the kitchen wall crying and almost screaming. Why, Why, Why?

As I sat in the crane cab alone, fifty feet above the steel mill floor, the tears began to trickle. Suddenly, my whole life seemed to jump out at me. Everything that had ever gone wrong seemed to pass in review. For the first time in many years, I thought about Jane Jones. She had been my childhood sweetheart. When her family joined our church, I liked her right away. I was in the sixth grade.

There were a few times in high school when Jane and I broke up, but when we did, she never dated anyone else. After I graduated from high school, I went to college in Grand Rapids, Michigan, for a year. Jane was a senior in high school, and when there was a special Valentine's weekend at the college, she came up for it.

After the banquet—it was February 14, 1966—I gave Jane an engagement ring. We were still engaged when I was drafted into the Army a year and a half later in July 1967. Jane wrote me every day while I was in training. When I left for Viet Nam in December, she still wrote every day.

Then in September of 1968, only three months before I was supposed to come home, we broke up. At first I thought it was just temporary, but she no longer responded when I started writing again. By the time I got home in December, she was engaged to someone else.

As I sat there in the crane, I remembered how long it had taken for me to "get over" Jane. But now it had been years since I had even a single thought of her. That night—eighteen years after we broke up—I sat in the crane and found myself asking God why that relationship hadn't worked out.

As tears dripped from my eyes, I began to think about my time in the Army. After basic training in Fort Leonard Wood, Missouri, I was sent to Fort Polk, Louisiana, for light weapons infantry training. With light weapons training, I knew I was headed for Viet Nam and would be on the front line.

Basic Training at Fort Leonard Wood, Missouri 1967

I spent twelve months in Viet Nam, and I saw dozens of fellow soldiers die. I saw friends with legs and other body parts shot off.

As a radio operator, my job was to carry a twenty-five-pound radio on my back for the company commander. Often I saw the sand around me kicking up from enemy gunfire, knowing any time, one of those *AK-47* rounds could find me.

My souvenir from Viet Nam was three pieces of shrapnel from an enemy mortar. I will carry it forever in my back, on the right side, just under my armpit. As I sat in the crane and prayed, I asked, "Why, God, did you let me live? Did I live so I could go through this bad time now?"

I asked God why I did dropped out of college after one year, which allowed me to be drafted in the first place.

And I thought about when I went to college on the GI Bill after I was out of the service. After getting a degree in pastoral theology, why did I suddenly drop out of church and set the degree aside? And why did I then continue my life as if I had never even set foot in the hallway of a church. Why? Why?

As my life passed in review, I thought about my divorce from Mary. She was a good woman. The divorce was my fault. I loved my three kids very much and I had really enjoyed raising them, but I lost custody of them when Chris was fifteen, Bob fourteen, and Becky "my baby" only six.

My divorce caused a lot of pain for my parents and others in the family. I was an embarrassment to them. I had lived in open sin, *terribly back-slidin'*, the Baptists would say. I had lost my family because I had turned my love to Judy. And now as I sat in my crane I asked God, "Why have I now lost everything? Why, Why, Why?"

I told God that I was sorry for everything I had done in my life that was wrong, that I was sorry I had ever hurt anyone.

I even thought about my bankruptcy after the divorce. After the lifestyle that I had been living before the divorce, I ended up losing everything. My name and signature had always meant something, but now my name was mud and my signature was worth nothing.

And to top it all off, I now had lost Judy, too.

Then I began to think about Nana, and the tears streamed down my cheeks. I had never really broken down and cried about Nana's death, but now the tears were rolling. I asked God why He had allowed one of His most precious children to suffer such a horrendous death. Nana was such a good person and she had died trying to serve Jesus. Why, Why, Why?

Why did our family, a good family, have to go through the suffering and the pain, especially my father who still has scars that will never go away? Why, Why?

Then I began to think about someone with many more problems that I had. I thought about Paula Cooper. I pictured Paula on her bed, slunk against the wall of her death row cell. I pictured her looking upward, to no place in particular. Tears were coming out of her eyes. She was saying, "What have I done, what have I done?"

She had ruined her life. For what?

I pictured Paula being very much alone. I knew her parents had not come to her sentencing hearing and doubted if they were supporting her now.

My mind flashed back to the day of the sentencing hearing when Paula was condemned to die. I thought about her grandfather being kicked out of the courtroom for wailing, "They're going to kill my baby; they're going to kill my baby."

I recalled seeing him led past me on his way out of the courtroom, with tears streaming down his cheeks.

Then I recalled Paula in the courtroom being led off to death row. Tears were streaming out of her eyes and rolling down her cheeks. I remembered seeing Paula wearing a light blue prison dress that had dark blue blotches because of her tears.

Chapter 15

The Epiphany in the Crane

And then I pictured Nana.

Nana

I pictured her in the beautiful photograph that was always included with stories about her in the newspaper. But as I sat in the steel mill crane that November evening, there was one distinct difference between what I was picturing and the beautiful photograph. I pictured Nana with tears flowing out of her eyes and rolling down her cheeks. At first I thought they might be tears of pain, but I immediately realized that they were tears of love and compassion for Paula Cooper and her family.

I knew that Nana would not have wanted Paula's grandfather to suffer the experience of having a granddaughter strapped into the electric chair and volts of electricity running through her until she was dead. And I didn't think Nana would want Paula killed for killing her—Nana had let Paula into her house to talk about Jesus.

I began to think about Nana's faith in Jesus, and I immediately thought of three things that Jesus had said about forgiveness. I recalled the Sermon on the Mount when Jesus said if we wanted our Father in heaven to forgive us, we needed to forgive others.

Then I thought about Jesus talking to the disciples and Peter asking Him about the number of times that we should forgive someone. Jesus answered, "***Seventy times seven***."

I knew that Jesus was not telling Peter that we should forgive four hundred and ninety times and then cease to forgive, but that Jesus was telling us that forgiveness should be a way of life.

And as I sat in the crane, I pictured an image of Jesus crucified on the cross. I pictured the crown of thorns dug into his brow. I envisioned His bloody hands and feet and the nails driven through them. I recalled what He said just before they killed him. Jesus said, "***Father, forgive them for they know not what they are doing.***"

I began to think that Paula Cooper didn't know what she was doing when she killed Nana. Someone that knows what they are doing does not take a twelve-inch butcher knife and stab someone thirty-three times. It was a crazy, crazy, crazy senseless act. I thought maybe the right thing for me to do was to forgive Paula. I told myself that I should try to forgive her.

Once again I pictured the image of Nana, tears rolling down her cheeks. There was no doubt in my mind that her tears were tears of love and compassion for Paula Cooper and her family. I felt Nana wanted someone in our family to have that same love and compassion. I felt the responsibility fell on me.

Even though I now realized that forgiveness was the right thing to do, I didn't have a bit of love and compassion. I thought how brutal Nana's death was, and I could see no way to come up with any love and compassion at all. But the tears I pictured in Nana's eyes affected me greatly. I felt that if I didn't try to generate some sort of love and compassion, then in the future, whenever I would think about Nana, I would feel guilty.

Not knowing what else to do, as I sat in the crane cab, I started praying again. By now my tears were flowing like a river. I begged God, "Please, please, please give me love and compassion for Paula Cooper and her family and do it for Nana's sake."

I started thinking about Paula. I could write a letter and tell her the kind of person Nana was and I could tell her about Nana's faith in God and her love for Jesus. I thought I could tell her about God's love and His forgiveness. I could also tell her that Jesus loved her and died on the cross for her.

At this point, things began to sink in. My prayer for love and compassion for Paula was being answered! And at that moment, I knew I no longer wanted Paula to die; I wanted to do whatever I could do to help her.

That night in the crane, I learned the most important lesson of my life: I learned the healing power of forgiveness. When God answered my prayer for love and compassion, the forgiveness was automatic. I knew I no longer had to try to forgive Paula, because the forgiveness had already miraculously happened. Forgiveness brought a tremendous healing.

It had been a year and a half since Nana's death, and whenever I had thought about Nana, it had been very painful, because I always pictured how Nana had died. I pictured her butchered on the dining room floor. This was the same dining room where our family gathered every year for Easter, Thanksgiving, Christmas Eve, birthdays and other special occasions. Picturing Nana's death had always caused me great pain and sorrow. But I knew that from that moment on, whenever I would think about Nana, I would no longer picture how she died. I would picture how she had lived, what she stood for, what she believed in and the beautiful, wonderful person that she was. I knew a miracle had happened to me and I knew that I would never forget how it came about. God gave me a tremendous peace, a peace that passes all understanding.

As I sat in the crane, I began to wonder why the change in me was taking place. I thought about the media involvement in Paula's case. I thought I might do an interview with a journalist some time about forgiveness. I also thought I might write an article about forgiveness or that maybe someday, a Sunday school teacher would tell her class about the grandson who forgave his grandmother's killer.

I even thought about how Oprah Winfrey might be interested in a white man who forgave the black girl who killed his grandmother. I thought I might even write a book someday and it could be made into a movie to help support my grandmother's issue of Christian education.

I began to think about family, friends and coworkers. I knew many would not understand the change I had just gone through. Yet, it was very important to me for my family to understand what had just taken place. I felt that it might take awhile, but since they were all Christians, I hoped they would eventually understand and agree. I knew my family had suffered greatly over Nana's death and I knew Nana loved everyone in the family. I knew that whatever I would do on behalf of Paula that I would have to be careful and try not to hurt anyone more than they had already been hurt. I knew Nana would have wanted it that way.

Before I left the crane that night, I made God two promises. The first promise was that any success that would come into my life as a result of forgiving Paula Cooper; that I would give God the honor and the glory. It wasn't anything I had done—it was because God had touched my heart.

The second promise I made was that any door that opened as a result of forgiving Paula, I would walk through it. I had no idea what doors God might open as a result of my night in the crane, but I knew if one did, I would walk through it. I would deliver God's message of love and compassion. I would talk about forgiveness. I would talk about healing. God would give me the words to say. He had promised me that in the Bible.

I had spent about forty-five minutes in the crane that night. The mechanics never did show up for their lifts. I walked down the fifty feet of stairs to the floor below. When I had gone up at the start of the shift, I was a defeated man. When I came down those same stairs forty-five minutes later, I felt victorious. I felt like a man with a mission!

Chapter 16

A New Life Begins

I knew that life would never be the same again after my night in the crane. I had no clue what was going to happen, but I just knew things were going to be different.

People have referred to my experience in the crane by different names. Some have called it an enlightenment experience; others have called it my conversion experience, others an epiphany. But I have always thought about it as my "*mountaintop experience*."

The Baptist's have a phrase, "*born again*." Although what had happened to me that night did not qualify as a Baptist "*born again*" experience, to me it almost seemed as if I had been born again. I had allowed my life to be changed. I allowed my mind to be changed because I allowed my heart to be touched.

Praying for love and compassion, learning about forgiveness, was to me the equivalent of finding the pearl of great price that Jesus talked about in one of His parables. In that parable, the one that found the pearl of great price sold all he had, so he could obtain that one great pearl. I felt learning the powerful lesson of forgiveness was that great pearl. I began to rethink all of my philosophies of life to see if they could pass through the filter of forgiveness.

I knew one thing, if love and compassion for all of humanity wasn't included as part of the answer, then to me it was not an answer. When I began to pray and ask God for love and compassion for all of humanity, my outlook on life changed and I knew I was pursuing God's way. I knew that it was God's message and that it was Jesus who had shown the way. Maybe I would never be the preacher that I had once wanted to be, but I knew that I could be one of God's messengers for one of His most neglected and misunderstood messages.

God had shown me the beauty of His love. I was able to answer for myself a few of the hard questions: Who am I? Why am I here?

There was no doubt in my mind who I was. I was a sinner saved by grace, and I was here because I had a timely message. I didn't know how I would get that message out, but I had promised God I would go through any door that opened. I had faith that He would open the right doors at the right time.

After "my night in the crane experience," I decided to call Kevin Relphorde, Paula's court-appointed attorney, to get Paula's address so I could write her. For the first time in weeks, I quit worrying about Judy. When I got home from work that first night, I called Mickey's Lounge where Judy was working. I told her I would like to talk to her when she got off of work. She said that when she got off work at midnight, she was going out with some friends. I asked her to call me when she got home.

I went to bed and fell right to sleep. When Judy called later and woke me up, I elected not to go next door to talk. I went back to sleep. Normally I would have talked with her right away, but things were different now. Our talk could wait until it was convenient for both of us. I wanted to tell her about my crane experience, but felt it could wait.

The following day, on my third call to Kevin Relphorde's office, I got through to him. After identifying who I was and the fact that I wanted to help Paula, Kevin told me that he felt it was too late to help Paula. I am sure he was wondering, "Where was this guy before we went to trial?"

I asked Kevin if he thought Paula would answer if I wrote a letter. He guessed that she would. That was good enough for me. He gave me her address but also informed me that he was no longer Paula's attorney, because she had been assigned a new attorney for the automatic death sentence appeal before the Indiana Supreme Court.

Before I started the letter, I prayed for the words to say. And I felt God's Spirit as I wrote. I told Paula who I was and how that through God, I had forgiven her. I shared Nana's faith, putting a strong emphasis on God's love and forgiveness. I told her I wanted to help her any way I could. I told her I would even be willing to travel or speak on her behalf.

I prayed that Paula would answer the letter.

The next day, I talked with Judy about what had happened two nights ago on the crane. It was difficult. Instead of coming right out and telling what had happened, I made it sort of a riddle. I told her that since she now had someone else that she was dating, and seemed to care about, and love, that I also had chosen someone else to care about and love. When I told her it was someone she knew of, she began to guess the names of every girl that we knew. Finally it was clear that she would never think of Paula's name in a thousand years. So I told her, "Paula Cooper."

Judy could not believe what she was hearing. When I explained that I really did have love and compassion for Paula, she said I was nuts and had "lost it." Then I told her about my experience in the crane, figuring that would clear it up for her. But when I finished the story, she still thought I was crazy. She figured the pressure since our breakup had been too great, that I had certifiably "lost it."

Then I talked with my good friend Wayne, from the bottom of my heart.

He responded to my experience the way that I had hoped. He confirmed my belief about what the Bible had to say about forgiveness. He said there was no doubt that forgiving Paula was the right thing to do because it honored God and Nana. But Wayne didn't say much when I talked about trying to get Paula off death row.

Ten days after I wrote to Paula, I got a reply. As I took the letter from the mailbox, I ripped it open and began reading before

I went into the house. Paula thanked me for writing. She said she didn't want my pity, just my forgiveness. She wrote that she had already prayed to God to ask for forgiveness. She said she believed that God had forgiven her. She said that it wouldn't be necessary for me to travel or speak on her behalf. She just wanted my friendship.

I responded with a lengthy handwritten letter, with tears hitting the pages as I wrote. When I finished I felt that God's Spirit had inspired me. One of the sentences I wrote still jumps out at me today: "Perhaps the greatest part of God's love is the forgiveness His love brings."

I took the letter to Judy's house before I mailed it. I felt that if Judy heard what I was saying to Paula that her heart could be touched, too. After reading to her the letter in tears, she looked me in the eyes and said, "You're nuts." She left the room and slammed the door. I had been working on getting our relationship back on track again and that didn't seem to help any.

It was time to talk to my parents. They had gone back to Florida for the winter, so I called them and told them that I had written a letter to Paula and that she had responded. After I read them what she had written I read them the "*inspired*" reply I was about to send to Paula. My parents were in total silence when I finished reading. Finally my mom spoke up. She didn't understand what I was doing and why. I tried to explain. My dad said they didn't agree with what I was doing, but he did say one thing that I still appreciate today. He told me, "Do what you have to do."

Then I sent the "*inspired*" letter off to Paula. In ten days she once again responded and said she was willing to have a visit. She gave instructions on how to go about getting on her visitor's list. She also responded to my request for her grandfather's name, address and telephone number.

I called the *Indiana Women's Prison* as Paula had suggested, and tried to get permission to visit Paula. I was denied special permission from the Assistant Superintendent, Dana Blank. Then I called Superintendent Clarence Trigg who said he didn't understand why I wanted to visit her. I tried to explain. After I told him I would write him a letter to explain in more detail why I wanted to visit Paula, he said that would be fine.

I prayerfully wrote Superintendent Trigg a letter and waited. He didn't respond. I finally called him up and he informed me he had not even gotten the letter. I told him that was no problem because I had kept a copy and would send it to him. After several more weeks, I still did not hear from him. When I called his office, he stated that he had gotten my letter; in fact he said he now had both copies.

But Superintendent Trigg said that he was not going to allow a visit because the Department of Corrections had a rule that would not allow the perpetrator of a violent crime to visit with the victim's family. I was stunned. All I wanted to do was to help Paula. I figured anything good I could do for Paula would be to the benefit of the prison.

Meanwhile, I called Paula's grandfather and we set a time to visit. Since it was almost Thanksgiving, I brought him a fruit basket. I was very nervous, but knew I was doing the right thing. Abraham Garron was a kind old man, and very gracious to me. We sat at the dining room table and looked at old photo albums for quite a while. He showed me pictures of Paula and her sister when they were very young. They were two very cute little girls. No one could have guessed from those pictures that one day, Paula would commit such a horrendous crime. I thanked him for his kindness and the nice visit.

When I wrote Paula about the fine visit with her grandfather, I also wrote my thoughts of "Thanksgiving and forgiveness." I suddenly felt they went hand in hand.

One day, at Mickey's Lounge, I ran into Tom. I hadn't seen Tom since Nana's death. The first thing he said to me was, "I hope the bitch burns!" Like similar comments from other friends, I realized it was his way of expressing condolences over Nana's death. I looked at Tom and told him, "I don't." He gave me a funny look and asked, "Why?"

I told him the story of my night in the crane. When I finished, he looked at me and said, "I hope she doesn't die either."

Chapter 17

The Answer Is . . .

Before we parted ways that night, Tom said, "You ought to write an article for the Gary ***Post-Tribune*** to let people know how you feel."

Two days later, I wrote that article, hoping to promote more dialogue about the death penalty and especially the executions of juveniles. I also hoped to get a religious dimension involved in the discussion by applying forgiveness to the subject. The article was called "**The Answer Is . . .**"

> The answer is love, prayer and forgiveness. Ruth E. Pelke lived and died knowing the right answer. She knew the Way and followed it.
>
> Why would God allow such a horrendous death to one of His most precious children? There can only be one answer and that answer is revival. We need revival in this country . . .
>
> Preachers—God is longsuffering and He is ready to pour His Spirit. He is ready for a revival. Now is the time for revival in the hearts of man. How do we reach hearts? Through the children. Children are our future. Children are most important.
>
> God allowed Mrs. Pelke's murder. Why? Could it be that God knew the case of Paula Cooper would gain the

> eye of the world? Could it be that He knew the ears of the world would be eager to hear what Paula might say? Paula Cooper can start revival fire by singing of the Glory of God.
>
> Pray for Paula Cooper.
>
> Love Paula Cooper.
>
> Forgive Paula Cooper.
>
> Paula Cooper is seeking a closer relationship with God and she has God's love and forgiveness. How about yours? She has mine. Ruth Pelke would want it that Way. I am her grandson.
>
> (Signed) William R. (Billy) Pelke

Neither the newspaper article nor my letter to Superintendent Trigg were the type of thing I would normally write, but I prayed a lot before I wrote them. I knew the letters might end up making me look like a religious kook, but after all, it was God who got me involved in this effort so I felt okay in mailing them.

Shortly after the "**Answer Is . . .**" article was printed, I saw Cuzzin' Judi. I thought of her songs of comfort at Nana's funeral. Cuzzin' Judi told me she had read the article, and then surprised me by saying that she didn't want to see Paula executed either. This was the first time I had seen Cuzzin' Judi since my experience in the crane. She seemed a bit skeptical when I first began to describe that experience, but by the time I was finished, we were both in tears and hugging each other.

How I thank God for Cuzzin' Judi. Now I had someone in my family who felt the same way I did. I knew Judi loved God and was a spiritual person. That was very important to me. Cuzzin' Judi knew that Nana would have had love and compassion for those four girls and that Nana would not have wanted Paula put to death. Christmas was coming . . . I felt that God had just given me my Christmas present through Cuzzin' Judi.

Each day, I checked the newspaper to look for letters to the editor. Strangely enough, after "**The Answer Is . . .**" was printed, all letters about Nana, Paula and the death penalty stopped. There was no dialog at all.

Paula and I exchanged letters about every ten days. I wanted to share with her the things that I felt Nana would have wanted me to say. I included different Bible verses that I thought were important. It was quite an experience to be able to write to someone who had done something so terrible, and yet know that I had God's love and forgiveness for that person. It was a great feeling.

My own horizons grew, and I learned that in addition to Paula there were thirty-two other juvenile offenders on death row throughout this country. I prayed for love and compassion for them and I found I no longer wanted them to die either. I became convinced that the death penalty for juveniles was wrong.

As I contemplated the magnificence of forgiveness, I became painfully aware that during my twenty years at Bethlehem Steel there were some people I worked with that I didn't like. I immediately thought of four people I had a problem with and didn't care for very much. The name of Jim jumped out at me. Ten years earlier, Jim and I had some words. When I heard him make a crude remark about me over the crane phone, I took my crane to the landing and came down the stairs to confront him.

On the way down the stairs, I coughed up a large "hocker," but instead of spitting it out, I slid it under my tongue. In front of five or six other people, I walked up to Jim and challenged him to make that same crude remark to my face. He did, and I planted the "hocker" between his eyes.

We didn't break into a fight because neither of us wanted to lose our jobs. But for the next ten years, whenever I would see Jim on my way in or out of the steel mill, I would look in the opposite direction and not even acknowledge that he existed as a human being. He did the same.

I knew that if I were to forgive Paula for killing Nana and yet still hold a grudge against Jim, I was being a hypocrite.

I knew I had to take care of that.

I saw Jim a few days later at work and I went up to him: "I'm sorry about my part in the event ten years ago. And I hold nothing against you." Jim said, "Apology accepted."

A few weeks later, I was grocery shopping and I turned into an aisle at the supermarket and saw Jim. Normally, I would have turned around and gone to another aisle, but not this time. I walked by Jim and said, "Hi." He responded with "hi" and we went on about our shopping. I was glad that I didn't have that bad feeling toward him anymore. I wasn't quite ready to make him my best friend and invite him over for dinner yet, but it was great to experience the process of forgiveness and be free of the hate.

I forgave the other three men at the mill I held grudges against. I knew it was the right thing to do.

I was totally convinced that Jesus was right. Forgiveness is the way to live. "***Seventy times seven.***" Since my "*mountaintop*" experience in the crane, I realized that forgiveness is a great way to live. Maybe that is why Jesus told us to live that way.

Chapter 18

The Italian Connection

One day, when my friend Wayne and I were at Judy's house, we got into a discussion about Paula Cooper. Both Wayne and Judy said they thought I was becoming obsessed with "this Paula thing." In fact, Judy said I was crazy and "losing it." Wayne agreed to a point. He said, "It's all right for you to forgive Paula, but now you're taking it too far." And he agreed with Judy that I was wrong to work to help her get off death row.

As we sat, I talked with the two of them from the bottom of my soul about how God had touched my heart on November 2, 1986. I told them again how a miracle had happened. It was very important to me for these two close friends of mine to believe that God had *actually* touched my heart and that a miracle had *really* happened that night up in the crane.

I said, "What, for instance, if Oprah Winfrey were to call and say that she wanted me to be on her television program to talk about my forgiving Paula Cooper—then would you believe that God had touched my heart in the crane and that a miracle had taken place?" Both agreed—it would be a miracle if Oprah were to call.

In February, I did receive a phone call, but not from Oprah. It was from Anna Guaita, a journalist from Rome, Italy. Anna said that she and a colleague would soon be coming to Indiana to do a story about Paula Cooper. They would be representing three newspapers, including Italy's largest, ***Il Messaggero***.

Anna told me of the great interest in Italy about Paula's case. She said that a group of students had started a petition drive to save Paula's life. Anna said that she had called the Gary ***Post-Tribune*** about their proposed trip to Indiana, and asked for recommendations for persons to interview for their article.

The ***Post-Tribune*** suggested that she contact Paula's new attorney, William Touchette; Patti Wolter, an investigator in Paula's case; and Paula's grandfather. Then, almost in passing, the person mentioned that a grandson of the victim had written an article about forgiveness a few months earlier.

In her phone call, Anna told me that Italians do not perceive Americans as being a very forgiving people. She asked if it would be all right for her to talk to me about it when they came to Indiana. We set a time and a date.

I was very excited that I would now have a chance to talk to a reporter and that I would be able to talk about love, compassion and forgiveness—talk about Nana, about Jesus, about why I didn't want Paula executed. I was very excited and I thanked God for the opportunity.

When Anna came to Indiana, we met at the *Holiday Star Plaza* in Merrillville. She introduced me to her colleague, Giampolo Polli. They expected the interview to last about thirty to sixty minutes. I brought with me the videotapes of the television news both when Nana was killed and when Paula was sentenced to death. I also had a tape of the ***60 Minutes*** program, which featured Paula's case. And I brought my scrapbook with newspaper articles, along with the dozen letters Paula had written me. We spent four hours talking.

During our lengthy conversation, Anna suggested that I start an organization of murder victims' family members *against* the death penalty. I smiled and said I had never heard of such a thing, and then asked if she had. She said no. Anna had been near tears during much of our interview. As she left, she promised she would pass along my greetings to Paula when she visited her in the Indianapolis state prison the next day.

The first in the series of articles in ***Il Messaggero*** and other Italian newspapers appeared February 20, 1987. The very next day, the Gary ***Post-Tribune*** headlined **Paper Says Pope's Help Asked for Paula Cooper**. William Touchette, Paula's attorney, had told Anna in his recent interview for ***Il Messaggero*** that, "I have just written the Pope, asking for his intercession. A word from him would carry great weight in our state."

In her prison interview, Paula had told ***Il Messaggero***, "I hope the Pope can help me." They also reported that Paula "had been in contact with the victim's grandson, who had forgiven her and sent copies of pages from the Bible."

The Paula Cooper case was attracting an amazing amount of attention in Italy. For example, a newspaper in Florence received forty thousand signatures opposing the death penalty for Paula. Paula's attorney, William Touchette, said, "Around the name of Paula Cooper has emerged a moral case that supersedes the boundaries of our country. I want to obtain a commutation of the death penalty to a sentence of sixty years in prison."

The paper also reported that Paula spent twenty-three hours a day in her cell in isolation and that when she could watch TV, she watched ***Swiss Family Robinson***. "I like that family. The parents never get mad and never hit their children."

When Anna was doing her interviews for the Italian newspaper, she talked with William Touchette, Paula's attorney, about me. He already knew from Paula that we were corresponding. Anna told him I wanted to meet him to see if there was some way he could help me visit Paula. Shortly thereafter, William Touchette called to invite me to have lunch with him and Monica Foster of the Public Defenders Office. Monica had been appointed to help Touchette with Paula's case.

It was a good meeting. I was confident that Paula now had two excellent people working to save her life. In fact, Touchette was getting ready to go to Italy to do a television program about Paula's case.

Then James Ricci called from the ***Detroit Free Press***. He had heard about me when he interviewed Anna Guaita and William Touchette.

When Ricci's article appeared, it was entitled "**Is This Killer Too Young to Die?"** The article included pictures of Paula, Nana, the Indiana Women's Prison and the electric chair at the Indiana State Prison in Michigan City. The article quoted Victor Streib (the Ohio lawyer researching the death penalty for juveniles), William Touchette (Paula's present lawyer), Judge Kimbrough (who had handed down the death sentence), James McNew (the deputy prosecuting attorney), my dad, Paula Cooper, and me. The only thing new was Prosecutor McNew stating, "I didn't argue to the court about deterrence. I don't believe in it anyway. What we are about is justice—justice for the victim, justice for the victim's family, justice for society." I felt it was very interesting that a prosecutor in favor of the death penalty would dismiss deterrence as a reason for the death penalty.

The Detroit paper quoted me saying I was determined "to do anything I can to get her off death row . . . I just want to show her God's love; I don't think she was raised with very much of it . . . Killing her would be wrong and two wrongs don't make a right."

Paula was quoted as saying, "Ruth Pelke is in my thoughts every day. I think about why did it happen. I can't see why . . . I try to figure it out." The article also said she occasionally reads the Bible.

Several weeks later, I got a call from William Touchette. He had returned from Italy and said there was some interest in my going to Italy on Paula's behalf. He asked if I would be interested in going if it could be worked out. I said I would.

Then I got a call at work from Francesca, a spokesperson for ***RAI***, the state owned television station in Italy. She said ***Domenica In*** was a popular Italian television show that combines entertainment and talk for six hours on Sunday afternoons. They wanted to schedule me with a translator during the current-events section of the show with a story on Paula. The show was to be hosted by Raffaella Carra, a television celebrity and actress. It wasn't Oprah, but it was the next best thing, with an audience of millions. I said I'd be happy to go. Praise the Lord, Hallelujah!

Chapter 19

Getting Ready for Italy

I couldn't wait to tell Judy and Wayne about my upcoming trip to Rome. But I wasn't in a hurry to tell my parents I was scheduled to leave for Italy on May 14, the second anniversary of Nana's death. I had two weeks to get ready.

I felt that going to Italy might be the most important thing that ever happened to me. As I prayed to say and do the right things in Rome, I decided to go on a fast. It was fourteen days until the TV program so I set fourteen days as my goal. I had fasted a number of times as a college student, the longest period being a week. But I felt I could do fourteen days. What I had learned about fasting was that it helped you to focus. Part of a spiritual fast is that, whenever you think about food, you are reminded to pray. I wanted to focus on getting out the message of love and compassion for all humanity. God had opened this Italian door and I wanted to walk through it the right way.

On Saturday morning, May 2, I woke up to a surprise. The headline in the Gary ***Post-Tribune*** read, **Kimbrough Death Hushes Courts.** Judge Kimbrough had been killed when his car ran into the back of a semi-trailer truck making a left-hand turn. The paper told how court employees were in shock, and once again revisited the Paula Cooper case calling it Judge Kimbrough's toughest decision.

Only hours before his death, Judge Kimbrough had been in conversation with Lake County Commissioner T. Edward Page.

Page reported, "That decision took a tremendous toll on him. He talked about how, if a re-sentencing hearing were held, it would involve him going through all those same emotions again."

Judge Kimbrough was to have escorted his daughter to her prom on Friday night.

A short time later, the ***Post-Tribune*** had the headline: **Judge Intoxicated at Time of Death.** Some people insinuated that his drinking had increased after the Cooper decision.

A week before I left was Mother's Day. I called my mom to wish her a Happy Mother's Day. Then I told her and Dad about the coming trip to Italy. They didn't understand why I was doing what I was doing.

Five days before I was to leave for Italy, the ***Post-Tribune*** ran a front-page headline: **Pelke's Grandson to go to Rome on Cooper's behalf.** They printed a very fuzzy picture of me. At the time I had a beard and it made me look like a terrorist.

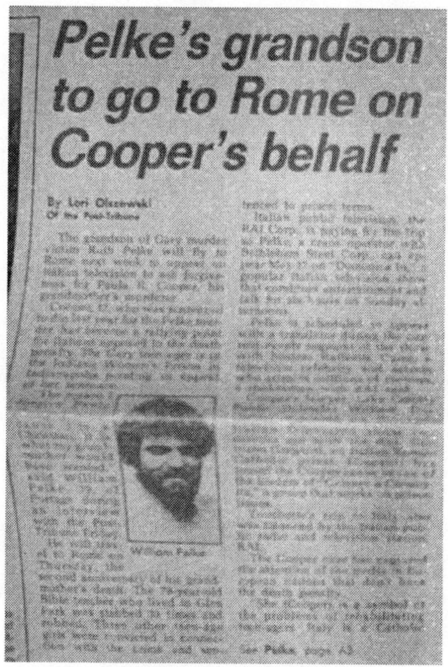

Pelke's grandson to go to Rome on Cooper's behalf

By Lori Olszewski
Of the Post-Tribune

[illegible]

William Pelke

[illegible]

Gary ***Post Tribune*** May 9, 1987

The article noted that Italian public television, the ***RAI Corp.***, would pay for the trip. And it told about William Touchette, Paula's lawyer, previously being on the same program with the Rev. Germano Greganti. He was an Italian Roman Catholic priest who had joined the Cooper cause and was one of the leaders of ***Carcere a Comunita***, a group working on prison issues.

I was quoted as saying, "In this area [Northwest Indiana], I'd say 95 percent of the people would like to see Paula burn and burn immediately. Basically I feel I'm alone in wanting to forgive Paula. It makes me feel good to know so many people in Italy feel the same way . . . I just feel that if you live as a Christian, forgiveness should be a way of life."

Italian interest in the Paula case was even expected to spill into some sort of demonstration of public support for Cooper when President Reagan visited Italy the following month, in June.

Judy and Wayne were both excited about my going to Italy, but the reaction at work was somewhat different. Suddenly, co-workers who had been very sympathetic to me during the period of Nana's death were now yelling at me. "Crazy" was one of the kindest comments. I always tried to respond by talking about love, compassion, and forgiveness. I had no problem talking about what the Bible has to say about forgiveness. I weathered the attacks just fine.

While I continued fasting and praying, ***NBC*** Channel 5 in Chicago came out to my house in Portage to do an interview. I tried to stay focused on my mission because this trip to Italy was not about me—it was about God's message of love, compassion and forgiveness.

Two days before I left, the ***Post-Tribune*** did another story. It was the front page of the local news section. The headline: **Should Cooper die? Victim's Family Divided**

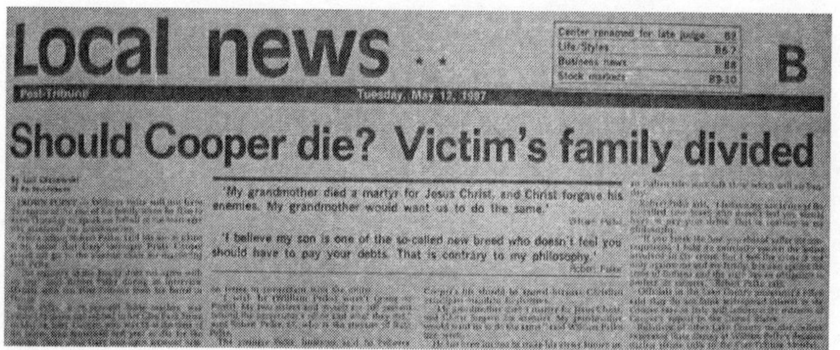

Local news

Center renamed for late judge	B9
Life/Styles	B6-7
Business news	B8
Stock markets	B9-10

Post-Tribune Tuesday, May 12, 1987

Should Cooper die? Victim's family divided

'My grandmother died a martyr for Jesus Christ, and Christ forgave his enemies. My grandmother would want us to do the same.'

'I believe my son is one of the so-called new breed who doesn't feel you should have to pay your debts. That is contrary to my philosophy.'

Robert Pelke

Gary ***Post Tribune*** May 12, 1987

The article stated how I would not have the support of the rest of my family when I flew to Rome to speak on behalf Paula.

The paper quoted my dad saying that I was alone in my belief that Paula Cooper should not go to the electric chair for Nana's murder. "The majority of the family does not agree with my son," he said from his home in Florida. "I wish he wasn't going to Rome. My two sisters and I are 100 percent behind the prosecutor's office and what they did."

There were two quotes in bold print at the top of the page under the headline.

The quote from my dad was, "**I believe my son is one of the so-called new breed who doesn't feel you should have to pay your debts. That is contrary to my philosophy.**"

My quote was, "**My grandmother died a martyr for Jesus Christ, and Christ forgave his enemies. My grandmother would want us to do the same.**"

I was not upset at my dad for his statement. My only thought was that I liked my quote better than his. What I had learned about forgiveness made it very easy for me to forgive my father for not understanding what I was doing.

On May 14, the second anniversary of Nana's death, I headed for Chicago's O'Hare airport. I had two stops to make on the way. The first was at the cemetery where Nana was buried. I took some flowers and said a prayer. Then I took a couple of pictures of Nana's gravesite and also a picture of the gravesites of Granddad and both his wives, Nana and Dorothy. They were buried side by side by side. Granddad loved both of them deeply.

Then I went to see Aunt Ruthie. Aunt Ruthie and Cuzzin' Judi lived together near the cemetery. As I explained to them what I was doing and why I was doing it, Aunt Ruthie seemed to understand.

Then Aunt Ruthie shared something very touching with me. She told me that when my dad had called her to tell her that Nana had been killed, that even before she hung up the phone, she forgave whomever it was that had killed Nana. Boy, was that a real blessing for me to hear, especially, now that I was on a journey to Italy to talk about forgiveness. We shed a few tears, prayed, and I headed to the airport in Chicago.

I had now gone about twelve days without eating. And where did they seat me on the plane? Right next to the galley. Up to that point, the fasting hadn't bothered me. But the aroma coming from the galley got my attention. It was just a constant reminder to keep praying.

I believed I was on a mission for God, with a unique opportunity to witness for Jesus Christ and the forgiveness he taught. I had no desire to see the sights while in Rome. My desire was to have God's power in my life and to touch hearts of others with love from Jesus. My prayer was to speak with God's wisdom and power to let others see God's love and forgiveness.

Chapter 20

Radio and TV in Italy

In Rome I was met by Francesca, the person I had talked to on the phone. Francesca and a couple of her friends from the TV station took me to an outdoor cafe to talk about the upcoming program. I had only juice. Francesca informed me of a rumor that the TV cameramen might go on strike, which would affect the program. They would know more the next day, they said.

After a press conference, we went to the television studio for a preliminary meeting with Raffaella Carra, a very beautiful woman in both looks and personality. I knew I would be comfortable with her when the actual interview came.

The following morning, the rumor was confirmed: the cameramen were going out on a wildcat strike and the program would be postponed. They suggested that I go back to the United States for now and maybe in a few weeks come back.

But I was concerned that if I went back to the United States, they might never call again, and I wanted very badly to do the show. I told them that I could get more time off work and stay until the strike was over. They left me alone for a few minutes in the studio where they had taken me to get my hair trimmed by their barber. When they came back they said it would be fine if I stayed until the strike was over. They said my ticket was open-ended—I could go back to the U.S. whenever I wanted. They also said they would take care of my food and lodging while I was there, and give me expense money in the amount of one million lire. I hadn't been in Italy long enough to know the exchange rate, but one million sounded good to me.

Bill and Raffaella Carra prepare for the
Domenica In program in Rome May 1987

It was then that I called off my fast. I had no idea when the program would take place, but I knew I was ready to get involved with Italian cuisine. My meals at the hotel were being paid for and I was ready to eat and stay awhile.

When I got back to my hotel room, I had three calls from Anna Guaita. She said I would be meeting with her and Father Greganti the next day. Father Don Germano Greganti was a cofounder of ***Don't Kill,*** an organization inspired by Paula's death sentence.

Father Greganti had spearheaded the drive to gather petitions on Paula's behalf. He intended to take me to a few schools to meet some of the people who had signed the petitions, which were now approaching almost five hundred thousand names.

Although I was no longer fasting, I continued to pray for strength, wisdom, courage, more love, more power and more faith. I asked for those things to bring honor and glory to God.

It was after 1:00 A.M. when the Gary ***Post-Tribune*** called me to talk about my activities in Rome. With the eight-hour time difference, the best time to talk to anyone in America from Europe was in the middle of the night. I ended up staying awake for about four more hours. I called Bethlehem Steel to get more time off of work. I also called Wayne, Judy and several other friends.

When Father Vito, a colleague of Father Greganti, met me in the morning, we took a bus to *Vatican City*. As his guest, I visited the *Vatican, St. Peters,* the *Coliseum,* and the *Italian Tomb of the Unknown Soldier*. We walked so much that day I got blisters, and didn't get back to my hotel until around 8:30 that night.

Bill with Father Vito Bracone at the *Vatican*

At 10:00 P.M. I received a call from the hotel clerk. He said there were four men in the lobby who wanted to meet me. I was already in bed, but I was curious. So I dressed and went down to the lobby.

The four gentlemen were all wearing suits and only one spoke English—poorly. His name was Italo. After he introduced me to his friends, Franco, Gheraldo and Gaitano, he explained that Gheraldo had written a book. The book had Paula's picture on the front cover along with a picture of the electric chair. The book was a play he had written. Although the play was not about Paula, it had been inspired by Paula's case. He gave me four copies of the book.

Gheraldo had read in the paper that I was in Rome, so he had driven one hundred miles to meet me. His friends, Italo, Gaitano and Franco, lived in Rome; he had picked them up before he came to meet me. Italo explained to me that the writer, Gheraldo, was a "chef."

Italo and Franco offered to take me sightseeing while I was in Rome. Italo graciously invited me over to his house the next evening to have dinner with his family.

The next day, I did an interview with *Radical Radio*. This really concerned me. What was *Radical Radio*? I was from a very conservative background and I knew my father would never understand me doing an interview for "*Radical*" *Radio*! Then I found out that the *Radical Party* was one of the major political parties in Italy. In fact, the *Radical Party* seemed to be the major organization pushing for worldwide abolition of the death penalty. I wasn't sure how much the *Radical Party* wanted to hear about Jesus and forgiveness, but it was an open door and I was going to go through it. I have no idea how much they eventually used of our taped conversation.

Italo and Gheraldo then took me sightseeing. After we went to a number of ancient and beautiful churches, I was taken to the *Trevia Fountain (Fountain of Coins)*. We went to a pizzeria for the noon meal. Italo then took me to the catacombs. Not only was I able to tell my story many times while in Rome, but I was also getting a first-rate tour.

That evening, I went to Italo's house for dinner and met his wonderful family, his wife Rosanna and daughter Emmanuelle. Both Rosanna and Emmanuelle tried very hard to practice their English while I was there, keeping an Italian-English dictionary in hand. It was a great deal of fun.

What an experience the next day! Father Greganti took me to do an interview on *Vatican Radio*. Father Greganti was around eighty years old and beloved by everyone around him.

I was able to speak on both the national and international segments of *Vatican Radio*, quite an adventure considering my conservative Baptist upbringing. But I enjoyed that interview more than any I had done, and felt very comfortable talking about love and compassion, the healing power of forgiveness, and Jesus. It was a rewarding experience to talk about Nana, and why I didn't want Paula strapped into the electric chair.

Bill with Father Don Germano Greganti
at *Vatican Radio*

The wildcat strike ended and ***RAI*** TV decided to film my segment in advance of the Sunday showing, so we did a taping. I was not really happy with the interview because I didn't really get to talk much about the healing power of forgiveness. But at least I had been able to get my message of forgiveness out on *Vatican Radio*. That was a consolation.

Then I had an offer from Gheraldo. He wanted me to be his guest for a week where he lived in the Province of Grosetto. I would stay with his friend Phillipo who owned an oasis near there. I found out then that Gheraldo was not a "chef" as I had first thought, but that he was a "chief." Gheraldo was the Chief of Police in Grosetto, the third highest political position in the province! Gheraldo told me that coming to Grosetto would be a wonderful experience and that he would line up a number of interviews. He knew I had a real desire to spread the message of forgiveness.

Phillipo's oasis overlooks the Bay of Talemone. (An oasis in Italy is a resort motel.) God blessed me with both a press conference and a television interview there.

Phillipo could not speak English but was a wonderful host. We went to Port Saint Stephen, and then to Salermo for a television interview. Phillipo was obviously a rich man, owning four oases, several campgrounds and three restaurants. When he drove me in his Mercedes to one of his restaurants, he had the chef bring out a loin of beef and had me tell the cook how thick I wanted my steak.

The day I left for home, there were three more articles in the Italian papers. One of the articles had a picture of Nana, Granddad and my niece Kim. During my nineteen-day stay in Italy, I had done numerous telephone interviews with the ***Post-Tribune*** back home because they wanted to report my daily actions in Italy. The ***Associated Press*** also called quite a few times. Also, ***CNN*** had a segment about my trip.

When Phillipo drove me to the airport in Rome, Franco met us there.

I had a wonderful time in Italy. The people I met were fantastic. I wished that I could have said and done more, but felt that it was all in God's hands. I did thank people wherever I went for signing the petitions and encouraging others to sign. I also hoped that someday I would be able to return.

My only disappointment was that I had not done better in getting out my message of forgiveness on the ***Domenica In*** program. Anni Crina of ***RAI*** TV called to say it was a good program and that I done great. It may have been a good program, but I had wanted to talk more of Jesus and forgiveness.

As I prepared to leave Italy, I held the hope that it would now be easier to get out the message of love, compassion and forgiveness. Before leaving, I had to settle the enormous phone bill for the hours of long-distance calls I had made while there. It came to about $700.00. The million liras allowance I had been given also converted to about $700.00.

Chapter 21

Public Emotions Still High

Both Wayne and Judy met me at O'Hare airport in Chicago.

They had saved the newspaper articles while I was gone. The ***Chicago Tribune*** said that the nature of a crime isn't the typical stuff of international crusades, but that is what the 1985 slaying of a Bible teacher has become. The article told my story of forgiveness that night in the crane. It quoted me: "My life has changed entirely since that night."

My dad regretted my going to Italy. He said, "I have a hard time accepting what he is doing. I don't know why he changed. Each girl received the punishment according to the law, according to her part in the crime. No one has the right to touch my family."

In an interview I had done with the ***Associated Press***, I was quoted as saying "Many people in the States want to see Paula get the electric chair. They think I'm crazy not to want to see her dead. If it were their grandmother they would want to switch on the power to the electric chair themselves. I have come here to lift up Jesus Christ's message of forgiveness and to thank all the people in Italy that have shown an interest in seeing Paula taken off the death row."

Wayne and Judy showed me a May 25 ***Post-Tribune*** article, which gave details of the ***Domenica In*** program. It told about Rev. Germano Greganti spearheading the petition drive that now had over five hundred thousand signatures. Spanish poet Raphael

Alberti had also read a poem, which he wrote out of his compassion for Paula Cooper being on death row.

With all these headlines and stories in the paper about my trip to Rome, the "**Voice of the People**" section in the ***Post-Tribune*** again sprang to life.

Rev. Bruce Ison of Hobart wrote:

> We don't need the Italians sticking their noses into our judicial system. Why would William Pelke go to Rome to ask for forgiveness? I never realized that Rome had the Omnipotent living there. I wonder if William Pelke will tell how his grandmother, the Sunday school teacher, had a butcher knife twisted into her body 33 times, then was robbed.

Christopher Griffin wrote:

> .... I do not believe that Paula Cooper and company should go unpunished. However, I do feel sorrow for them because they have been reared in an environment that condones violence and abuses liberty. I felt pity for Judge Kimbrough, for, even when laws conflicted with his humanity and beliefs, he was bound by law to render judgment. I have compassion and sympathy for the families and loved ones of the victims who lost their lives in terror. My faith comforts me and lets me believe that they, the victims, are now OK.
>
> I admire William Pelke. He has shown us all how to be free.

Betty J. Fain of Portage wrote:

> Our society tries to use every excuse to explain why this killer should not die. In the case of Paula Cooper, the excuse is that she had a bad childhood. Does that give everyone who was emotionally or

physically abused as a child the right to kill someone that only had the best interest for her and many other young people?

I cannot understand how Ruth Pelke's grandson can have so much compassion for Cooper. I feel I am a Christian, too, but I feel absolutely no forgiveness for Cooper, John Wayne Gacy, Alton Coleman or any other killer that kills just for the pure pleasure of killing.

Laura L. Adams of Lakes of the Four Seasons wrote:

. . . . I have a better idea than Cooper or William Pelke, Ruth Pelke's grandson who is attempting to save Cooper's life. I think that we should unleash Cooper and the thousands like her on the people of Italy and let them worry about saving her.

Maybe we Americans can start a trend. Whenever we have young adults murdering for pleasure, money or just plain amusement, we'll just pack them up and send them to Italy and let the Italian people 'rehabilitate' them.

I figured that since some of these "**Voice of the People**" articles were mentioning me by name, it was time for me to write once again. The article was titled "**The Ways of Mercy**":

The eyes of the world are on the Paula Cooper case. The Italian press carried the death sentence of Paula Cooper in its headlines. Many other countries, such as West Germany, Australia, Holland, England and Austria, have followed the case with great interest. Their interest focuses on one question: Will America murder its children?

If the answer is yes, then America will suffer another black eye in a portrait that has already been maligned.

European countries look up to America as a great leader and yet most are shocked that Americans will allow their children to be killed. Currently there are 36 Americans on death row for crimes committed while they were juveniles. Paula Cooper was 15.

Where was society when Cooper kept asking for help? Where were the Christians? The death penalty is society's easy way out! Out of sight, out of mind and also no more bills to pay.

To show Paula that killing is wrong, many want to kill her. Many want vengeance. The Bible tells us that vengeance belongs to God and not us.

Jesus said an eye for an eye and a tooth for a tooth was from the days of old. Christ said He was bringing a new way to live. To love one another was to become a way of life, forgiving all evil done unto you.

Jesus said to love those who hate you, to love those who persecute you and do all manner of evil against you.

Jesus said that if we don't forgive others, then our Father in Heaven would not forgive us.

Paula Cooper committed a terrible crime. It was a terrible crime that deserves punishment. It deserves stiff punishment. Indiana also has a 60-year life sentence available as an alternative to the death penalty.

Paula Cooper showed no mercy to Ruth Pelke, but let's not follow in Paula's error. Mercy on her life is the answer. Ruth Pelke lived her life under the grace of God. God's grace is also sufficient for me. The amazing thing about God's grace is that it is completely undeserved. His love, forgiveness and mercy are freely given to us. Will no one show love and forgiveness to Cooper? Jesus died for her, too.

How will God judge a country that murders its children?

A short time later, on June 5, 1987, Paula Cooper became a rallying point for Italians who staged a demonstration near Venice for the benefit of visiting President Reagan. Members of the Italian *Radical Party* demonstrated outside the hotel where Nancy and Ronald Reagan were staying. The sign-carrying demonstrators did not have access to the portion of the hotel where the Reagans were staying. Two members of the Italian Parliament asked to speak with Reagan during his visit to Italy to present a resolution calling for the end of the death penalty in the United States.

The same month, on June 20, Father Vito came to Indiana to visit Paula. He spent two hours talking with her. According to the ***AP***, Bracone, in broken English, said, "In the talk that we had for a couple of hours we feel that she's full of life. The first thing she asked me was to pray for her and she asked me to hold her hands while I was praying." Father Vito carried petitions signed by more than eight hundred thousand Italians and other Europeans to deliver to Indiana Gov. Robert Orr.

When I got a call from an ***Associated Press*** reporter, he told me that the ***AP*** wanted a story about my trip to Italy. We met at Mickey's Lounge where Judy worked. The interview turned out to be the best one yet. The article was carried in newspapers around the country, and was nearly half a page, including a picture of me holding the Bible I had bought to give Paula. The Bible was engraved "To Paula, In memory of Nana."

The article noted the strength of my father's opposition. "I knew it was going to be something a lot of people weren't going to understand," I said, "but it was something in my heart I knew was right. I don't want to hurt anybody. I don't want to hurt anybody in my family. If they don't understand it, I'll try to explain it to them as much as they are willing to listen."

If Paula would get off death row, her sentence would then be commuted to sixty years, which under Indiana state law, she could be free after thirty years in prison. "But," I said, "if Paula doesn't escape the death sentence, I know what I will do, and I've known it since day one. If she's got to die, I will walk hand in hand with her to the electric chair, if she wants me to."

Chapter 22

Paula's Case a Symbol

Shortly after that ***AP*** story ran, I got a call from ***Good Morning America*** asking if I would do a segment about juveniles on death row. I flew to New York and joined two others as guests of ***ABC's*** legal analyst, Arthur Miller.

After I had a chance to tell my story, we were asked the hypothetical question about how would I feel if a teenage terrorist destroyed a plane with hundreds of people aboard? Would I then want the death penalty? I said no—I was against the death penalty, but not only for juveniles, in all cases.

Stories about the death penalty and Paula's case continued to be in the news. Indiana State Representative Earline Rogers was successful in getting the Indiana legislature to change the age limit for which a person could be sentenced to de ath upwards to sixteen years old. But the legislature specifically stipulated that Paula Cooper was still under the old law; this new law would not affect her.

Lake County Criminal Court Judge Richard Conroy, who had replaced Judge Kimbrough on Paula's case, held a hearing on July 23 to see if there were any conflicts of interest in his taking over the Paula's case. Paula told Judge Conroy, "I just want to ask you to please keep an open mind. I know you haven't had this case long, but you seem to be fair so far. If you can tell me you'll be fair, that's good enough for me."

I was present for the hearing. Once again, the media told how in spite of all my attempts, I had not been able to visit Paula at the *Indiana Women's Prison* in Indianapolis. They told about the Bible I had for Paula and about how I hoped to visit with her while she was in Lake County because the rules were different. I was hoping to give her the Bible that I had taken with me to Italy. It now had hundreds of signatures.

When I went to the Lake County jail, I was told my name was not on the visitors' list. Monica Foster, Paula's attorney, said she would have Paula put my name on the list, so that I could visit the next day. But the next day, Paula was taken back to Indianapolis. The visit didn't happen.

In August of 1987, the ***AP*** reported that Paula Cooper would turn eighteen in prison without a birthday party. A group of forty Italians demonstrated outside the U.S. Embassy in Rome to mark her eighteenth birthday, and demanded clemency for her. Officials at the *Indiana Women's Prison* simply canceled any plans for a party.

Then Pope John Paul II came to the U.S. Without elaborating, he told reporters while en route to Miami that he might ask President Reagan about Paula. When the ***Associated Press*** story ran in the Gary ***Post Tribune,*** it carried the headline, **Pope, Reagan, May Talk of Cooper.** Pope John Paul II and Reagan met twice on September 10—but there was no indication of whether Paula had been mentioned or not

William Touchette, Paula's attorney, said, "There is widespread support for Paula's case also in other European countries, but it is nowhere like in Italy, where the organization has come from the very grassroots. The Catholic Church stresses the importance of the family and the upbringing of children. Italians realize how important parents are. When confronted with such parents as Paula's, they are troubled when they understand the background of her crime."

Reagan greets pope at Miami airport

Pope, Reagan may talk of Cooper

Gary ***Post Tribune*** September 11, 1987

Paolo Pietrosanti, an organizer of the demonstration at the U.S. Embassy in Italy and a member of the *Radical Party*, stated, "She is a symbol of those in the world who are fighting the death penalty."

Meanwhile, Lake County prosecutor Jack Crawford continued to defend his decision to seek the death penalty against Paula. When Paula pled guilty to the crime, Crawford refused to drop his death penalty request calling the crimes "terrible and senseless." The ***Vidette-Messenger*** repeated how Crawford had originally wanted the death sentence for all four girls involved in Nana's murder.

In September, the announcement came of the hearing for Paula's automatic appeal before the Indiana Supreme Court; it would be held in the spring. William Touchette and Monica Foster, Paula's lawyers, were hoping that Paula's "extremely, extremely violent" family life would lead the Indiana high court to overturn their client's death sentence.

"Her family life was just an abomination," Foster said. "When you grow up being nothing but tortured and beaten, it affects how you look at life. The state is asking that Paula Cooper be executed for what happened in one day of her life. The defense attorney's job is to show the rest of her life. Not to legally justify or excuse the crime, but to show why it happened."

Paula wrote to Pope John Paul II, according to his press secretary. The letter was hand delivered to the Pope in Detroit at the conclusion of his ten-day trip. She told the Pope she wanted to live and asked him to help her, "even if it's nothing but praying for me. Maybe someday I can contribute more to society than just time and help someone make a difference. You know it would help me also."

By now over one million signatures had been signed on Paula's behalf and that had given her hope.

Paula also told the Pope, "I feel that a lot of people have misunderstood me concerning remorse. I feel it every day because it's really hard for me to feel good about myself when I'm dealing with so much. But I believe if more people would look a little deeper maybe they will see what I really feel and how sorry I really am."

"She feels, I think, a spiritual closeness with the Pope," said Monica Foster, "because of the support she got in Italy and the way he interacts with young people."

Chapter 23

The Pope Gets Involved

On September 26, 1987, Pope John Paul II urged clemency for eighteen-year-old death row inmate Paula Cooper. Joaquim Navarro Valls, spokesman for the *Vatican*, said, "I affirm that the *Holy See* and the *Holy Father* have, through confidential channels, put forward their views, aimed at obtaining clemency for Paula Cooper, underlining the human and humanitarian aspects of the case."

The announcement followed reports earlier in the week that the Pontiff might have interceded on Cooper's behalf either during his visit with Vice President George Bush in Detroit or through the offices of Indianapolis archbishop, Monsignor Edward O'Meara.

Gov. Orr of Indiana, in a prepared statement, said, "I express my appreciation to the Pope for his concern for humanity, but until the judicial system has completed its work and the [Indiana] Supreme Court has taken action in the matter, it would be inappropriate for me to intercede."

Jack Crawford, the prosecuting attorney, immediately responded to the news of Papal intervention. He was totally against it. Crawford, himself a *Roman Catholic*, issued a delicately worded statement: "I respect the *Holy Father's* concern for human life and human rights. However, I am disappointed he has chosen to involve himself in a matter which is largely secular and legal rather than religious."

Then Crawford added, "Paula Cooper has been accorded every right guaranteed her by the constitution and laws of the state of Indiana. The appropriateness of her sentence should be determined by the courts, according to the law, removed from outside pressure and influences."

Gov. Robert Orr responded five days later. Orr said he appreciated the humanitarian instincts of Pope John Paul II and thousands of Italians who have asked him to spare Ms. Cooper from the state's electric chair. Orr repeated his plan not to intervene until the case has been reviewed in appellate courts. He added, "The Italians who have pleaded for clemency for teen-age murderer Paula R. Cooper ignore the brutal nature of her crime . . . I haven't heard directly from the Pope. If I do, I will respond by attempting to convey to him that I share his concern from a humanitarian standpoint, but I do have governmental responsibilities to carry out."

One week later, I was headed to Italy again. This time it was to Milan, for another TV program about Paula Cooper. Once again, ***RAI*** TV was sponsoring my trip.

Eliza Tesser, with ***RAI*** in New York, said, "***RAI*** also invited Lake County Prosecutor Jack Crawford to be on the show, but he didn't want to go." She said no one from Crawford's office was willing to go, and added that the show would also feature a prison interview with Paula Cooper via satellite from Indianapolis.

Meanwhile, I was still trying to visit Paula. An ***UPI (United Press International)*** reporter told me that the state would not grant my request because of my father's position. By this time, Paula and I had exchanged dozens of letters. I was quoted, "I'm doing this in Nana's honor. It's what I feel she would want me to do. I feel she was a martyr for Christ. She was serving Jesus Christ by letting Paula and her friends come into her home for Bible lessons."

When I got to Milan, it was a beautiful fall day. Unlike my last extended trip to Italy, this one would last only twenty-four hours. The TV program was called ***Giallo***. The host was a well-known personality, Enzo Tortora. When Paula was interviewed on satellite from her jail cell in Indianapolis, she expressed shock by the concern shown for her by thousands of Italians and Pope John Paul II "because all my life nobody cared for me."

A telephone survey during the Milan program showed 71% opposed to Paula being executed; 12% of the viewers said Paula should die in the electric chair; the rest said they didn't know.

After the Papal support for clemency and my second visit to Italy, a new round of letters to the newspaper began.

Carey Robertson of Crown Point wrote:

> I do have a suggestion for [Italians]. If she means so much to them, give her to them. Let them feed her, clothe her, and shelter her. Ruth Pelke and her family deserve justice, and in my opinion that comes from lethal injection or volts of electricity (both work too fast for my liking).

The Rev. William V. Spiffy of Aurora, New York, wrote:

> As a Roman Catholic priest, originally from Whiting, Indiana, and now living in upstate New York, I find it difficult for Crawford, who is also Roman Catholic, to say that "(the Pope) has chosen to involve himself in a matter which is largely secular and legal rather than religious." Crawford should know that the bishops of the United States, as well as the bishops of Indiana and every major religious leadership body of Christian and Jewish faiths, have spoken out against the death penalty as a matter of public policy influenced by moral and religious values. When people's lives are involved, so are morality, religion, and ultimately, the church.
>
> What Paula Cooper was convicted of doing was, without doubt reprehensible and evil. What the state of Indiana wants to do is just as reprehensible and evil.

Don J. Baron of Crown Point wrote:

> It seems almost ludicrous the Pope would take a special interest in Paula Cooper.
>
> With all due respect, I suggest the pontiff venture a step further and put his money where his mouth is. Taxpayers would appreciate relief from the $30,000 annual cost of maintaining Cooper in A1 condition. 'Do not pass go but proceed directly to the Vatican,' please.

The main juvenile case in the U.S. courts at this time was Wayne Thompson. He was fifteen when arrested with three other men for the 1983 shooting and stabbing of Charles Keene in Amber, Oklahoma.

Thompson was now on Oklahoma's death row, and his case was before the U.S. Supreme Court. The general argument was that executing juveniles is cruel and inhumane punishment, based on interpretations of the Eighth Amendment of the U.S. Constitution.

Victor Streib of Ohio, a co-counsel for young Thompson, had just written a book called ***Death Penalty for Juveniles.*** The day that Streib's book was released was the very same day Thompson's hearing was held before the U.S. Supreme Court.

And also on that very same day (November 9, 1987) ***USA TODAY*** published an **"*Inquiry*"** on the topic of teenage killers. In his lengthy interview for this feature, Streib was asked, "How did Paula Cooper, at age fifteen, convicted of murdering an elderly Sunday school teacher, become such an international case?" He said:

> When they found out that we had a 15-year-old on death row and that Indiana at the time had a minimum age of 10, a lot of Western European countries began to say, "Geez, how barbaric are you over there? You would put 10-year-olds on death row, and you've actually got a 15-year-old on death row.

When ***USA TODAY*** asked, "Do you think we're too hard on juvenile murderers?" Streib replied:

> Some would paint Paula Cooper, or maybe other juvenile murderers as saints, who have simply had their hand in the cookie jar. That's wrong. They're all serious offenders who've committed very serious crimes.

USA TODAY asked, "On the whole, does society gain or lose from executing its youth?"

> It just doesn't work. And we ought to do away with it. That's before you get to the fact that it costs three or four times as much to execute one of these kids as it would to keep him in prison for life. You can put somebody in prison for life, or 40 years, for about $800,000. That assumes $20,000 a year to keep them in prison. The average cost of an execution is about $3 million.

Streib then explained:

> It's primarily because the death penalty trial takes three or four times as long as a case in which the death penalty is not involved, simply because it's more complicated. The appeals will take 10 to 12 years, through lots of courts, lots of attorneys, while a non-death penalty case usually is not appealed more than once or twice.

Along with its lengthy article, ***USA TODAY*** ran the beautiful picture of Nana that has become so dear to me. There were also pictures of Paula and author Victor Streib. The issue of juveniles and the death penalty was not going to go away. It had been a year since my night in the crane. An unbelievable year.

Chapter 24

No Visit with Paula

When I met Mike Sutherlin, the Indianapolis attorney who did volunteer work for *Amnesty International*, he asked me to document my unsuccessful efforts to visit with Paula. I wrote Mike a very long letter that detailed my futile attempts to get permission to visit Paula.

The no-visit battle continued when Paula's attorney, William Touchette, called me to say that Father Vito was coming from Italy for a visit with Paula. Touchette suggested I ask permission to accompany Father Vito. *Indiana Women's Prison* Superintendent Trigg again turned me down.

So I wrote Indiana Governor Orr to ask his help. Within weeks, I had a letter from the Indiana Department of Corrections to say my case would be reviewed.

When I received a call from Larry Levenson, a reporter with ***UPI***, I was told the real reason why Supt. Trigg had turned me down again: members of my family looked unfavorably toward the idea of my visiting Paula. I later found that my father and his two sisters had been called by the Indiana Department of Corrections. One aunt felt it was OK for me to visit, but my father and the other aunt did not.

Then I contacted Indiana State Senator William Costas. I eventually found out that the IDOC (Indiana Department of Corrections) felt that a visit by me would cause them embarrassment, because the whole case was such a politically sensitive issue. The attention Paula's case was receiving in Italy was no doubt an embarrassment. But Senator Costas felt that if I would have a personal meeting with prisons Commissioner Shettle, a visit would be possible. Jean Thurman, president of *Project Equality and Justice* wrote state Commissioner Shettle a letter on my behalf. It was never answered.

After several calls to Commissioner Shettle ("he's out for lunch" and "he's out for the day" and "out of town till after the weekend"), I finally spoke with an IDOC representative, Mr. Vaughn Overstreet. He summarized the IDOC position for refusing me a visit with Paula: First, I was not a lawyer and therefore couldn't help Paula. Second, a visit would not be in the best interests of the institution. But when we talked further, a third idea surfaced: He suggested that I had perhaps become "an international celebrity" through the case. Noting that my expenses to Italy had been paid, he said, "See what I mean?"

My next call to Commissioner Shettle's office was the final one. The secretary informed me that my case was settled, the IDOC position was as Overstreet had stated and further discussion was closed.

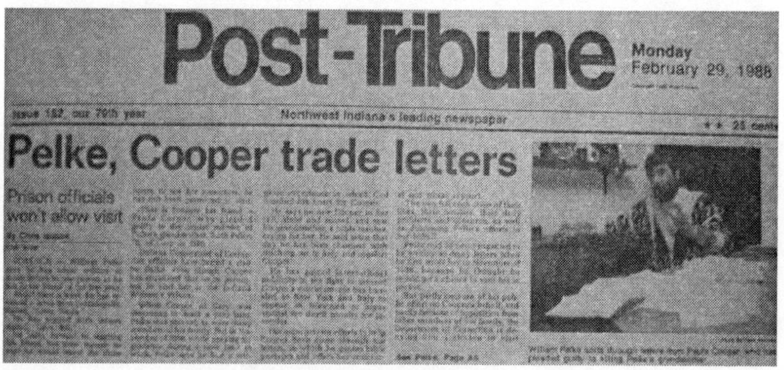

Post-Tribune

Monday
February 29, 1988

Northwest Indiana's leading newspaper

Pelke, Cooper trade letters

Prison officials won't allow visit

Gary ***Post Tribune*** February 29, 1988

Then Chris Isidore, a reporter for the Gary ***Post-Tribune*** contacted me to do a story on why I was not allowed to visit. When his article appeared, it was headlined "**Pelke, Cooper Trade**

Letters." Nine months earlier, when I went to Rome, the frequent letters between Paula and me were reported as routine fact, and raised no questions. Now it was the headline.

The reporter summarized my experience in the crane, my attempts to prevent Paula's execution, my international interest against death penalty for juveniles, and my letters offering Paula emotional and moral support and how they often included Bible passages.

Then came the real reason for the story. It chronicled my attempts to visit with Paula. I expected some negatives in the article, but was surprised to the extent. Vaughn Overstreet, executive assistant to the Indiana Department of Corrections was quoted:

> "[Pelke] is using this to forward his own interests . . . two free trips to Italy where Cooper's case has attracted great attention. [These trips to Italy] suggest that there are benefits from talking to Paula Cooper other than effecting a reconciliation between family and perpetrator . . . ."

He also cited objections to the visit from members of my family. My aunt Fran was quoted as saying.

> "I don't want to get into any of Bill's monkey business. The family is opposed to it . . . . He's getting a lot of free publicity . . . ."

And then came the biggest pisser of all when Overstreet said,

> "If something would go wrong [during a visit], if he's not emotionally stable, it would be the department's responsibility . . . ."

Questioning my emotional stability on the front page of the newspaper was to me a "low blow." I wondered why the state of Indiana did not question my emotional stability when I was drafted into the U.S. Army and sent to Viet Nam where I carried an *M-16* rifle as a light-weapons' infantryman.

And I was a grandfather myself at this point, yet they were making a big deal that my parents and an aunt did not want me to do something. It also struck me as ironic that they were going to use my two trips to Italy as a reason I couldn't visit, even though I had been attempting to visit with Paula for six months before I was offered the first trip.

But some fairness soon followed. In her letter to the ***Post Tribune***'s ***"Voice of the People,"*** Cuzzin' Judi Weyhe wrote:

> [Your reporter] interviewed family members who stated that the family did not support Bill and accused him of trying to get publicity for himself.
>
> Ruth Pelke was my grandmother, too, and I support Bill in his efforts to save Paula Cooper from the death penalty, and in no way support accusations that he is self-serving.
>
> Paula Cooper's death would accomplish nothing, but Bill's message of love and forgiveness speaks loudly to us all. I have seen his message of forgiveness touch other lives. I do believe my grandmother forgave Paula even while she was dying. Bill is motivated by his memories of a loving, Christ-like grandmother to save Cooper from the death penalty.

God Bless Cuzzin Judi!

Chapter 25

Indianapolis, Albany, and *S.O.L.A.C.E.*

In May, I was invited to the Indiana capitol, Indianapolis, to participate in a press conference about Paula's case. Father Vito Bracone came from Rome to visit Paula and he was hoping to visit with Indiana Gov. Robert D. Orr. Although Orr was out of town with a previous commitment, Father Bracone and members of the human rights group *Amnesty International* delivered to the governor's office petitions with nearly two million Italian signatures urging Orr to commute Paula Cooper's death sentence.

At the press conference, Father Vito talked about his visit with Paula. He said that they talked mainly about her family and what she was trying to do with her life. "I see a lot of changes in her life. I think she feels much remorse for the crime she committed."

Father Vito also told the press he was unsure why Paula's case has attracted so many Italian supporters. They believe the U.S. government is violating international human rights agreements by instituting the death penalty for juveniles. Father Vito said that youth groups involved in human rights issues in Italy began the petition drive for Paula in November of 1986 after hearing about her case. As news spread about the petition drive, signatures were collected through churches, schools, universities and media announcements.

Michel K. Sutherlin, spokesman for the local *Amnesty International* group, reported that they would try to get the 1989

Indiana General Assembly to repeal the state's death penalty law. "It's not that we have no sympathy for the victims, but you don't rape rapists and you don't burn arsonists."

Then I had a chance to tell my story at the press conference. Afterward, Magdaleno Rose-Avila approached Father Vito and me and introduced himself. He was director of *Amnesty International USA*'s death penalty program. He told us of *Amnesty*'s campaign to abolish the death penalty; he asked Father Vito and me if we would like to attend *Amnesty's Annual General Meeting (AGM)* the very next weekend in Atlanta, Georgia.

He said we could lead the anti-death penalty march. He said that *Amnesty* would pay the expenses. Father Vito and I looked at each other and smiled—we began to plan the trip. Although I didn't recognize Magdaleno's name at the time, he was the one from *Amnesty* who had written me after I was on ***Good Morning America.***

With this invitation to Atlanta, I could feel God's hand moving in my life. I felt this conference would be a very important part of the whole scheme of life as I continued on my journey. Life was great—except for my relationship with Judy. We had broken up again, and each time seemed so much harder than the time before. I moved to the other side of town—it was too difficult to live in the duplex next door to her. My heart broke whenever I saw her with someone else. But I wasn't about to let true love go without a struggle.

Shortly thereafter, Judy graduated from nursing school, the first person in her family to ever earn a college degree. Her mother invited me to the all-day open house, but Judy had suggested it would be best to come in the daytime and then leave with her kids, so all would avoid meeting "Mike" in the evening.

But the "open house" was the same day as the *Amnesty* march in Atlanta. I knew I had to take the journey to Atlanta, and hoped that whatever relationship with Judy was left could weather the situation. Since I was convinced I was on a mission for God, I felt He would work out the problems. I put my trust and faith in Him.

When Father Vito and I went to Atlanta, we led the march and addressed the rally. I met grass roots anti-death penalty activists from *Amnesty* groups around the country, including a girl named Elissa. At the closing dance on Saturday night, Elissa informed me that her sister had been killed a few years earlier but she didn't want anyone to get the death penalty for her sister's murder. Our stories had a lot in common. We had a long conversation as we shared a ride to the airport on Sunday when the conference ended.

Bill and Father Vito lead the *Amnesty International* march in Atlanta, Georgia 1988

When I got back to Indiana, Elissa called to ask if I would like to help start an organization of murder victim's family members who were opposed to the death penalty. Then I remembered the words of Anna Guaita, the reporter from Rome. She had said that I should start an organization of victim's family members against the death penalty! I knew I wasn't qualified to start one, but sure would be happy to help someone else do it. I had a one-week vacation coming up in August, so I set up a meeting with Elissa during that time. I agreed to drive to Elissa's house in Albany, New York. And she agreed to put together a meeting of people she thought would have good ideas and be supportive of such an organization.

Cuzzin' Judi said she would like to go with me to Albany for the meeting. We planned a route that would take us through Detroit to see my sister Dottie and her family, then through Canada, stopping at Niagara Falls, then to Albany.

It was a long but wonderful journey for us. It seemed like a spiritual voyage, as we looked forward to the meeting in Albany. Somehow, we both knew it was very important.

I knew that some of the leading anti-death penalty activists in the country would be there in Albany and I was curious to find out what I could do in the movement. I wanted to be used; I felt I had something to offer.

Leigh Dingerson was at the Albany meeting. She was Executive Director of *NCADP*, the *National Coalition to Abolish the Death Penalty*. The *NCADP* is the major organization in the country whose sole purpose is abolition of the death penalty. Leigh's presence gave a real strength to our meeting.

Marie Deans was also at the Albany meeting. Marie was with the *Southern Coalition of Jails and Prisons*, a group providing resources for death row inmates in seven southern states.

When Elissa had invited Leigh Dingerson of the *NCADP* to the Albany meeting, Leigh had told her about Marie. Marie had started a small support group of murder victim family members who were against the death penalty. Her mother-in-law Penny had been killed and Marie was surprised that so many people expected her to want the death penalty for the killer. She realized there were other victim family members who felt as she did and realized the need for a support group. This informal group traded names and wrote letters to each other.

Most of the members were from Virginia but there were a few others from across the country. The group was started back in the '70s

Elissa called Marie and asked her to come from Virginia to the meeting in Albany. Elissa and I chipped in the money for Marie to fly to New York. We knew it would be important for her to be there.

And Jonathon Gradess was at the Albany meeting. Jonathon

was the director of the New York Public Defenders Office. He was also involved with the *NCADP* and had a great reputation in the abolition movement. We knew we could count on Jonathon's wisdom and good advice.

And Pat Bane was at the Albany meeting. Pat, a librarian from Syracuse, New York, had been friends with Marie, and was in her victims group. Pat's Uncle Ashley was killed in the 1950s. Pat had always been supportive of Marie's idea of wanting murder victims' families involved in the abolition movement.

Also in Albany was Camille, a lady from Atlanta, Georgia. Her son was one of those killed during the notorious string of child murders in Atlanta. Camille felt that the wrong person had been arrested for her son's murder, and became an outspoken opponent of the death penalty.

Amnesty International, Pax Christi and several church denominations were also represented at the Albany meeting. Cuzzin' Judi had a great interest in what was taking place, but wanted to observe from a distance. She chose the kitchen for her spot to observe. She volunteered to cook and cater for our two days of meetings. She wanted to make sure we were all well fed.

Since Elissa had called the Albany meeting, she started the program. After introductions all around, she shared the agenda for the weekend.

We spent two wonderful days of planning, plotting the future, and making decisions. There was complete agreement in the group that within the abolition movement, there needed to be a strong and active organization made up of murder victims' family members. That was why we all came to the meeting.

Marie talked to us about her group, *Murder Victims Families for Reconciliation*. She wanted it to grow, but told us she just hadn't had the time or money to do what it would take. Almost every second of her time was already spent trying to keep the *Virginia Coalition of Jails and Prisons* from going under. It was her job to raise money and gather the resources to help those on death row with the latter stages of their legal appeals. That took all of her time and effort. So Marie welcomed with open arms any new people who wanted a viable organization.

Marie had a list of names and some newspaper articles with stories of murder victims' family members talking about forgiveness, reconciliation, and opposition to the death penalty. In her collection of articles, she had the ***AP*** interview of my story that I liked so well. The article had made it around the country.

Marie was willing to place her organization into new hands, in hopes that its work could be better carried out. The Albany group chose Elissa and Camille to be responsible for running the organization.

The last major item we had to deal with was the name for the organization. To someone unfamiliar with the name, *Murder Victims Families for Reconciliation* was a bit much to handle. Although Marie originally wanted to stay with that name, she and everyone one else liked Elissa's suggestion: ***S.O.L.A.C.E.***

The name *SOLACE* was the exact feeling we wished to get out to family members. The letters for ***SOLACE*** stood for ***S****urvivors* ***O****f* ***L****oss* ***A****gainst* ***C****apital* ***E****xecutions.* Marie smiled and said she was sure her members wouldn't mind that name change.

We all thought this was great. *SOLACE*—murder victims' family members uniting for a strong stand against the death penalty. With *Amnesty International*, the *NCADP* and other groups helping us, it sounded like a "can't miss" thing. Elissa and Camille said they would take on the responsibility we were asking of them. I pledged to do all I could.

Cuzzin' Judi and I headed back to Indiana. It had been a wonderful time for both of us. Instead of stopping halfway home and getting a hotel, I just kept driving. I was wide-awake and "pumped." And Cuzzin' Judi wanted to get back for work. I just kept driving and thinking about all that had happened in Albany.

After dropping Cuzzin' Judi off in the wee hours of the morning, I drove the last leg home. When I walked into my apartment, I played my answering machine for the first time in days. The first message was, "Mr. Pelke, this is the ***Oprah Winfrey Show***. We would like to talk with you about being on a show we are planning on the subject of forgiveness. Would you be willing to come talk about forgiving Paula Cooper? If you are interested, please call as soon as possible."

It was 6:00 A.M. and I knew Wayne would be up. I called him, and then played the taped message from ***The Oprah Show***. When he heard it, he exclaimed, "Hallelujah, Amen—it's a miracle." He remembered the discussion we had had with Judy. We had all agreed that if Oprah ever called, yes, it would be a miracle!

Imagine, if you will, a tear or two in my eyes.

Chapter 26

The Oprah Show. . . and Judy

Several days later, Cuzzin' Judi and I drove to Chicago for ***The Oprah Show***. I had not been praying for this, but it sure was an answer in part to my prayers and thoughts in the crane on the night of November 2, 1986. Oprah's show was called "**Forgiving the Unforgivable.**"

The guest for the first segment of ***The Oprah Show*** was "Mother Henry," from Gary, Indiana. She told the amazing story of her son's death and how she had befriended the murderer.

In the second segment, there were three new guests. Oprah started talking with the young lady sitting next to me, SueZann Bosler. SueZann and her father, the Rev. Billy Bosler, had come home from an afternoon of Christmas shopping. When Rev. Bosler answered a knock on the door, a person entered, attacking her father with a knife. SueZann came from the back of the house and saw what was happening. She came toward the attacker to help her father, who had fallen to the floor. The man then stabbed her several times in the back, and she fell to the floor. As her father tried to get up to help her, the attacker began stabbing him again. As SueZann struggled to her feet, the attacker stabbed her in the head three times.

SueZann's father died. She was left for dead, but miraculously survived.

SueZann told Oprah how the perpetrator, James Campbell, was arrested seven days later, and eventually convicted. Although SueZann's testimony in court helped convict Campbell, she said she didn't want him executed. The state of Florida sentenced him to death anyway.

Then she started talking about forgiveness, and how her father was against the death penalty. In fact, he had once told her that if anyone were ever to kill him, he would not want the killer put to death.

During SueZann's interview with Oprah, several pictures were shown on the monitor. One was a smiling Reverend Billy Bosler, one of SueZann with her dad, and several of the aftermaths of the attack on SueZann. The stitches on her baldhead looked like a horseshoe had been woven into her cranium. The tip of the knife had broken off in her brain, and she now has a plastic plate implanted in her skull because it had been fractured into so many pieces.

There was also a picture of James Bernard Campbell.

Reverend Billy Bosler's favorite song, *"Let there be peace, and let it begin with me,"* had become SueZann's crusade song. I was deeply impressed by this girl and her message of love, forgiveness, and peace.

Then it was my turn. After hearing SueZann's story, I almost forgot I had a story. But when Oprah asked me about Nana, I had a chance to talk about Nana and the kind of person she was. I told how she loved to tell young children stories from the Bible.

I told Oprah how Nana was killed and told about Paula Cooper being sentenced to death. I told about November 2, 1986, my night in the crane. Oprah made a few comments about forgiveness. She talked about how it sets you free and gives you peace.

I had brought pictures with me, too. On the monitor they showed a picture of Nana with Granddad, my mom and dad, my sister and her family, my ex-wife Mary and me with our three children. They also had a picture of Paula and of the memorial Bible I had brought with me.

The Pelke Family 1983

Others who had stories of forgiveness joined us. For example, a mother whose son was killed by a drunk driver told how she had comes to terms with the incident and eventually forgave and befriended the driver. She told how they now travel as a team and speak to high school students about drinking and driving.

Then Oprah said that since this program was about forgiveness, it would only be fair to give some time to those who said they would never forgive.

Two ladies told their stories. One story involved a death of a daughter; the other involved severe physical injuries. Both women said they would never forgive the perpetrator. And both told how miserable their lives have been ever since the incidents happened.

All of the stories presented that day were tragic. But I felt most sorry for the two ladies who could not forgive.

Judy didn't see ***The Oprah Show***. Judy was now working at a hospital and I had really hoped she would walk into a patient's room, glance at the television set, and see me on the show. I figured if she did, it would boggle her mind. As it turned out, her sister Carol saw the program and called Judy. Being on the program was a reassurance to me that God was still on the throne.

But Judy and I were not happening. I talked with her on the phone a few more times in the following weeks, and whenever she asked how I was doing, I always let her know how torn up and broken-hearted I was. Finally, I told her I needed to get over her and that it would be best for me if we didn't talk anymore. It hurt too much.

Two weeks later, Judy's ten-year-old daughter, Taniya, called to talk about a minor problem she was having at school. She had known me since she was three, and knew how I felt about her mother. This was Taniya's way of letting me know she missed me.

A few hours later, Judy called to talk about Taniya's call. Then we talked about her boys, Jamie and Kennie. And we admitted we missed each other . . . and talked for several hours more. Before the evening was over, she came over to see me. Not only did we agree to get back together again that night—we decided to get married within the next six months!

It just so happened that a television team from Italy was in Northwest Indiana making a documentary about the Paula Cooper case that weekend. When the leader of the group heard Judy and I just gotten engaged, he suggested we take our honeymoon in Italy when we did get married. He told us we could have free use of his apartment.

When Judy and I were married, we took him up on his offer. When we arrived in Italy, Father Vito and Italo once again befriended us—we had to buy only four meals during the entire two weeks in Italy! I was also involved in media events dealing with the Paula Cooper case during the honeymoon.

God was wonderful; life was good. Now if only they would take Paula Cooper off death row. At least Judy had come to the point where the fact that I forgave Paula was no big deal. She realized that it had helped me heal. Although she still thought I was crazy for trying to save Paula's life, she considered it my business and let me do what I had to do. I thanked God for that.

Chapter 27

Court Appeal . . . and Overturn

In early 1989, the new governor of Indiana, Evan Bayh, said he would not consider intervening in the Paula Cooper case until the appeal had run its course. Former Governor Orr had also said it would be inappropriate for him to intervene while Cooper's case was still under appeal.

The oral arguments for the appeals case were to be heard before the Indiana Supreme Court on March 1, 1989. I was invited to come to Indianapolis for the hearing by the television program ***PM Magazine***. They were doing a story about juveniles and the death penalty and wanted to interview me. I had intended to go to the hearing anyway. Father Bracone also came back to Indianapolis for the hearing and also was to be interviewed by ***PM Magazine.***

The Indiana State Hall of Justice in Indianapolis, was packed with an audience of reporters, students, and others wanting Paula taken off death row. Seven members of "*Thou Shall Not Kill*," Father Vito's group, were there. Over two million signatures had now been gathered asking the state of Indiana not to kill Paula.

I knew that William Touchette was going to be there as Paula's attorney, but was surprised when I found out that Victor Streib was going to be Paula's second attorney. The attorneys told the media they saw a glimmer of hope that the Indiana Supreme Court might spare Paula's life.

Victor Streib made a great presentation why Paula should not be executed. I didn't see how the five Indiana State Supreme Court justices could disagree with him.

Supreme Court Justice Brent Dickson openly questioned whether Paula was a victim of legislative discrimination under the new state law that protected every young teenager from the death penalty—except her. In their presentations, both Touchette and Streib twice told the justices, "Indiana has never executed anyone as young as Paula Cooper."

They also argued that the United States Supreme Court has almost forbidden the execution of anyone before age sixteen.

Then State Deputy General Gary Secrest argued for the state of Indiana. He said, "The legislature solved the age problem last year by passing a law setting the minimum age at sixteen." He said, "Cooper was excluded from that protection because the law doesn't affect anyone who committed a murder before last year."

Justice Dickson questioned how they could exclude the very person whose predicament inspired the new law.

When the day of oral arguments ended, the five justices said they would deliberate and issue a decision in the near future.

During the four-month wait for their decision, I attended the *AGM* of *Amnesty International.* It was held in Chicago, and the work of *S.O.L.A.C.E.* was highlighted. SueZann Bosler was there; so was Elissa.

At a *SOLACE* event in Boston a few months earlier, there had been a special showing of the documentary film, ***The Thin Blue Line.*** It was the story of Randall Dale Adams, the wrongfully convicted Texan who came within seventy-two hours of being executed. Sam Reese Sheppard was at that event and he heard about *SOLACE.* He joined with us at the annual *Amnesty* meeting in Chicago.

Those who were old enough could remember the sensational 1950s trial of Dr. Sam Sheppard. When Sam Reese Sheppard was seven years old, his father was arrested and convicted of the murder of his wife. The state of Ohio sought the death penalty, but the jury sentenced him to life. After Dr. Sam had spent ten years in jail, F. Lee Bailey, a brilliant young attorney, took on the case. The U. S. Supreme Court declared the sensationalized trial a mockery of justice and ordered a new trial for Dr. Sam. In the second trial, Dr. Sam Sheppard was found not guilty; however, there were still a few people in the Cleveland area who felt he was guilty. After staying out of the public eye for many years, when Sam learned of *SOLACE*, he decided to step forward and get involved with the issue of the death penalty. Sam also dedicated himself to proving his father's innocence and finding his mother's killer. Sam's father died a few years after his release from prison.

It was great to meet Sam and I knew that his well-known family name would help *SOLACE*.

Also during the summer of waiting for the court's decision on Paula's death sentence, the May 30, 1989, issue of ***Woman's Day*** magazine ran an article **Should We Execute Kids Who Kill?** The first page headlined, **Paula Cooper Never Had a Chance**. It showed a stamp-sized picture of the black-and-white mug shot of Paula when she was first arrested. There were two larger pictures of Paula in color showing her as a beautiful young woman. In bold print it said, **Paula Cooper, now 19, is on death row for a murder she committed at 15.**

The second page of the feature article had a black-and-white picture of Nana, headed by the bold caption **Ruth Pelke Never Had a Chance.**

The article included several quotes from Paula that I had never heard or read before. She said, "One day my mother be nice, the next day she be angry and then the next day she be real strange-acting." Paula also said that although his father beat her, it was her mother who egged him on. "I'm not really sure why she get mad at us. We did everything we was supposed to do, but it just wasn't never enough for her . . . She get mad at us and he'd beat us. 'Be a man,' she'd tell him. 'Take care of it' she'd say. And he took care of it."

She also said he beat them with an air-conditioner extension cord. "He'd triple it up and go to work. It got to the point I was so used to it I didn't cry any more."

The article also said that when Paula was fourteen, she was held and interviewed briefly at a mental institution. Paula said, "This woman, she asked me have I ever considered committing suicide and I told her, 'Yeah,' I say, 'everybody consider committing suicide.'" Paula was then released without treatment.

The article also reported Victor Streib as saying, "Recent trends show the American public is becoming more and more uneasy with the idea of executing young people as a matter of public policy."

And the American Bar Association stated, "The spectacle of our society seeking legal vengeance through the execution of children should not be countenanced by the ABA."

In the ***Woman's Day*** article, former South Carolina State Representative D.L. Aydlette stated, "If a person is capable of committing a heinous murder, I don't care if he's twelve or eighty-two."

Jack Crawford, the man who had prosecuted Paula said, "It would be difficult for me to imagine a twelve-year-old able to form the necessary intent. Paula is that rare exception of a fifteen-year-old who knew what she was doing."

The ***Woman's Day*** article also stated, "Those who resent paying tax dollars to maintain killers for decades may be surprised to learn that depending on the jurisdiction, it costs four to ten times more to execute a killer because of all those appeals than it does to maintain them."

The article closed by quoting me as saying, "If the trial were today, I would testify that my grandmother was a very forgiving person. I am definitely convinced that my grandmother would not want Paula Cooper on death row."

On July13, 1989, I was in the foreman's office at the steel mill. As I was talking on the phone with my wife Judy, she said there was a beep on "call waiting." I held, and when Judy came back on the line she said it was a man from the ***Associated Press*** who wanted to talk with me. So I told her to give him my work number and I hung up.

A few minutes later, the phone rang. The man identified himself as being from the ***AP*** and said, "Mr. Pelke, the Indiana Supreme Court, on the automatic appeal for Paula Cooper, has set aside her death sentence and given her a sixty-year prison term." He asked for my comment.

The first words out of my mouth were "Praise the Lord!" Then I then went on to talk about love, compassion and forgiveness. I talked about Nana and her love for Jesus. I talked about how glad I was that Paula would not be executed. I told how I was glad I would not have to keep my commitment of walking hand in hand with her to the electric chair.

I called Judy back and told her the news. I told her if anyone else called to have them call me at work. In the next hour and a half, I had more than a dozen calls from around the country. All were media people, except Marge Byler, the *Amnesty International* mid-west regional director in Chicago. She had heard the news and just wanted to let me know how happy she was for me and for Paula.

The rest of the calls were from a half-dozen television stations, several radio stations and some newspapers. They got the same story each time. "Praise the Lord!" was always my first comment. I went on to talk about love, compassion and forgiveness. I talked about Nana and her faith in Jesus. It was a great day!

The next day, the newspapers around the world were filled with the story of Paula Cooper's death sentence being overturned. The Gary ***Post-Tribune*** articles took over half of the front page with the heading **Ruling Spares Cooper.** There was a colorful picture of Paula taken in 1988, and a black-and-white picture of her mug shot from 1985. There was the black-and-white picture of Nana they always used, plus a picture of Father Germano Greganti with Father Vito Bracone and Paula taken during a visit, and a picture of the late Judge Kimbrough.

There was a time line showing a history of the case along with several other articles. One was titled **Decision Prompts Joy, Disappointment** and another was titled **60-Year Term Set**.

Post-Tribune

Ruling spares Cooper

A history of the case

60-year term set

Decision prompts joy, disappointment

Gary *Post Tribune* July 14, 1989

Indiana Chief Justice Randall Shepard had written the unanimous decision (5-0) that spared Paula's life. He wrote, "Now that Indiana law establishes 16 as the minimum age for the imposition of the death penalty, Paula Cooper would be both the first and last person to be executed in Indiana for a crime committed at the age of 15. This makes her sentence unique and disproportionate to any other sentence for the same crime."

The Indiana Supreme Court also said that a U.S. Supreme Court decision in the 1988 Oklahoma case of Wayne Thompson showed that four justices believe "It is cruel and unusual punishment to execute a juvenile convicted of a murder committed before the age of 16. One justice believed it was unconstitutional to execute a juvenile unless the death penalty itself identifies a minimum age for the death penalty."

Indiana Attorney General Linley Pearson, who represented the state, said, "The court's ruling effectively quashes any appeal efforts to return Cooper to Indiana's death row. It would be a futile effort, I'm sure. Because the Indiana Supreme Court ruled on constitutional grounds, it would be impossible for anyone to be executed under the age of 16 in this state. In a sense, they foreclosed the ability of the state to even take the Paula Cooper case to the [U.S.] Supreme Court. If they had not decided on Indiana constitutional grounds and just used the federal, I'm sure the [U.S.] Supreme Court would have been very interested in taking that case," said Pearson.

Jack Crawford, former Lake County Prosecutor, who was now the new Hoosier Lottery director made no comment. A spokesperson from his office said, "He won't talk about it."

Lake County Prosecutor Jon E. DeGuilio expressed his disappointment and considered appealing the ruling, although he admitted it was unlikely the court would reverse a 5-0 decision.

Neither former Governor Robert Orr, nor his successor, Evan Bayh, issued an opinion on Paula's case. Bayh's wife, Susan, told a group of Merrillville high school students that her husband favored the death penalty for Cooper, but later Gov. Bayh said his wife had misrepresented his position.

Prison superintendent Clarence Trigg reported, "It was a joyous occasion for Paula; she jumped up and down." He also stated that she didn't want to talk to anybody until she talked to her attorneys. She was just overjoyed about the decision.

Monica Foster spoke on Paula's behalf. "The superintendent of the prison was the first to tell her. As I understand it, she wasn't even able to speak to him. I got there about twenty minutes after that, and it was just very emotional—she was crying and shaking. Monica said Paula realized she must serve thirty years of the sixty-year sentence before she would be eligible for parole.

Monica said, "She accepts that. She realizes she needs to be punished for what she did, and she's always been very remorseful about it . . . I think she wants to get on with her life, even though she knows that will be within the confines of the Woman's Prison. One of the things she's anxious to do is start going to classes. As a member of the general prison population—once she's off death row—she'll be able to attend classes, and she's real excited about that."

Monica told reporters, "She wants to try, as best as she can, to make up for the mistakes that she's made."

William Touchette, Paula's lawyer, said, "We won! I'm elated, relieved. I'm very happy for Paula. I'm just so relieved that this is over. It was not an easy case. She's particularly happy to get off death row. She's been in isolation for over three years. She was able to go out only twice last summer. She's very happy the court did this and is looking forward to living the life of a normal prisoner. We never questioned her guilt. We knew all along she was going to be punished and deserved to be punished. We were attacking the death penalty."

Kevin Relphorde, the Gary lawyer who had represented Paula at her trial three years earlier, said, "I'm elated. It doesn't mean they are slapping her wrist and saying she can go home. She'll be there at least thirty years. I never did think the death penalty was in order."

Relphorde also stated that he wished Judge Kimbrough were alive to enjoy the decision. "This is something that didn't sit well with him. He took it to his grave . . . I wish he was here to see it."

Interestingly, both Touchette and DeGuilio agreed on one thing: they both doubted that the enormous amount of American and Italian publicity had directly influenced the Indiana appellate justices. Touchette pointed out that the publicity did help inspire the change in state law, which was a keystone in the states reversal. Touchette also said, "The international pressure we've seen in Paula's case is the kind of thing that influences state legislatures, but not courts."

Paula's case had become an international *cause celebre*. The next day, the Indiana Supreme Court decision was the top story on Italian TV and radio, because Paula Cooper had become a symbol of the international struggle against the death penalty.

USA Today in a one-paragraph story said in part: " . . . Cooper had the backing of Pope John Paul II and William Pelke, the victim's grandson. 'That's what my grandmother would have wanted,' Pelke said. 'She opposed killing.'"

Whoever would have thought, the Pope and Pelke in the same sentence?

The Chicago ***SUN TIMES*** quoted me as saying I was "very happy that Paula would not face the electric chair. I believe it would have been morally wrong to have taken her life. Defending Cooper was something my grandmother would have wanted me to do."

That's basically what got me involved. I felt my grandmother would have had love and compassion for Paula. I, along with several members of my family, believed that my grandmother had forgiven Paula even as she was lying on the floor dying.

CHAPTER 28

New Letters, New Directions

Yet another round of letters to the editor began! Virginia Williams of Valparaiso wrote in part:

> I am so appalled with what I read in the newspaper . . . . Oh, yes, she had a good lawyer and using the Lord always helps, but does it really? One of the commandments is "Thou shall not kill." I say a person who doesn't want death shouldn't go against the commandments. Life without parole is too good for her.
>
> . . . . Why not let Richard Speck and John Hinckley free, or why punish or kill anyone. How does one decide who to fry and who not to?

Arthur Lemke from Hammond wrote another letter. This time he said:

> The law should be set, and once it is set then it should be carried out, no matter what the age. It is time we stop babying these punks and show them that the law is for them and jail is for them no matter if they're 15 or 17, because if the laws are not enforced, there will be a lot of punks getting their heads shot off.

> The high courts have gone too far when they can say a killer should not die in the chair and that it's OK to burn the flag. This makes me think we need a new Supreme Court.

Ned J. Marich of Portage also disagreed with the ***Post-Tribune's*** editorial and Indiana's Supreme Court decision. He wrote:

> If we are talking about the constitutionality of our laws, then isn't it only proper to ask what kind of "constitutional" protection under the law did Pelke, and other innocent victims like her, have?
>
> .... The wheels of justice turn in a strange manner whenever politics get involved.

Gary Galloway, a columnist for the ***Post-Tribune*** had written several articles dealing with his personal perspective on Paula's case. After the State Supreme Court decision, he had a front-page column, which said, in part:

> One of these days Gary's famous butcher Girl is going to miss the death row limelight.
>
> Her name will have dropped out of the newspapers.
>
> Her painted face will have disappeared from the TV screen and colorful magazines.
>
> The Italian liberals will have confused themselves with another unworthy cause.
>
> William Pelke will have gone off somewhere to talk to the squirrels.
>
> "She won't be the Queen Bee anymore," Clarence Trigg said Friday about Paula Cooper. "She will be just another inmate.
>
> She will be able to associate with other inmates.
>
> That could be a problem.
>
> Cooper can be a creep.

> Trigg said she has been an occasional disciplinary problem since arriving at the prison. He blames part of her insolence and bad attitude on a big head from the extensive media interest in her death-penalty case.
>
> Critics of the death penalty, including Pelke's grandson, William, said Cooper was too young to die. Last week the Indiana Supreme Court agreed and ordered her sentence vacated and remanded her case to re-sentencing to 60 years.
>
> Cooper has assured Trigg she won't be a problem once she is released from death row and joins the other inmates.
>
> Meanwhile, Trigg said, Cooper stays where she is, missing out on another glorious Indiana weekend out of doors.
>
> There will be plenty of others, assuming Cooper doesn't sting the wrong inmate with her Queen Bee attitude, which could trigger another round of notoriety.

Obviously, not everyone was happy that Paula would be getting off of death row, but I was very happy.

I called the prison and talked with Superintendent Trigg to ask about visiting Paula. He told me to call back when Paula was off of death row and in general population. He said at that time he would give me permission to visit with Paula, though all the paperwork to move her could take several months.

So I called the prison several months later when Paula had been moved to general population. But Trigg was no longer at the prison. Dana Blank, who had been the assistant superintendent back in 1986 when I first tried to see Paula, was now the superintendent.

My request to visit was turned down once again. Paula informed me that Dana Blank had no intention of letting me visit her as long as she was the superintendent. Back to square one. I didn't call the prison anymore.

As happy as I was that Paula was now off death row, there

was a bit of wistfulness over the fact that Paula's case would no longer have media exposure. During the long months of radio, newspaper and television exposure, I had had numerous opportunities to speak out about love, compassion and forgiveness. I was afraid these opportunities would now come to an end.

Then I heard about a two-week event that would be taking place in Florida the next spring. It was billed as a *Pilgrimage for Life*, sponsored by four organizations: *Amnesty International (AI)*, the *Southern Christian Leadership Conference (SCLC)*, the *National Coalition to Abolish the Death Penalty (NCADP)* and the *American Friends Service Committee (AFSC).*

I was not yet familiar with *AFSC* but understood it was a Quaker organization that was opposed to the death penalty.

The *Pilgrimage* would be a two-week march, beginning at Starke, Florida, the state's death row site, and ending at the burial site of Dr. Martin Luther King, Jr. in Atlanta, Georgia.

The *Pilgrimage* was billed as "an event to help enlighten the spiritual community about the issues of the death penalty." Since it was for spiritual reasons that I was opposed to the death penalty, I felt I should go. I scheduled my vacation six months in advance so I would be free to go unless I changed my mind.

As the time approached for the march, Judy was not really happy about my decision. She said that since Paula was off of death row now and we were married, we should take our vacations together and I shouldn't go running around the country without her.

And she didn't want to spend her vacation time on a march against the death penalty. She felt the death penalty was still proper in certain cases.

Judy asked me a lot of questions. Who is going to be there? Where will you sleep? What will you eat? I had to admit to her that I knew none of the answers. I just knew I needed to go.

She asked me if I would consider going for just one week. I told her I didn't know which week to pick. Finally after much discussion, Judy gave me her love and blessings to go for the whole two weeks. I was very grateful for that.

When the time came, Judy helped me pack my bags and gave me a wonderful send off. I filled my van with gas and began the one thousand-mile drive from the Chicagoland area to Gainesville, Florida, where the marchers would be gathering. I drove straight through, stopping only a couple of hours near dawn outside of Chattanooga, Tennessee, to catch a little sleep. I stopped in Valdosta, Georgia; at an outlet mall my mother had told me about to buy a pair of shoes to march with.

As I drove, I prayed and meditated a lot. In some ways, I felt guilty about my arrival on the abolition scene. My very first venture against the death penalty was the big press conference in Italy. I knew that many people had been fighting the death penalty for years and had never even had a single opportunity to speak on television or talk to a reporter.

These were the people who were doing the grass roots work against the death penalty. I felt like I had never paid my dues as a grass roots worker and this would be my opportunity. I determined that I would go to the *Pilgrimage* with the attitude of a servant. I decided to do whatever I could to help once I got there.

CHAPTER 29

The Florida-Atlanta March

When I crossed the Florida state line on the morning of May 5, 1990, I turned on the radio. The first thing I heard was news about an execution that had taken place shortly after midnight.

Jesse Tafero had been electrocuted in Florida's electric chair in a botched execution. Flames leaped several feet from his head. The switch was turned three times before the execution was complete—the wrong kind of sponge had been put into the headpiece. According to the news reports, Tafero and his common-law wife were sentenced to death for the murder of two Florida highway patrolmen. His wife's death sentence had been commuted to life.

When I arrived in Gainesville, I went to the address I had been given. It was the office of *Pax Christi*, a sort of peace wing of the Catholic Church.

In the registration room, I introduced myself to the lady sitting behind the table. She said she knew who I was, stood up and gave me a hug. She introduced herself as Sister Helen Prejean.

Sister Helen was one of the organizers of the *Pilgrimage* and would be spending the full two weeks with us as a spiritual advisor.

All the marchers, supporters and organizers met that night for a meeting. When I got there, I recognized Mike Radelet, whom I knew from *Amnesty International*'s annual meetings. I walked over to Mike, who was talking with a lady. He told her, "This is Bill Pelke." She held me tightly and began to cry.

I held her in my arms until the weeping subsided. I guessed that she might be the mother of Jesse Tafero, the man who had just been executed. She was.

At the meeting, Jesse's mother, Kaye addressed our group. She said that Jesse had told her about our march and had asked her to come and wish God's blessings on us. I will never forget her tears that night. What a way to start our march against the death penalty.

The next morning, we met at the state prison in Starke, Florida, the site of Florida's death row. Our group of over a hundred formed a large circle and held hands.

People in the circle took turns reading a list of names of all those on death row in Florida. Then we began our march.

The organizers had rented four vans for the march. Each one was equipped with a CB radio. My van also had a CB, so it also became part of the official caravan.

Since my van was the only one with a trailer hitch, one of my duties was to pull the trailer of dual porta-potties wherever we went. Each vehicle in the caravan had a CB radio "handle"—mine was "*Porta-Pottie Bill.*"

As we marched alongside the highway, we began singing. We had with us a group of *Hutterites*, from a religious community in New York. They sang songs and choruses with some of the most beautiful voices I had ever heard. Unfortunately they were with us only the first few days of the march.

As we marched, I got to know people like Laura Van Voorhis, a Church of the Brethren volunteer from Indiana and Pajama Lady, a clown from Maine.

There were also a few people I already knew, like Sam Reese Sheppard.

Sam and I were the only murder victim's family members to do the full two-week march. As we marched, Sam and I talked about how we were uncomfortable with the way things were going with *SOLACE [Survivors of Loss Against Capital Execution]*. Over the last six months, we would tell people about *SOLACE* and give the phone number to them. They would report back telling us that they could never reach anyone. They said when they left a message no one would return their call.

Elissa was planning to join the *Pilgrimage March* as we approached the Atlanta area. Sam and I were looking forward to meeting her and working out a way that *SOLACE* could be more effective. We hoped to get some of the problems solved. I wanted *SOLACE* to move forward; I hoped things would work out when Elissa arrived.

As we walked from city to city, the media would always come to check out the marchers. We were instructed to direct them to Sister Helen.

When Sister Helen would talk to the media, she would refer to us *Pilgrims* as a "*tricky group.*" She would explain how we had young and old—a sixteen-year-old girl and a seventy-two-year-old man. Sister Helen would tell how we were black and white, believers and non-believers, former military and former war-resisters, death-row family members and family members of murder victims all marching together. We were indeed a "*tricky group.*"

We spent only a few days in Florida because we soon crossed the border of Georgia. We sang that we were on our way to "Big A Town," Atlanta. By now our marching group had shrunk to thirty core marchers

In each city, the journalists were always interested in the fact that two murder victim's family members were on a march against the death penalty. Sister Helen would alternate sending reporters to Sam Sheppard and me.

As we went from city to city, we had rallies at different churches. We even stopped at a few places where anti-death penalty activities were strong. We stopped in Americus, Georgia, and met with the *Koinonia Community*. We also met with *Jubilee Partners, New Hope House*, and the *Open Door Community*.

Before we came to Americus, we had an unnerving experience. It was late at night and we were traveling down a long lonely stretch of highway. A pickup truck seemed to be keeping tabs on us, reminding a few of the *Pilgrims* of the movie ***Mississippi Burning.*** All the guys from *SCLC (Southern Christian Leadership Conference)* and a few others of our group stayed up all night when we arrived in Americus, just to keep guard on our group. Fortunately there were no problems.

The first few nights of the march, we slept on the floors of churches that were kind enough to open their doors and provide lodging. Floors proved to be too hard for me and I ended up sleeping on the reclined bench in the back of my van. For a few nights, we stayed at a very nice state park in Georgia. There were cabins with comfortable beds.

We would march from seven to fourteen miles each day. Usually, we would stop for lunch alongside the road. Twice we went to black Missionary Baptist churches that fed us fried chicken for lunch. I really liked that.

As we marched and talked, I began to get a real education about capital punishment and about the death penalty abolition movement. I learned, for example, that there were no rich people on death row. The people with little or no money quite often ended up with poor legal representation. In other words, when it came to capital punishment, those without the capital got the punishment.

I heard about cases where all white juries sentenced black men to death. I heard the story of an attorney who referred to his client as a "nigger" to the jury, only to find out later that the defense lawyer was a member of the *KKK*. His client was, not surprisingly, sentenced to death.

I also began to learn about innocent people who had been sentenced to death. Professor Mike Radelet, who was co-writing a book called ***In Spite of Innocence***, told us of documented cases where twenty-three people had been put to death since the turn of the century by this country, only to find out later that they were innocent.

I learned statistics that documented the cost of executions. I learned it is three to four times more costly to execute a person than to keep them in prison for a lifetime—a statistic that many people find hard to believe but true because of massive costs of a capital trial and the appeals process. At least the United States Supreme Court recognizes that the penalty of death requires more safeguards than a normal sentence of prison time.

I found myself marching down the Georgia highways with people who had loved ones on death row. For example, Melanie Bloom from California had a son on death row at San Quentin. Another girl had a brother on death row and yet another had a father on death row.

The state of Georgia is beautiful in the month of May. But as we marched, especially in the cities, we always seemed to have someone keeping an eye on us. Not only did they keep their eye on us but also their camera: the *GBI (Georgia Bureau of Investigation)* would sit in their cars at intersections and take pictures and videos of us.

We always had the help of the local law enforcement officials as we paraded through various cities. They were always very professional and courteous. But it was a bit unnerving to have the *GBI* always filming us.

The middle Sunday of the march was May 14—the fifth anniversary of Nana's death. I had told my story to a number of journalists on the march and many of the individual marchers were aware of my story, but I had never told it to the entire group.

Sister Helen said it would be okay for me to speak to the group that Mother's Day Sunday. I'll never forget standing on a balcony in front of a guardrail, addressing the *Pilgrims* and others who had gathered for our rally.

Bill speaks in Macon, Georgia during the *Pilgrimage March* on Mother's Day, May 14,1990, the fifth anniversary of Nana's death

It was a special time for me and I felt very close to Nana. I knew she would be pleased with what I was doing with my life; my talking about Jesus would have pleased her. I continued to keep the two promises I had made God that night in the crane: for any successes, I gave Him the honor and the glory, and I continued to go through any door that would open.

We *Pilgrims* were all aware of Sister Helen's story of meeting a man on death row and being his friend and spiritual advisor. She had witnessed his execution. In fact, she had done this several times with different men. One of the men she had been seeing, Dalton Prejean (no relation to her), had a Louisiana execution date set during the *Pilgrimage*.

Sister Helen was troubled as to whether she should leave the *Pilgrimage* and join Dalton for his last day or stay with us. Arrangements had been made for someone else to take Sister Helen's place with Dalton, but I think she was beginning to feel a bit guilty about not being with him. It was definitely bothering her.

Since Dalton had told her to stay, Sister Helen decided to stay with the *Pilgrims.*

On the night of the execution, the whole group joined hands with Sister Helen. Later in the evening, about five or six of us got in a small circle with her, trying to give her comfort. We joined hands and prayed.

We had a problem when we got to Jackson, Georgia. The city would not give us a permit to march. They would give permits for marches only on Mondays and Wednesdays, and we were coming through on Tuesday.

We had a meeting with all of the *Pilgrims* to decide what to do. There was some talk of civil disobedience, but several representatives of organizations sponsoring the march expressed strong reservations against it.

After hours of discussion, we decided against civil disobedience. Donna Schnewies, a nun from Kansas, gave a great talk about how this march was not the place for civil disobedience.

On Wednesday, we arrived at Waycross, Georgia. The *Pilgrims* split up into several groups to visit different churches. I went with about ten others to a Missionary Baptist Church for the weekly prayer meeting. I was asked to tell my story. The only white folks there were *Pilgrims.*

I had never told my story in a Baptist church, but when I started to speak, I felt right at home. When I would say something like, "God told us to forgive seventy times seven," there would be a loud chorus of Amen. Whenever I would say something from the Bible and say, "God said," the "Amens" would ring out. It inspired me. I almost got to preaching.

Sam Sheppard and I were really looking forward to Elissa arriving so we could talk about what was happening with *SOLACE.* We were both greatly disappointed when we got the word that Elissa was not going to be able to come. It was beginning to look like *SOLACE* hardly existed any more.

I called Judy daily while on the march. I told her some of the exciting things we were doing and about the wonderful people I was meeting. I wished she was there and I let her know it every time I called.

Judy was going to have a long weekend off work at the end of the *Pilgrimage*. Even though she didn't like flying, she agreed to fly down and meet me in Atlanta for the last four days of the march. I met her at the Atlanta airport.

I began introducing Judy to new friends I had met over the previous thirteen days. It is amazing the bonding that takes place on an event like this. Everyone loved Judy. Of course, they knew a lot about her even before she came.

When Judy joined the *Pilgrims*, we were still ten miles outside of "Big A Town." Judy marched with us into Atlanta.

In Atlanta, on Saturday, we had our big march downtown to the burial site of Dr. Martin Luther King, Jr. Death penalty abolitionists from around the country joined us for that last weekend. We marched into Atlanta with three hundred people carrying banners, signs, and cardboard caskets representing people who already had been executed.

We sang and chanted. Jack Hill, Jr., an old civil rights veteran, led us in our chants. He had had a lot of experience marching with Dr. King. A megaphone aided his loud booming voice.

As I walked along beside Judy, I noticed she was singing the chants, too. My heart was touched to hear her shouting the response to "What do we want?" She would yell in unison with the rest of us, "**No more death penalty**."

In response to "When do we want it?" she would yell back "**Now**." Tears came to my eyes as I watched her sing and shout the march lyrics. I had never pressured Judy to be against the death penalty; now it appeared that she had arrived. It was a joyous occasion for me.

During the two weeks of this march, I increasingly realized that I would be an abolitionist for the rest of my life. I knew that as long as people were being executed anywhere in the world that I would have to speak out against it. On the

Pilgrimage March, I dedicated my life to the abolition of the death penalty.

Shortly after I came to that conclusion, Rick Halperin announced that there would be a march in Texas the next year. Without even thinking, I responded that I would be there.

On Saturday, our last night, we met at the Ebenezer Baptist Church in Atlanta, Dr. King's church. It was packed to overflowing. About twenty people were asked to speak, limited to a period of five minutes each.

I was the third speaker on the list, right after Dr. King's daughter, Yolanda. It was one of the greatest honors of my life to stand behind the same pulpit that Dr. King had spoken from.

I held up the Bible that I had gotten for Paula. I talked about love, compassion, the healing power of forgiveness, and God's blessing . . . and my five minutes were finished.

Bill speaks from the pulpit of the late
Dr. Martin Luther King, Jr. at the Ebenezer Baptist
Church in Atlanta, during the *Pilgrimage March*

The *Pilgrimage* was a great success. We had the opportunity to speak to a lot of people at churches. The great press coverage helped us reach thousands with our message abolition. We passed out a lot of educational materials and we also each received a great personal education about the death penalty. We were all greatly inspired.

When Judy and I got in the van and headed for home, I realized two things. First, that I had found new family, the abolition family. Second, Judy had become an abolitionist. That was the best news of all.

But as we drove back to Indiana and our jobs, there was the growing concern: **What has happened to *SOLACE*?**

Chapter 30

Washington and Wayne

Marie Deans, the founder of *Murder Victims' Families for Reconciliation (MVFR)*, began receiving complaints about the lack of response from the *SOLACE* office. Marie felt she owed it to the original members of *MVFR*, as well as the new murder victim family members we were identifying, to have an organization that would respond to the members' needs.

Marie decided she would get *MVFR* back on track. All I had wanted was an organization of *victim's families* to be successful in the abolition movement—I had hoped that *SOLACE* would be that group. I decided to have memberships with both groups.

That fall, the *NCADP (National Coalition to Abolish the Death Penalty)* held their annual meeting in Washington, D.C. Judy and I decided to go and make it a bit of a family vacation. We took three of our kids, Becky, Taniya, and Kennie.

The *NCADP* gives an annual honor to the *Abolitionist of the Year*. This year the award was going to Marie Deans and Rev. Joe Ingle for their work with the *Southern Coalition of Jails and Prisons*. The *Southern Coalition* helped raise money for legal research and obtaining lawyers for those on death row.

Many of the *Pilgrims* of the Florida-to-Atlanta march also came to the Washington conference. The *NCADP* had been one of the sponsors of the *Pilgrimage* and the only national organization that I was aware of whose sole purpose was abolition of the death penalty.

We met a lot a great people at that conference. When Judy met Marie Deans, they instantly hit it off. It was great to see Marie share the *Abolitionist of the Year* award with Joe Ingle, whom I had met at my first *Amnesty AGM* in Atlanta, Georgia, a few years earlier. I admired the way they lived their lives devoted to a cause.

Five murder victims' family members were at the conference—Pat Bane, Teresa Mathis, Sam Reese Sheppard, Marie Deans, and me.

As the conference ended, Marie called the five of us together. She said that since the five of us always seem to show up at abolition events, she wanted each of us to be on the *Murder Victims Families for Reconciliation* board, to help it get incorporated. *MVFR* also needed help in getting its non-profit status with the IRS, for people to claim deductions for donations.

I thought back to my night in the crane, and my promise to go through any door that opened. This was, of course, another open door to go through. I was honored that Marie asked me to be on the board. It brought the *SOLACE* era to a close.

The trip to Washington, D.C. was great for the family. One of the sightseeing trips we made was to the Viet Nam Memorial. The wall brought back a lot of memories, especially when I located the names of some of the men I knew and fought with who were killed during the war.

Both Judy and I had to get back home and back to work. At work, it seemed that whenever I walked into an office at the steel mill, someone would want to get into a debate about the death penalty. A person would invariably say what about so-and-so? Look at what they did. Shouldn't this person get the death penalty? I would always say "No."

One day, my friend Wayne Crawley and I walked into an office together and someone started talking about the death penalty. I started talking about the Bible and what *Jesus* had to say when he was confronted with the issue.

Wayne spoke up and said that the Bible supported the death penalty. I was upset, but I was not going to debate with Wayne in front of the others. The Bible reference he gave to support his feelings was Romans 13:4.

That passage is talking about how God has ordained the rulers of government to be over us. The verse in the *King James Version* (*KJV*) says, "For he is the minister of God to thee for good. But if thou do that which is evil, be afraid; for he beareth not the sword in vain: for he is the minister of God, an avenger to execute wrath upon him that doeth evil."

When I had a chance to get alone with Wayne, I explained it to him. Yes, it does talk about a *sword* and *executing*, but a closer look shows it is not talking about the death penalty. *Sword* was a word used often in the *KJV* of the Bible to represent a sign of *power*. In this section of scripture, the apostle Paul (the writer) was saying that God has ordained that rulers are over us. The rulers have the *power* (sword) to *execute* (carry out) laws and bring down wrath on evildoers. It has nothing to do with *executing people*.

I asked Wayne to please not differ with me anymore when we were in a public setting because I didn't want to argue with him and wouldn't, even if he were wrong. I asked him to talk to me in private on matters we differed. Several weeks later, he came to me and apologized. He said I was right.

Chapter 31

The *TASK* March

The night before I was to leave for the *TASK (Texans Against State Killing) March* in April of 1991, I was talking to Wayne. I said, "Wayne, Judy can't get off work to go. You ought to go with me."

To my surprise he said, "I think I will." I'll never forget the reaction of his wife, Molly.

She said, "Wayne, why are you going? You are *for* the death penalty!"

Wayne said, "I know, but I want to see what Bill is up to."

I already had my airline ticket, but it was too late to get a reasonably priced ticket for Wayne. So we filled up the van with gas and took off for Texas. I wasted the money on my airline ticket, but felt it was worth it for Wayne to go.

We drove straight through to Huntsville, where all Texas executions take place. The march started off with a rally that first night outside what they call the *Walls Unit*. Wayne and I got there a little late and missed the first part of the rally.

When we got there, Sam Reese Sheppard was speaking. Sam pointed to a clock over the *Walls Unit* entrance and noted how the clock was no longer working. He stated that it unfortunately symbolized the justice system in Texas: it was no longer working because of all of the executions that were taking place there.

Rick Halperin had managed to get *Amnesty International* to

help sponsor this Texas march. When he saw Wayne and me, tears came to his eyes. He was moved by the fact that we had driven over twelve hundred miles to get there. Some of the participants in this march had also been on the Florida-to-Atlanta *Pilgrimage*, old timers like Mike Kennedy, Pajama Lady, November Belford West, Dave Harper, and Jack Hill, Jr.

Then I heard about Larry Robison, who was on death row in Texas. His parents, Ken and Lois Robison were on the march, as well as Larry's brother Steve, and his sisters Carol and Sharon.

As we marched, Larry's mother Lois spoke to us about his situation. When Larry was twenty-one years old, he began to have some problems, and was diagnosed as a paranoid schizophrenic. His parents were told that Larry needed long-term treatment.

Since Larry was twenty-one-years old, insurance coverage for him had run out. It would have cost about $200 a day to take care of Larry. Ken and Lois were both schoolteachers and could not afford that kind of money.

They took Larry to another hospital, which kept him for thirty days. Ken and Lois were told that if Larry were violent, they could keep him longer, but since Larry had never done anything violent they had to let him go.

Ken and Lois took Larry to a third hospital, a veteran's hospital. Larry had served in the Air Force, but he had been suddenly discharged.

The veterans' hospital kept Larry for thirty days, and then told Ken and Lois that because there was no insurance, they must release him. Once again they were told that if he ever did anything violent that they could get him the long-term care they admitted he needed.

Then Larry did do something violent. In a psychotic episode he killed five people. It was a heinous crime, with one of the people beheaded. Larry said he heard "voices from God" telling him to do it. He was convinced that he was doing them a favor by sending them to a "higher level."

Larry felt after he killed the five that he also would be taken to this "higher level." He waited and waited, but after several hours realized he was not going to a higher level. He realized that all that was happening was that he was sitting with a lot of blood and a bunch of dead people.

Ken and Lois were horrified that their son could have committed such a horrible crime. They had great compassion for the victim's families, and wanted to tell them of their grief. They assumed Larry would spend the rest of his life in a mental hospital. At least there he would get the help he so desperately needed.

But the state of Texas had other plans. Larry was found guilty of capital murder and sentenced to death. Ken and Lois could not believe that the state of Texas was going to kill their mentally ill son. When the death sentence verdict was read, Lois went into shock and passed out. She was taken by ambulance to the hospital where she was a patient for four days.

Ken and Lois then got involved with the prison reform group *CURE (Citizens United for the Rehabilitation of Errants). CURE* had taken a stand against the death penalty. Ken and Lois also got involved with the *National Coalition to Abolish the Death Penalty* in order to meet people who might be able to help save Larry's life.

Now they were marching with us to draw attention to Larry's case. Larry's brother Steve was a great help to the marchers, especially with maintenance of the vehicles.

Our march was deep in the heart of Texas, the state that has executed more people than any other state in the country. We were scheduled to march from Huntsville to Bryan, College Station, Brenham, Caldwell, Rockdale, Taylor, Bastrop and finally Austin.

Soon there were some new murder victims' family members on the march. For example, Sherri Dye, whose mother had been killed, joined us for a few days. Judge Bill Allshire's brother was murdered; Bill spoke for us at a rally.

When we got to College Station, home of *Texas A & M*, Jack Healey, the Executive Director of *Amnesty International*, was the keynote speaker at our rally.

On the third day of the march, Wayne came up to me and said, "You know, Bill, this death penalty stuff is wrong. I can no longer support it."

Well, Hallelujah! Tears again. After four and one half years and many hours of discussion, Wayne finally saw what I had been talking about!

This Texas march was not as well organized as the Florida-to-Atlanta *Pilgrimage*. For example, we had only a little media coverage. Once again, however, the media was fascinated by the fact that murder victims' family members would march and take a stand against the death penalty. Sam and I spoke as members of *MVFR*. We let the media know that there was a national organization of victims' family members who did not want the state to kill in our name.

One day, as we were driving along in a caravan, I was riding with Bob Gross. I noticed he was looking in the rear view mirror and then said "Oh no!" as he began to slow down and pull over to the side of the road. Bob told me that in the mirror, he was watching our porta-pottie trailer cross over the highway and pass the car that had been pulling it!

Fortunately, the porta-pottie did not hit any vehicles before it crashed on the other side of the highway. Since we were already running a bit late for our speaking activity and no damage had been done, we decided to retrieve it on the way back.

We could imagine some of the jokes that were tossed around, or the newspaper headline if they became aware of the incident. We could see it now: **"Abolitionist's Spread Their S—All Over Texas!"**

Wayne and the others returned later to salvage the trailer. It turned out it wasn't near as bad as we had thought. I was happy for Wayne's sake.

According to the ***Austin American Statesman***, our Texas march encountered the great middle ground, the people who alternate between support of and opposition to the death penalty. Rick Halperin was quoted as saying, "Support for the death penalty is a mile wide and an inch deep."

The article also mentioned that we met people who disagreed "fiercely" with our stand. For instance, Mike Budell, a Brennen gun shop owner, told the ***Statesman***, "I think these people fell out of a tree." Budell, dressed in cowboy clothes, stood with a friend inside his place of business. "I just don't understand what they're trying to do. There has got to be a death penalty. What are you going to do? Put them in jail, feed them all their lives and let them watch TV in the air conditioning. Wish I could do that."

One lady pulled up to the marchers and yelled, "What do you want to do with people who kill children?" We did not respond to her because our policy was not to respond to any confrontations during the march.

As we approached "Big A Town" (This time it was Austin) more and more people began to join us. During the middle part of the march, we had dwindled to a core group of less than thirty, but our numbers began to grow as we approached Austin.

As we neared the Austin city limits, Wayne looked at me and said, "We should do something like this in Indiana." I looked at Wayne and laughed. Only a week ago, he was for the death penalty and now he was talking about doing an Indiana march against it. He felt we could do a much better job of organizing; for example, we could make sure we didn't run out of toilet paper.

Then I began to think about *MVFR* and felt that if murder victim's family members would lead an event, that many other abolitionists would stand by our side and support us.

When I saw Sam Sheppard, I told him that Wayne and I wanted to do an event in Indiana. Sam looked at me and said, "So, you'll be the big cheese." I looked at Sam and said, "*MVFR* will be the big cheese." Sam smiled and with a big grin said he thought that would be great.

I had to talk to Bob Gross. Bob had helped organize both the Florida-to-Georgia *Pilgrimage* and the *TASK March*. Since he was from Indiana, I figured that if Bob would help to organize in Florida, Georgia and Texas, surely he would help organize in his home state, especially for murder victim's family members. Bob worked part time for the *National Coalition to Abolish the Death Penalty*. He worked out of his home in Liberty Mills, Indiana, which was also used as the field office for the *NCADP*.

We told Bob what we wanted to do: a two-week event starting

off in Michigan City where Indiana has their death row, and ending at the state capitol in Indianapolis. We did not want the event to be a march. In Texas, we sometimes were marching over fifteen miles a day and by the time evening came and we went to a meeting, everyone was very tired. We told Bob we wanted to *caravan* to speaking locations. If we didn't spend so much time walking, we could get into more locations to speak.

Also, on the Texas march, we spent a lot of time packing when we would change our lodging location. It seemed like we moved every day or two. We wanted to be able to stay at one place for a longer period of time. The state parks that we had stayed in on the *Pilgrimage* and the Texas marches had been good deals, so we told Bob that we would like to stay in one state park in the northern part of Indiana the first week and one in the southern part the second week.

Then we told Bob that we felt we needed two years to organize the event. We even came up with a catchy phrase—**"Indiana—*the Place to Be in '93.*"**

Half of our group on Saturday was at Houston-Tillison College in Austin. The other half was at another college across town. Both colleges were about the same distance from the Texas state capitol building. Both groups left the colleges simultaneously and began to march to the capitol.

The all-morning rain had put a bit of a damper on things. We were wearing our rain jackets when the march began. But as we moved along toward the state capitol building, the rain began to slacken, and before long, it went away.

The plan was for both groups to arrive simultaneously from opposite directions at a street that led to the state capitol. Upon meeting, we would both turn together and go the last few blocks to the Texas capitol building itself.

The sun came out just as we peaked on a hilltop and saw the other group coming towards us. There was electricity in the air. We had marched from Huntsville to Austin, and now we were about to arrive for the final rally.

As the other group approached us, we could see their banners and hear their chants. When we merged, we formed a much larger group than I had imagined.

With our voices unified, we turned and headed toward the capitol. We boomed out our chants saying that the death penalty must go. We had two flags with us: the state flag of Texas and the flag of the United States. Since I was a veteran, I was asked to carry the United States flag. It was an honor. When we got to the capitol, we found a large number of additional supporters waiting for us.

It was a gigantic rally. Sissy Farenholt, a former candidate for governor of Texas was one of the speakers. Ashanti Chimurenga, the new *Amnesty International* program director to abolish the death penalty, also spoke. A country singer by the name of Steve Earle sang a song he had written called "**Billy Austin**," about a death row inmate.

After the rally, we joined hands and made a huge circle. We sang out chants and hand in hand we moved inside the state capitol building. We moved through the lobby and then came back outside. It was the greatest day I had ever spent as an abolitionist.

Chapter 32

A Name and a Voice

All the way home from Texas, Wayne and I talked about **"Indiana—*the Place to Be in '93.*"** Boy was I excited. I couldn't wait to get home to tell Judy.

We knew that Bob Gross would be the key to making a successful event. He had the experience of the two previous national marches and he had connections within the abolition movement. The fact that Bob lived in Indiana was maybe the most important element of them all.

I needed to check with Marie Deans as soon as we got back to Indiana. I told Marie what Wayne, Bob, Sam and I had talked about, and she was in favor of it. She told me what she wanted to accomplish with *Murder Victims' Families for Reconciliation* was to get it on the map within the abolition movement.

I told Marie that after **"Indiana—*the Place to Be in '93*"**, I was sure that *MVFR* would be on the map. Since our board was five members and three of us already agreed, I knew it was a "bingo."

The next step was for Bob to get the *National Coalition to Abolish the Death Penalty* to support the event. Leigh Dingerson, the Executive Director of the *NCADP* said that the coalition might be interested in supporting an educational event. Bob and I said, "No problem—we will make it an *educational* event."

The dates were set for June 4-20, 1993. The two previous marches had been during the school year making it nearly impossible for students and teachers to attend. Both events had been held in the South where it was too hot to do a summer event. Indiana has great weather in June.

One of the first things Bob wanted to do was to form a steering committee. Bob knew several people in Indiana who might be interested. Laura Van Voorhis, who had been on the Florida-to-Atlanta *Pilgrimage*, was one of the first to volunteer.

The name **"Indiana—*The Place to Be in '93*"** was a catchy phrase early on in the planning, but Bob felt it was necessary to come up with a better name for the actual event. I reluctantly agreed.

During a steering committee meeting in Indianapolis, Bob presented us with a number of words and combinations of words for a new name. We needed to come up with a name that told what we were all about. We were not a *march* and needed to make that clear. We looked at words like *tour, pilgrimage, journey* and others. We also wanted to have a second word describing what we were about. We looked at words like *compassion, reconciliation, hope, understanding* and others.

Scott Schiesswohl from the *Indiana Council of Churches* was the first to put the words *journey* and *hope* together and say them out loud. ***Journey of Hope***. It was perfect. It described exactly what we were about.

Bob also felt we needed a subtitle to go with the ***Journey of Hope*** name. After some deliberation on phrases like from "*fury to forgiveness*," "*anger to reconcili*ation" and others, we came up with "***from violence to healing***."

Perfect. Now we had a name: ***Journey of Hope . . . from Violence to Healing***.

Different people on the committee had different jobs. Bob and Laura took on most of the work. My job was to promote the *Journey* and promote *MVFR*. Most people were not even aware that *Murder Victims' Families for Reconciliation* existed.

MVFR did not have a brochure, so I began to work on one.

Bob Gross had given me a number of copies of old newspaper articles about victim's family members who were opposed to the death penalty. From these articles I came up with some quotes for the brochure. I chose ones from Coretta Scott King, Robert Kennedy, Norman Felton, Marietta Jaeger and Marie Deans. For example:

Marietta Jaeger, whose daughter was kidnapped and murdered: "To say that the death of any other person would be just restitution is to insult the immeasurable worth of our loved ones who are victims. We cannot put a price on their lives. That kind of justice would only dehumanize and degrade us because it legitimizes an animal instinct for gut-level, blood-thirsty revenge."

Coretta Scott King: "As one whose husband and mother-in-law have died the victims of murder assassinations, I stand firmly and unequivocally opposed to the death penalty for those convicted of capital offenses. An evil deed is not redeemed by an evil deed of retaliation. Justice is never advanced in the taking of a human life. Morality is never upheld by a legalized murder."

Robert Kennedy: "Whenever any American's life is taken by another unnecessarily—whether it is done in the name of the law or in defiance of law . . . in an attack of violence or in response to violence—the whole nation is degraded."

I also had a quote from another murder victim, Jesus, who said, "Whosoever is without sin cast the first stone."

The brochure explained what *MVFR* was all about. It also told about plans for the coming *Journey of Hope* in 1993. I was going to the *NCADP* annual conference in Seattle, Washington in the fall of '91 and I wanted the brochure ready to hand out there.

When Wayne and I were driving to a steering committee meeting in Indianapolis, a few weeks before the Seattle conference, he saw my rough draft. He was quite impressed, and said that it should be printed first class. He said he would pay for it. It would cost around $400 for the first fifteen hundred printed.

The brochure was not ready to be picked up from the printers when I left for Seattle, so Wayne picked it up and had it express mailed. It was beautiful. I felt inspired working on it, and the final product showed it. I passed out the brochure at a plenary session on Saturday night.

Mike Radelet came up to me after the session and gave me a check for $50, the first money that we had received for *MVFR* and the *Journey*. The *MVFR* board decided that I should be the treasurer and that my home address should be used at least temporarily as the headquarters for *MVFR*.

During the conference, Bob arranged for me to be part of a workshop for religious organizing. I told about plans for the *Journey of Hope* in Indiana. After the session, a young lady came up to me and told me that she was from New York. She said that her church took three offerings a year to help special causes. She felt her church would like to help the *Journey*. That was exciting news. We sure could use the money.

Bill announcing the upcoming Indiana *Journey* during a conference in Indianapolis 1991 ***Indianapolis Star*** Photo

In December of 1991, I spoke to a prison reform group in Indianapolis and included the story about the *Journey* coming to Indiana. In the audience was a reporter from the ***Indianapolis Star***. The next day, the paper headlined that *Murder Victims Families for Reconciliation* was going to have a tour in Indiana. Although it was still a year and a half away, I knew the *Journey* was going to be a success. Praise God.

The article had a photo of me giving the thumbs up sign to someone in the audience after they made a positive remark.

In January of '92, I was asked to go to Nebraska to help lobby for an anti-death penalty bill. Nebraska was gearing up to execute Wili Otey. After I had a chance to meet with Wili, I spoke in Omaha and in Lincoln at churches, schools and on a radio talk show at the University of Nebraska. Each time, I told about the coming *Journey.*

In February, I spoke about *MVFR*, and the upcoming *Journey* at a workshop for the regional *Amnesty International* conference in San Francisco. Pat Clark, executive director of *Death Penalty Focus of California*, who followed me on the panel, mentioned that several people in her family had also been murdered. She did not generally speak about the death penalty from a victim's family point of view however.

When I got home, I called Marie and told her about Pat Clark. I told her we had a new member of *MVFR*. Not only did we have a new member, but a very talented one, who was already giving her all in the movement.

I began compiling a mailing list containing names and addresses from the *Indiana Coalition to Abolish the Death Penalty, CURE* Chapters around the country and a list of *Amnesty* staff members. I also included names from the Florida-to-Atlanta *Pilgrimage*, the Texas *TASK March* and those on Indiana's death row.

I sent out a mailing to about 250 people that were on the list and told them about *MVFR* and about the *Journey of Hope* coming to Indiana. Each person also received a brochure. About $400 was sent back to *MVFR* as a result of the mailing—it was the same amount as the brochures had cost. Praise the Lord.

One of the mailings went to a Sister Francita of Memphis, Tennessee. Sister Francita wrote and said, "I received the communication for *MVFR* . . . . Sounds great. I am interested mainly because of your 'weapons of choice'—love, compassion and forgiveness . . . . We need the murder victims' families' ***voice***."

I was planning to edit a newspaper for *Murder Victims Families for Reconciliation* to advertise the coming *Journey of Hope*. I now had a name for an *MVFR* newspaper, thanks to Sister Francita: it was ***"THE VOICE."***

Later that summer, I drove to a Minnesota regional meeting of *Amnesty International*, dropping Judy off at her brother's house in Wisconsin. He lived about an hour from where we were meeting. Bob Gross and I made a presentation about plans for next year's *Journey of Hope*. Toni Moore, the new director of *Amnesty International's* regional office in Chicago was there. Toni and her assistant Maureen Kelly were delighted to hear that the *Journey* was taking place in their region. Both volunteered their help and the help of their office. What a *coup* that trip was.

Planning for the *Journey* was basically three groups of two: Bob and Laura working out of Liberty Mills, Indiana; Toni and Maureen working out of Chicago; Wayne and myself working out of Portage, Indiana. We met every two months for the first year and then more frequently as the time for the *Journey* approached.

Meanwhile, I was still working fifty-six to sixty hours a week at Bethlehem Steel and traveling a lot on weekends.

I began accumulating articles for ***THE VOICE***. Although I had no experience in this sort of thing, I did have desire. The headline under ***THE VOICE*** read **"*THE VOICE* OF LOVE, COMPASSION & FORGIVENESS."** The subheading read, **"Dedicated to Abolitionists, Murder Victims' Families and Death Row Inmates.**" I found stories about people like SueZann Bosler, Marietta Jaeger and Sam Reese Sheppard and put them in the paper.

I also had a section called "The Ins and Outs of the Mailbag" containing letters to the editor. The "Ins" were death row inmates and the "Outs" were abolitionists. The first ***VOICE*** had death row inmates from Indiana write for the "Ins."

I had received a mailing from the *NAACP* Legal Defense Fund that contained the names of death row inmates around the country. In some cases I was able to get ID numbers and addresses, so I added those to *MVFR*'s mailing list.

I also inserted full-page advertisements for free from abolitionist organizations like *Amnesty International, NCADP, CURE*, and *AFSC* . . .

I reprinted an article that had been in the ***Hospitality*** newsletter. It was the last statement from Warren McCleskey who was executed by the state of Georgia at 3:18 A.M. on September 25, 1992. Warren spent thirteen years on death row, convicted of participating in an armed robbery in which Officer Frank Schlatt of the Atlanta Police Department was killed. Minutes before he was electrocuted, Warren spoke these last words:

> *I would like to say to the Schlatt family I am deeply sorry and repentant for the suffering, hurt and pain that you have endured over the years. I wish there was something I could do or say that would give comfort to your lives and bring peace to it. I pray that you would find it in your heart to forgive me for my participation in the crime that caused the loss of your loved one. I want you to know that I have asked God to forgive me and pray in my heart that you will forgive me. I pray that you will come to know the Lord Jesus Christ and receive his peace that passes all understanding. I know that is the peace that you are looking for; I know that is the peace that you desire; I wish that this execution could give it to you, but I know it won't. It will give you temporary satisfaction. The only peace you will forever have, that is lasting, that will never depart, is found in the light of God with Jesus Christ.*
>
> *I want to say to my family, be strong, courageous, and remember the things I shared with you today. Do*

> *not hold any bitterness toward anyone; do not have any resentment toward anyone. This is my request for you, that you be forgiving to all. I pray that you will go on with your lives* and *that you will keep God at the center so that he can direct your paths.*
>
> *To all the brothers whom I leave behind, I pray that you will remain strong in faith, and I pray also that you will not forsake the faith for what is about to occur to me. Stay strong and focus on God and on God's words; continue to fight and keep your hope alive and know that this is not the end for me. This is only the beginning to all blessed hope for eternal life. To all my brothers, take care, I love you all.*
>
> *The thirteen years I have been here on death row have been very productive years—years in which God has moved in my life and has inspired me to touch other lives. That is the service that will never be forgotten; that is something that will always live on. I know that many people have been longing and waiting for this moment in which the McCleskey case will end, but I would like to say to you that the McCleskey case will never end . . .*

When I first read Warren's last statement, tears came to my eyes. When Wayne came over, I had him read it. He had the same reaction. I knew I would have to print it in ***THE VOICE***.

I promoted the coming *Journey of Hope* in ***THE VOICE*** and Bob Gross had a special four-page insert that was *Journey* specific. In it, Leigh Dingerson of the *NCADP* wrote:

> We declare that opponents of the death penalty and family members of murder victims will no longer accept the roles of adversaries. We will no longer accept that those whose lives are shattered by violence should put back the pieces through revenge. We will no longer accept that those who oppose executions are insensitive to the anguish that violence causes in our society. We will

> no longer cooperate with the legal and social systems that cast us as antagonists, because in fact we share a common commitment—a commitment to end the violence, a commitment to justice. The *Journey of Hope* is a *journey* on common ground . . . . By joining us on the *journey*, you will help pave that common ground.

Joe Ingle added:

> As someone who works with the condemned and has been with many of them up to their moment of killing by the state, I find it appropriate and inspiring that murder victims' families recognize their solidarity with the families of those who face judicial killing. The *Journey of Hope* is a signal to the nation that the answer to murder is not more killing.

Magdaleno Rose-Avila wrote:

> We must create a new road of hope . . . by walking it.

I had a lot of help from a local printing company. The owner and one of his assistants spent a lot of time helping me. We had ten thousand copies made of the first twenty-page edition. Our mailing list was now over three thousand, but I wanted extra issues to be able to pass out to advertise the *Journey*.

We had a great response to the first issue of ***THE VOICE***, and I answered each person who responded. About fifteen hundred of the first mailing had been sent to death row inmates, and half of those responding were death row inmates. It was my goal to inform those on death row about the *Journey of Hope*, and hoped they would let their families know. I knew that death row families would be a natural support system for the *Journey.*

Chapter 33

Little Susie Jaeger

I first saw Marietta Jaeger when her car pulled into my driveway on October 18, 1992. She had called for directions to my house to be at a meeting arranged by Bob Gross. He had a video crew from the *Mennonite Conference* lined up to tape a discussion by members of *Murder Victims Families for Reconciliation.*

I marveled as Marietta told her story . . .

Twenty years earlier, Marietta, her husband Bill, and their five children set out for a dream vacation they had waited many years to take. They bought a new van for the venture. When they got in the van, Marietta led the family in a short prayer thanking God for this opportunity and she prayed for their safety. Then they left Detroit, Michigan, and headed west.

After a wonderful time in the Black Hills, they headed for Montana to meet up with Marietta's parents. Her mom and dad had a camper and they were already set up, waiting for Marietta's family to arrive at the campground.

After dinner and conversation at the campground, Marietta put the children to bed in their tent. She kissed each of the children good night. Susie was the youngest and her bed was against the far wall. When Marietta leaned over to kiss her, her lips were barely able to graze across Susie's forehead. Susie got out of her sleeping bag and said, "No, momma, like this" and she gave

Marietta a big hug and a kiss on the lips. She then scampered back into her sleeping bag.

The children went to sleep in the tent while Marietta and Bill went to her parents' camper. A short time later they went to sleep. At two o'clock in the morning the children woke up Marietta and told her that Susie was gone.

When Marietta got to the tent to try and find out what was going on she saw a big rip in tent on the side where Susie was sleeping. A short distance from the tent they found the stuffed animals Susie slept with.

The police were immediately called and they began to search the area looking for Susie. The FBI was called in to help investigate. There was no trace of Susie.

A massive search of the area found no clues. The local media gave the case a lot of attention, hoping that maybe someone had seen something that might help. A reward was offered; posters were put up all over the area.

At one point, the searchers turned their attention to the river that ran alongside the campground. They began to drag it for signs of Susie's body. Marietta told us, "The boat would move and it would stop. Every time it would stop, my heart would stop because I was so afraid they would find Susie." But as Marietta watched, it began to dawn on her that she might never see Susie again.

Marietta's family stayed in Montana for a month hoping to find Susie. There had been a call a week after the disappearance from a man who said he had kidnapped Susie and he said he wanted a ransom for her return. The man had not left clear directions as to how to deliver the money and the deal was not consummated. After three additional weeks, Marietta and her family returned to Detroit.

One night, as Marietta was getting ready for bed, she told her husband she was so upset with the kidnapper, that even if he were to return Susie right now, alive and well, she could strangle him for what he had done to their family. She told Bill she could do it with her own bare hands and do it with a smile on her face.

As soon as Marietta uttered those words, she knew that was not how God would want her to respond.

As Marietta sat on my couch, the cameras kept rolling as she told of the wrestling match she had with God that night. The wrestling match lasted almost all night and, of course, God won. Marietta finally surrendered to the idea that she needed to have compassion for this sick man and try to forgive him. She began to pray not only for Susie's safe return, but began to pray for the kidnapper.

She prayed that God would do something good for him each day. If he were to go fishing, she prayed that he would catch a big fish.

As the one-year anniversary of Susie's kidnapping drew near, a newspaper from Montana called Marietta at her Detroit home and told her that their readers were interested in knowing how Marietta was doing. When Susie was first taken, the story had captured the attention and hearts of the people in Montana.

The interview was supposed to run on the one-year anniversary of Susie's disappearance. Inadvertently it ran one day early. In the story, Marietta had mentioned that she wished she could talk to the kidnapper.

At two in the morning, one year to the hour of Susie's disappearance, Marietta's phone rang. Marietta had the presence of mind to turn on the tape recorder the *FBI* had given her and record the conversation that took place.

The man on the other end of the line identified himself as the man who had taken Susie. Marietta asked him if she was all right. He answered that she was.

Marietta then asked him if they could have Susie back. The man responded that it would be rather difficult since he had gotten used to her. Marietta then asked if Susie had been hurt. The kidnapper said that she had been hurt a little bit when he had taken her out of the tent but that was all.

Marietta flooded him with questions: How are you keeping her? Is she getting any education? How are you fixing her hair? What kind of clothes is she wearing?

Marietta then surprised the man as well as herself with her next response. She asked him if there was anything she could do for him. He responded that he wished there were. The man was completely taken off guard by Marietta's concern and compassion for him.

At this point, he began to reveal some details, which later proved to be valuable. Bill had gone across the street when he realized that it was the kidnapper and called the FBI so that they could trace the call. Marietta kept the kidnapper on the line for over an hour. The trace was botched, however, and the location of the call could not be found.

There was enough information on the tape, however, for the *FBI* to know that the caller was a previous suspect by the name of David (Last name withheld at Marietta's request). David had been given a lie detector test when Susie was kidnapped, but had passed it and was no longer considered a suspect.

Marietta worked with the *FBI*. She agreed to meet David in person while wearing a hidden tape recorder. They hoped that David would reveal some more information so that an arrest could be made. Marietta agreed to help the *FBI* if they gave her the assurance they wouldn't go for the death penalty, but instead seek life in prison without parole and with psychiatric help.

During his meeting with Marietta, David didn't reveal any helpful information, but while he was talking with Marietta, the *FBI* searched his property and found enough evidence to arrest him. After being assured that the officials would not seek the death sentence, David admitted that he killed Susie and that the killing occurred about a week after he kidnapped her. He also admitted killing several other young people.

Within twenty-four hours of being locked in his cell, David committed suicide. This is not the ending that Marietta wanted. Marietta did visit with David's mother because she knew that his mother had been unaware of David's activities and was now in great pain herself. Marietta wanted to comfort her and let her know that she held no animosity towards her.

Today, two decades later, Marietta's children are all grown and

Marietta travels around the world talking about forgiveness and works to abolish the death penalty.

As I watched Marietta talk and share her story, I knew that I had found a new soul mate. I praised God for meeting Marietta. Marietta had dealt with the question that is often asked by death penalty proponents, "What if someone killed your child, wouldn't you want that person to get the death penalty?"

Marietta answers that question very eloquently.

Marietta also says that she has been accused of not loving Susie very much because she forgave the killer and didn't want the death penalty for him. I have come to find out that this is a common accusation made to victims' family members who don't want the death penalty for the person who killed their loved one.

Many people think that if you don't want the ultimate penalty available, then you just didn't love your murdered family member very much. A member of my family, whom I love dearly, told me I must not have loved Nana very much because of what I was trying to do for Paula.

It was great to know that Marietta was planning to be on next year's Indiana *Journey of Hope.*

Another participant in this discussion and taping session was Maxine, a crane operator with me at Bethlehem Steel. Her son had been killed less than a year earlier. Maxine realized that the taking of more lives was not the answer.

Then JoMarva Bell talked about her loved one being killed, and how the death penalty was not the answer.

Next, Cuzzin' Judi talked about Nana and how she was convinced that Nana would have forgiven the girls involved in her murder. Then Judi said that she believed Nana was in heaven and Nana would want to greet those girls in heaven some day.

Of course I talked about love, compassion and forgiveness. The filmed conversation lasted three hours and the film crew got it all. We had talked and shared as if they weren't even there.

Then the film crew went to Washington D.C. where they were able to tape Marie, Pat Bane and Sam Sheppard in a discussion with each other. After a wonderful job of editing, we had a great piece to give to prospective churches and schools with hope they would want a speaker to come and talk to their organization about next summer's *Journey of Hope.*

The very next month, November of '92, *the National Coalition to Abolish the Death Penalty* had their annual meeting in Chicago. It was a wonderful coincidence that the conference was held in the same region where next summer's *Journey of Hope* would be held.

One of the main features at the *NCADP* conference was a discussion of the upcoming Indiana *Journey.* In a plenary session, we were able to tell of our plans: Bob Gross, Toni Moore, Marie Deans and I spoke.

Bob Gross did an excellent job in all areas of organizing. He was helped greatly by his wife Rachel and their two children Heidi and Anna. Wayne and I had told Bob right from the start that we wanted this to be a first class event and Bob went first class all the way.

Bob Gross made banners and used other mementoes at the convention to publicize the *Journey* . . . and to also help raise some money. We had *Journey* t-shirts, coffee mugs, buttons, book bags and printed materials available. We also had copies of the first issue of ***THE VOICE***.

The *Journey of Hope* was getting closer; we were turning the calendar to 1993.

Chapter 34

The *Journey* Gets Closer

The Riverside Church in New York, took a special Easter offering and decided to split it with three groups. The *Journey* was one of them. We got a check for $4,500. Praise the Lord! It was from the church that the young lady had told us about at the Seattle *NCADP* conference.

Pat Bane, the *Murder Victims' Families for Reconciliation* secretary, wrote a thank you letter to the church. We were able to use part of that money for our second issue of ***THE VOICE***. We reprinted her thank you letter in the paper. The second edition was a little easier to work on than the first because, after the first mailing, people sent a great deal of material we could work with.

With help, once again, from the printing company, the second issue was even classier than the first. Once again we had ten thousand copies printed even though our mailing list had only grown to four thousand. About seventeen hundred of these went to death row inmates for whom we had names, ID numbers and addresses.

The *Journey* steering committee was beginning to meet every three weeks. Every other meeting was held at my house in Portage. The meeting in between was usually held in Indianapolis, although once we held it in Lafayette. Wayne always rode with me for the trips south. He didn't always contribute a lot at the meetings, but his gift of presence was valuable.

That spring, I went to a *CURE* meeting of the northwest Indiana chapter. *CURE* was opposed to the death penalty and I was hoping for their members to support the June *Journey*. At the meeting, I was asked to speak about the upcoming *Journey* plans.

Charlie Sullivan, the Executive Director of *CURE* based in Washington, D.C., was in Indiana for that meeting. When the meeting was over, Charlie came up to me and told me about a national *CURE* board meeting they were having soon in Dune Acres, a small subdivision off Lake Michigan, right next to where I worked at Bethlehem Steel! Charlie invited me to come and make a presentation about the *Journey* to the board members of *CURE*.

Wayne and I went to that board meeting, showed our video clip, and talked about plans. There I met Lois Williamson, chairperson for the *CURE* board. Lois was also a murder victim's family member. When I asked her to come to the *Journey*, she said she would. Charlie and the *CURE* board also pledged their support.

That spring, I received a visit from Sheldon Himelfarb, who identified himself as a producer of television documentaries for ***Yorkshire TV*** in Great Britain. He told me he was a friend of Charlie Sullivan. Sheldon said he was looking for a good subject on which to do a documentary and, a week earlier, had asked Charlie for ideas.

Charlie told him about the *Journey*. Sheldon and I began to talk about the people who we knew were coming on the *Journey*. Sheldon was especially interested in the forgiveness aspect of many of our members. Sheldon left my home with a list of ten people that he wanted to visit to talk about possibly of being interviewed for the documentary. Sheldon felt that the ***Discovery Channel*** would fund a program about the *Journey*. Cool.

Sheldon then visited a number of people on that list. He visited Aba Gayle from Santa Barbara. Aba Gayle's daughter was murdered and the person who committed the crime was on death row in California. Aba Gayle had forgiven and befriended the man. Sheldon then visited with Sue Norton from Arkansas City, Kansas. A man called BK had killed Sue's father and stepmother. Sue forgave BK during his trial. She did not want him sentenced to death; nevertheless BK was sentenced to die by the state of Oklahoma.

Sheldon also talked with SueZann Bosler. SueZann was working as a beautician in Florida. Sheldon was quite impressed with her.

He also was very interested in Marietta's journey, but was concerned about getting involved in her situation because ***ABC*** was working on a script for a TV movie about her story.

Sheldon was impressed with the people he met, and made his proposal to the ***Discovery Channel***. He called a short time later with discouraging news: the ***Discovery Channel*** did not have room in their budget to cover the Indiana *Journey*. However, he said that the ***Discovery Channel*** was interested in doing a program on *forgiveness* and would have money in the budget for something the following year.

I had really hoped that the *Journey* would be documented. It would have been great if the ***Discovery Channel*** had done it. Oh well! Not everything happens as you want. I had learned that lesson.

One spring evening, I received a call from Wayne. He said to turn on the television and watch the TV program ***Prime Time***. It was about a woman on death row in Texas and a church that was trying to help her.

The woman's name was Karla Faye Tucker. As I started watching, they were interviewing people from this church. People were testifying how Karla in prison had converted to Christianity. Not only had she converted but also she had gone through a remarkable life change. Her Christian testimony was having a positive effect, not only on this church group, but also on other prisoners incarcerated with her, her prison guards and people from all over the world.

It was amazing to me to see so many Christians saying this woman should not be put to death. Most of the Christians I had been associated with were calling for the death penalty. I remember Jerry Falwell once saying that we should try to save the souls of those on death row and then execute them!

This ***Prime Time*** program also interviewed one of the prosecutors who helped send Karla Faye Tucker to death row. He had a total change of heart when he saw the tremendous change that had taken place in Karla. He said it would be a travesty for her to be executed.

The program also showed this church congregation singing, praying and shedding tears for Karla. I was impressed. Then suddenly the unexpected happened. A man identified as Ron Carlson, the brother of Karla's victim Debra Thornton, was interviewed. With tears in his eyes, Ron told how at one time he wanted to kill Karla Faye himself. He said that for seven years, he had such a hate and anger for Karla that he wanted to take a pick ax and plunge it into her, because that is how Karla had killed his sister.

Ron told how he had been an alcoholic and a drug abuser and tried to self-medicate the pain he felt after his sister's death. His father had also been murdered in a separate incident. Then Ron converted to Christianity. He proclaimed that this conversion saved his life.

Ron said he knew immediately that he must forgive Karla Faye. He did. He didn't know if Karla's conversion was genuine but he wanted to write her and let her know he had forgiven her. They exchanged letters and eventually visited. When they visited, Ron knew that Karla's faith was real and the same Jesus was in both of them.

When I saw this program, I knew I had to get in touch with Ron Carlson. Since I had Karla Faye Tucker's name and serial number on our death row mailing list, I wrote Karla Faye and told her about seeing the program. I told her about the coming *Journey* and my interest in getting in touch with Ron. I sent Karla a paper and brochure to forward to Ron.

Several days later Ron called. We had a wonderful conversation. When I invited Ron to come to the *Journey*, he said he would try to come. He was excited to hear about a group like *Murder Victims' Families for Reconciliation.*

A week before the actual start of the *Journey*, I began a fast. I hadn't fasted for longer than one day since I had gone to Italy the first time six years earlier. I prayed a lot for the safety of the Journeyers, and that God would make the *Journey of Hope* a success. It seemed like a successful *Journey* was the most important thing in the world to me, except, of course, Judy and the rest of my family.

The Sunday before the *Journey of Hope* began, the ***Indianapolis Star*** gave media attention with a front-page story, including a full schedule of *Journey* events. The article headline was **3 Who Have Been Touched by Murder Unite in Stand Against Death Penalty.** The subtitle was **Love-Filled Memories Stronger Than a Desire to Bring About Revenge.** In-depth interviews with Marietta Jaeger, Sam Reese Sheppard and me included my saying, "Murder is a horrible crime, but there has to be some other way than the death penalty."

The ***Sentinel News*** also quoted me saying, "The death penalty is a political issue. Americans are tired of violence; elected officials try to address that. But taking a person and killing them does not mean you're tough on crime or that you're going to be successful in eliminating it. The death penalty is not working."

In the ***Journal-Gazette*** I said, "I don't believe this *Journey of Hope* will change the death penalty immediately because it is a political issue. But what we want to do is educate the majority of people who still approve of the death penalty. We want to teach love and compassion."

The ***South Bend Tribune*** has a wide circulation in the Michigan City area where our first rally would be held. They quoted Bob Gross: "The *Journey of Hope* is coming to Indiana because we need to make it clear the death penalty's not just a southern problem." The article told how we had started planning the event two years ago, after the Texas march, and that we "were certain that abolitionists would stand by *Murder Victims' Families for Reconciliation* and help us have a successful event." The article went on to say how the planning also involved other groups, such as the *National Coalition to Abolish the Death Penalty, Amnesty International, the National Black Police Association* and several religious organizations.

The South Bend article also mentioned how local-organizing committees had formed in a dozen cities in Indiana and border states. It told how events would vary from city to city, but the primary focus in each will be the stories told by members of *Murder Victims' Families for Reconciliation.*

In telling about the founding of *MVFR*, Marie Deans told the ***South Bend Tribune***, "We just want to tell our stories and let our positions be heard. We want people to know how we got here, and why we stay here." Marie said she felt the *Journey of Hope* could counter the destructive message of revenge and hatred that she felt the death penalty represented.

On June 1, the day the **South Bend Tribune** article was printed, and only three days before the beginning of the *Journey*, I went to visit Richard Huffman, a death row inmate whom I had been visiting for several years.

When I left the prison and went across the street to the parking lot, a man came running out of the prison and began calling to me. It was a member of the prison staff; he said that the warden wanted to talk to me.

I walked into the office and Warden Jack Farley introduced himself. Then he offered me something to drink, but I politely declined. He informed me that he was aware of the events that would be taking place in a few days across the street from ***his*** prison. He was concerned and wanted to know what to expect when the *Journey* arrived.

Barry Nothstine was also in the office. I had dealt with Barry on several previous occasions. One time was when I was unsuccessful in getting death row inmates' prison ID numbers so I could send each a mailing. Another time was when I attempted to visit another death row inmate. They only allow you to visit one person on death row and I had been visiting with Richard for several years, so my request to visit someone else was denied. When Barry saw me leaving the prison grounds, he had notified Warden Farley that I was there.

I explained to Warden Farley what was going to happen on our day in Michigan City. I told him we would be gathering about a mile from the prison near city hall. I told him we were going to march to the rally site across the street from the prison.

Since it was one of my responsibilities to line up the events of that day, I was able to give Mr. Farley a complete picture of our planned event. I told him who the speakers were and about a band that would be playing several sets of human rights music. I informed him that we would be there three or four hours and then leave. I told him that we had plans for a program in Gary later that night. I let him know we were a non-violent group and had no intention of causing trouble.

Mr. Farley seemed quite relieved. He looked at me and smiled as he said, “I guess I can cancel putting the men with rifles on the roof tops.” I was 99 percent sure he was just kidding.

One day before the *Journey* was to begin, I picked up Sam Reese Sheppard and Rick Halperin at O’Hare airport in Chicago. We stopped at a *Ponderosa Steak House* in Gary on the way to my house. I broke the fast by pigging out on the buffet.

We drove to Indianapolis to get five rental vans. Two of the vans went to the state park where we would be spending the first week. The rest of the vans came on to my house in Portage where the majority of the people would be meeting. All those coming in through Chicago would be spending the day in Portage. Those coming from the south through Indianapolis would be going directly to the state park.

The *Journey of Hope* was finally about to begin.

CHAPTER 35

Journey of Hope: from Violence to Healing

We had reserved a nice shelter at Woodland Park across the street from where I lived in Portage. This would be a great place for people to gather as they came in from around the country to start the Journey. One slight problem, it was raining cats and dogs. So, instead of people going to the shelter, we just had them come over to our house.

Sister Helen Prejean was one of the early arrivals. Random House was scheduled to release her book, ***Dead Man Walking . . . An Eye Witness Account of the Death Penalty,*** the first of June. Sister Helen told them she would be in Portage, Indiana on the fourth and that they should send the first case of books there. A big box arrived shortly before Sister Helen did.

As soon as Sister Helen entered my house, I said, "Look what came for you!" She opened the box and took out a copy of her new book. It was the first time she had seen a final printed copy. Everyone was excited

People began arriving from all over the country. Effie Johnson, a dear old lady from Nebraska, was driven to Portage by her son. He left and went on back to the Cornhusker state, leaving Effie in our hands.

Mike Penzato, whom I had met at *Amnesty* functions, was there. I had gotten to know him pretty well at a recent *TOT (Training of Trainers) Amnesty* session in Chicago. At the *TOT* I talked a lot about the upcoming *Journey* and Mike decided to see what all the talk was about.

Abe Bonowitz arrived. He had rented a car and driven from Ohio. Pajama Lady was there from Maine.

Shirley Dicks and her daughter Marie drove up from Tennessee. It wasn't long before we had a full house. It had rained all day so we never did go to the park across the street. My wife Judy and Cuzzin' Judi took care of the food. We had fried chicken from the best chicken place in town and some wonderful homemade macaroni and cheese.

That Friday evening, I was supposed to speak at a Jewish Temple in Gary for Rabbi Halperin (no relation to Rick). The rest of the group was to go on out to the state park where Bob Gross was waiting.

The group in Portage was ready to get on with the *Journey* right away and ended up going to the Temple with me. Abe, who is Jewish, did a reading at the service. We were able to talk about the *Journey* and everyone was introduced. Each person gave their name, where they were from, and why they had come on the *Journey*. It was a wonderful start for everyone.

In late evening, we went as a caravan of eight vehicles to the state park. The drive was slow because of the rain, and took an hour and a half. We met the others who had been waiting for us. Bob had planned a group meeting for all the Journeyers, but because we arrived so late, most of that plan had to be scraped.

But thank God, the *Journey of Hope* had begun!

Saturday morning we had an early wakeup call for the drive to our morning meeting site at Indiana death row at the Indiana State Prison in Michigan City. It took an hour to get there. We were delighted that the media came out in force, and interviewed a lot of us before we began to line up for the one-mile march to the prison.

Nearby, a small group of six women stood together with signs protesting what we were doing. Their signs said: **Help NIPSCO,** [the local electric power company] **Send 54 Murderers to the**

Electric Chair, and **Take Murderers off Death Row—Give Them the Chair.**

As we marched, we chanted, **"Abolition, Yes, Yes! Death Penalty, No."**

We marched to the rally site at the prison with only one incident: one person leaned almost the full length of his body out of a passing car yelling, "Kill them all!"

Amnesty International's Toni Moore helped me emcee the rally. I introduced Rick Halperin, who gave a great historical talk about the death penalty.

Marietta Jaeger talked about her daughter Susie's death and her own personal journey "from fury to forgiveness, from revenge to reconciliation." She said that those who hold on to hate only give the murderer another victim. "I am now convinced that the only whole, healthy and holy way to respond is forgiveness," she said.

Lois Williamson, the chairperson for *CURE*, spoke. She said forgiveness was freedom for the soul. Lois's nephew and husband had been killed in separate incidents and their killers sat on death row in Pennsylvania. Lois said, "If you don't forgive, then you've given them another victim because it tears up your life."

Lois told how the words of her eight-year-old granddaughter made her reflect on the injustices of the death penalty. Her daughter had seen a television news program about a man who was executed for killing a policeman. Her granddaughter asked, "Who's going to kill the guy who kills him?"

The group protesting our march toward the Indiana death row had now grown to a dozen.

One of the protesters carried a sign that said: **Murderers Don't Want To Be On Death Row: Dawn Didn't Want To Die**. It was carried by Fran Van Meter, from nearby Merriville, whose daughter Dawn had been killed. Fran came with several other relatives to say, "No murderers should live, and no victims die un-avenged." Fran said that her twenty-year-old daughter Dawn had been slashed and beaten to death eleven years ago. She could not understand how an organization called *Murder Victims' Families for Reconciliation* could even exist, much less organize this rally.

The ***South Bend Tribune*** later reported:

> The Merriville woman talked quietly to Prejean for at least 20 minutes, while some of her relatives taunted speakers at the anti-death penalty rally.

Later, Sister Helen said that Fran Van Meter's greatest concern is not that someone die for her daughter's death, but that the killer—who has never been charged with murder—never kill again. "That's not bitterness. That's from love."

Sister Helen then gave the keynote address. She talked about her book ***Dead Man Walking*** and what led to the writing of it. She talked about the two men whose execution she witnessed in Louisiana, about their families and the families of their victims.

Sister Helen said she saw firsthand how wrenching the issue is. "The book shows both sides," she said.

When Sam Reese Sheppard spoke, he told how the state of Ohio seeking the death penalty for his father had affected his life. Sam talked about his concern for the children of those on death row.

November West read a poem she had written and Pajama Lady had a few things to say.

We ate a picnic lunch that Cuzzin' Judi and my wife had helped put together. It was a great afternoon. Press coverage was fantastic. The music was super. The weather was beautiful. The film crew that had done the promotional piece advertising the *Journey* was there, and Judy also videotaped the rally for the archives. It would have been nice if more people had shown up.

Our Saturday evening stop was Gary, Indiana, for a service at the St. Monica / St Luke Church. In our free hours before that meeting, a few of the *Journey* vehicles stopped by the beautiful Dunes State Park on the shore of Lake Michigan.

At the evening service, the mayor of Gary welcomed the *Journey of Hope*. After several people from the *Journey* spoke, it was time for one of the special moments that I knew awaited us. Our guest speaker was Rev. Bernice King, daughter of the late Dr.

Martin Luther King, Jr. Bernice began her talk by calling *Murder Victims' Families for Reconciliation* "one of the most important organizations in America." She praised those taking part in the June 4-20 *Journey of Hope* for "setting a higher standard of compassion, forgiveness and non-violence."

She said, "I lost my father and my grandmother to violence, yet I cannot accept the judgment that their killers deserved to be executed. Sometimes I struggle with my feelings of anger, but then I remember that my father was a Christian minister who preached a message of forgiveness and non-violence."

Being a daughter of a minister and an ordained Christian minister herself, she said she is called to "love the evil-doers even as I deplore their deeds. This isn't easy."

She pointed out how Christianity offers forgiveness as a way to reach spiritual wholeness. "Revenge and retribution can never bring about healing," she said. "Every act of violence leaves in its wake the seeds of more violence. We have to make something positive come out of the tragedies we have faced. Forgiveness is a positive, transforming, healing force."

Rev. King said she was opposed to the death penalty not only for moral reasons but also for social reasons. She talked about innocent people on death row. "The death penalty makes irrevocable the miscarriage of justice. Is it worth the death of even one innocent person to execute two thousand five hundred who are guilty?"

She said that the death penalty sets an example of brutality that makes us, as a country, "a little less humane, and more willing to take human life again. If we are ever going to have credibility for moral leadership in the world, we will have to abolish the death penalty."

Then Bernice said to all of us taking part in the *Journey of Hope*, "I salute you for your bravery. Your efforts will reap a great victory for humanity—a more just and loving America."

A church choir sang and a local group did an ethnic dance. It was a great night and a wonderful start to the *Journey*. Then we made the one-hour drive to our cabin site at the state park. It was late by the time we got to sleep.

Journey members present Rev. Bernice King
an Indiana *Journey of Hope* t-shirt at
St. Monica/ St. Luke Church in Gary

I had to leave early Sunday morning to speak at a church in Goshen, Indiana, while other Journeyers were traveling to cities all over Northern Indiana. Wayne and I drove to Goshen. There were no major highways, mostly two lane roads with a lot of ninety-degree turns. Some of the small towns we went through were Amish, with horses and buggies everywhere. We had to drive very slowly at times and it took almost two hours to get to the church. We had allowed only seventy-five minutes so we were about fifteen minutes late. Several people were out front waiting for us.

After the service, we drove to Elkhart to pick up SueZann Bosler. She had been at her sister's house and spoke at her sister's Brethren Church, and would now be joining the *Journey* for the first time. We headed back to Tippecanoe State Park and were late for lunch. Cuzzin Judi had roasted some turkeys, and saved a turkey leg for me. Delicious.

There was a collection of area newspapers at the campground. All of them gave major coverage to our march and rally. There were many interviews and a lot of statistics about the death penalty.

In the afternoon I drove to East Chicago to speak to a group of young people at the *Catholic Worker House*. Mary Hutchison ("Hutch"), an elderly lady and one of our steering committee members from Gary, was there. She had her ex-son-in-law, John Gorak, drive her. John supported the death penalty, but he was moved by the presentation.

On Sunday evening, we had a fundraiser at the home of Helen Boothe, where the *CURE* board meeting had been held. Sister Helen was the guest speaker along with four *Journey* participants. Other *Journey* folks were once again spread out at churches all over Northern Indiana.

Several members of the media had come to interview Sister Helen. There had been tremendous coverage in all the local Sunday papers about our march the previous day. The ***South Bend-Tribune*** featured a colored 10" x 6" picture of Sister Helen and Fran Van Meter, the protester Sister Helen had talked with. In the photo they had their arms around each other.

But Sister Helen did not show up by the time the meeting was to begin because she had taken a wrong turn and didn't realize it until the highway came to an end twenty miles down the road in the wrong direction. She had to turn around and come back.

When she arrived, she was wearing a shirt that said: "Abolish the death penalty: Just do it." Sister Helen spoke and read some from her book.

Sister Helen talked about how her personal journey had begun. She told how her order, Sisters of St. Joseph of Medaille, took a stand to be on the side of the poor and to work toward social justice. She explained how, at the urging of a friend, she had written Patrick Sonnier, a death row inmate in Louisiana. "I didn't know then how it would change my life," she said.

Sister Helen went on to explain how her efforts have drawn national attention. The media exposure at first was not welcomed by her religious order. "Some sisters had questions, but they have been very supportive," she told the group.

She explained how—although she was opposed to the death penalty—she supported life without the possibility of parole for people who commit heinous crimes.

"Serious crimes do merit serious punishment," she stated. "People need to feel safe. But when people are educated about the death penalty, support for it drops."

She closed her talk with the statement, "The death penalty has nothing to do with solving crime. It's a random act of vengeance. It's almost always used against poor people and frequently against people who kill white people."

When the Gary ***Post-Tribune*** wrote their article about the fundraiser, they quoted me saying, "Sister Helen was the inspiration for the *Journey of Hope*."

Again it was late when we arrived back at the Tippecanoe River State Park on Sunday evening. Monday promised to be another great day, especially for me, because we were headed to the Glen Park section of Gary where Nana had lived.

The first thing I did in the morning was to go to a local radio station for a one-hour interview and call in program. Then I met up with most of the rest of the Journeyers at *Lew Wallace High School*. This is the school where the four girls that killed Nana had attended.

The school officials were very pleased that the *Journey of Hope* was coming to their school. *Lew Wallace High School* had suffered a real black eye when four of their students were involved in such a terrible crime. Assistant Principal Paul Freeland said, "That tragedy has been a cloud over the school and the students . . . this is the beginning of a healing process."

Cuzzin' Judi rarely talked about Nana's death, but this was also a special occasion for her. Students who were there for summer school were ushered into a room we had set up with banners and posters. We showed them the *Journey* video clip and then Judi and I talked about the very emotional subject of Nana's death, forgiveness and the death penalty. I held Cuzzin Judi's hand while she spoke.

We entertained questions from the students. One of the girls responded to me by saying, "you must have a big heart." I looked her in the eyes and said, "I have a big God." In turn she replied, "I believe in God, too, but I don't believe anyone has a right to take a life." Once again I looked her in the eyes and said, "Exactly!"

At the end of the session, we presented the school with a plaque to be placed near a tree that we were about to plant on the school grounds. The plaque read: **In the spirit of love, compassion and forgiveness, given in memory of Ruth Pelke, presented by the *Journey of Hope . . . from Violence to Healing*, June 7, 1993.**

We all held hands. We said a few words and all took turns putting a shovel full of dirt onto the tree planted in Nana's memory. The idea of planting the tree was Bob Gross's. Bob also came up with the idea of planting trees in each city that we went to in memory of all the victims of murder. Bob said, "It's a way of making a statement of hope and life and pointing the way toward reconciliation and healing rather than a cycle of vengeance."

Bill and Cuzzin' Judi Weyhe participate in a memorial tree planting service at *Lew Wallace High School* in Gary, where Paula and the three other girls attended

The ***Post-Tribune*** had a big color picture of Mike Lawson of Indiana placing a shovel full of dirt on the tree. Mike's brother, a newspaper boy, was shot to death. Mike made the statement, "There's no sense for me to want to have anyone killed, to see someone else go through the pain that I did."

We used a church recreation center in the Miller section of Gary for relaxation when we had breaks during that Monday. I went there for a while and played basketball with my stepsons Kennie and Jamie, Taniya's boyfriend Tony and several other Journeyers. All three stepchildren were told that they must come with us on the *Journey* because we were not about to leave them 'home alone'. I did tell them they could bring their dating companions if it was all right with their parents. Each parent said okay, so we added Tony, Tori and Dede to the list of Journeyers.

Monday night, we had a special session at *Indiana University Northwest*, located in the Glen Park section of Gary. It was advertised as a concert and speaking event. Charlie King, a folk singer well known for his music on human rights struggles, was the featured artist. I spoke after his first set and then SueZann spoke after the second. There was not a dry eye in the house when SueZann finished speaking. She told about the Bible she had gotten in hopes of giving it to James Campbell someday. She asked people to sign it. It was the first time that most people on the Journey had heard SueZann speak. Everyone was moved beyond words.

As usual, we arrived back at the campground late. And as usual, we had a group meeting to discuss that day and what would be happening the next. It was also a good time for people to share.

After these evening meetings, many of the Journeyers would build a bonfire, sit around and talk. We got to know each other better, while drinking a beer or soda and attempting to "solve the major problems in the world" as we enjoyed the fire.

Chapter 36

Surprises Every Day

As we headed for South Bend, home of *Notre Dame*, on Tuesday morning, I had my first chance to talk in depth with George White. When I asked George why he had come on the *Journey of Hope* he told me his story . . . .

George was vice-president and general manager of a building supply company in Southern Alabama. One night, after store hours, George received a phone call at his home. The caller apologized for calling George at home, but explained that he had an emergency. The circuit breaker for his freezer had gone out and he needed a replacement right away.

George and his wife, Charlene (whom he called Char), were about to go out for dinner and a movie. Char's mother was babysitting the children. George and Char agreed that they could meet the man at the store in fifteen minutes, get him the circuit breaker, and then go on to dinner.

When George and Char arrived at the store, no one was there, so they went inside and waited. In five minutes, there was a knock on the door and George went to answer, expecting to meet a grateful customer. Instead, a man wearing a ski mask and holding a gun in his hand confronted him. He demanded money from the safe. George opened the safe and gave the man the money inside. Then the man wanted to go into the showroom to get money out of the cash registers.

George told him there was not any money inside the registers but the man giving the orders had the gun. As they walked through the door to the showroom, George turned back towards the gunman to find out where he should go first. Char tripped and suddenly the gun fired. George said it fired again . . . and again . . . and again . . . and again . . . and again. George had tried to wrestle the gun away.

The next conscious thought George had was lying on the floor in pain. He had been shot three times. George saw his wife on the floor and thought she was dead. He got up and went to call for help. He heard Char cough. He went to her and put her head on his lap. She never coughed again; she died in his arms.

George had lost his wife to murder and the two children had lost their mom. Tom was twelve years old and Christie was five. But their nightmare did not end there. Sixteen months later, George himself was arrested for the murder of his wife. But George had faith that the legal system would work and he would be found not guilty.

Fourteen months later, after a trial that the Alabama Court of Criminal Appeals later called a mockery and a sham, George was convicted of first-degree murder. The prosecution sought the death penalty. George said the all-white jury saw him as one of their own and he felt they lacked the guts to send a white man to death row . . . so they sentenced him to life in prison. George said if he had been a black man he would be on death row today or already electrocuted in Alabama's electric chair.

George spent two years and 103 days in a southern Alabama prison before he was released by order of the Alabama Supreme Court. He was to be tried again. Then evidence came forward to prove his innocence beyond any shadow of a doubt. Some of that evidence had been sitting and molding in the prosecutor's office. George spent a total of seven years in legal limbo. He credits a country lawyer by the name of Paul Young, who took his case for $1, and was finally able to prove his innocence.

George said he learned what hate is. He hated the man who killed his wife and he began to hate people within the system that had let him down. George said he realized that all that hate was killing him, too, and he had to let it go. He wanted healing. George told me that hate is a continuation, not an ending.

George said that for seven years he had a love-hate relationship with God. He hated God but God kept on loving him.

George had brought his son Tom to the *Journey*. George is a tall man, 6'4", but Tom overshadows George, standing 6'8". Tom was getting ready for his junior year at *Lynchburg College* in Virginia where he had a basketball scholarship.

When Tom met Sam Reese Sheppard, there was a natural bond. They had been through similar experiences. Both of their mothers were killed and their fathers wrongly convicted by the state.

George was now working with death row inmates through the *Alabama Prison Project*.

In South Bend, as we were ready to begin our march toward *Notre Dame*, John Gorak suddenly entered the building where we were meeting for final instructions. John Gorak was the man from Gary, who favored the death penalty, but had driven his ex-mother-in-law, Mary Hutchison, to several of our sessions. Now he was full of anxiety, something obviously on his mind. He told me he wanted to speak to the group.

John had heard SueZann Bosler speak the night before at *Indiana University* in Gary. John said he was deeply touched by her message and the message of the love and compassion shown by the Journeyers. John wanted to let us know that he was finally able to see the light. He also wanted to read us a poem he had written during the night; he said he hadn't slept at all.

John had served ten years with the U.S. Marines, with two tours in Viet Nam. He said he had now found peace within himself because of us and he had made the sixty-mile drive to tell us. He did not know where to find us in South Bend. But sure enough, he saw several Journeyers standing on a corner passing out flyers with a listing of the day's events. He asked where our base was for the day and located us.

SueZann was making a difference! We were all making a difference. I envisioned the *Journey of Hope* being like what the

Bible says about sowing seed: sow good seed; you will bring forth good fruit. I had seen good fruit come out of some past events, but this was the quickest fruit I had ever seen! It was great for the rest of the people on the *Journey* to see the good that was already happening. We were ready to start the march into South Bend.

But heavy all-day rains on Tuesday had washed away many of the local supporters of the South Bend march against the death penalty. Only twenty local activists joined the forty regular *Journey of Hope* travelers. In spite of the weather, media camera crews, radio stations, and newspapers still covered the day. South Bend mayor Joseph E. Kernan proclaimed the day set aside to support the families of murder victims, and he endorsed the *Journey* philosophy of reconciliation and forgiveness instead of retribution.

During the evening service, there was a terrible storm. We heard a loud noise and some of us ran to look outside. A large tree had fallen down in the parking lot. Fortunately, none of our cars were damaged. When we drove back to the state park, it finally stopped raining, in time for our late-night group meeting and bonfire. Day five had dampened our marchers, but not our spirits.

First thing Wednesday morning, the *Journey* headed to Goshen, Indiana, in Mennonite country. To make the ecumenical service scheduled for 8:30 A.M. we had to leave the state park by 6:45, heading for the Elkhart County courthouse. Rev. Wanda Callahan, director of *HOPE (Hoosiers Opposing Executions)*, was the leader.

Wanda Callahan knew most of the fifty-five men on Indiana's death row. She visits twenty-two people regularly, and another twenty on occasion. She's a spunky woman, nearing her seventieth birthday.

Wanda told the ***Elkhart Truth***, "I'm a Christian minister and I don't believe in taking life. But even if I weren't a Christian, I couldn't believe in the death penalty . . . we don't rape rapists." When people tell Wanda, that she should considered the sensible thing of slowing down or giving up her ministry, she replies, "I don't know how to quit. These guys are my friends. You don't quit being a friend just because money is tight or you're a little scared to drive." Wanda explained that the Lord has a way of providing for her needs just when it seems there's no more money for gas or stamps or a phone call.

On several previous occasions, I had spoken publicly with Wanda and had also met her wonderful husband Callie, before he died. Wanda was thrilled with the *Journey* coming to her area.

Another important Elkhart area participant was Ruth Andrews. Her mother, Helen Klassen, had been murdered in her home in 1969. Ruth organized in the Elkhart area before the *Journey of Hope* came to town. "I believe that violence begets violence," she said. "The opposite is also true: Love and forgiveness will have the same ripple effect. Then there will be more opportunities for love and forgiveness."

Wanda Callahan was the emcee for the ecumenical service. SueZann Bosler spoke first, and talked about the Bible she had for James Campbell. "I have people sign it. I will take it to him to show that I really do forgive him and love him from the bottom of my heart."

Rev. B. Pat Butler, pastor of Elkhart's First Presbyterian Church said, "Capital punishment is not just an issue of life vs. death for offenders. The issue is a hit-man mentality that is out for punishment and hate. I am opposed to the mind-set of 'getting even' even more than I am against putting someone to death as a punishment. Grace is the opposite of getting even. Let there be more grace."

All those gathered began to sing *Amazing Grace*. Then I had a chance to talk once again about forgiveness. George White spoke after me and said, "For society to say to me, my children, my family, that execution would heal the wounds of our loss is a damnable lie. What began as an act of violence should not be memorialized by an act of vengeance."

After the ecumenical rally, Judy and I left with Ed and Mary Ruth Weir of Georgia to meet with the *Mennonite Board of Missions*. I had met Ed and Mary Ruth during the Florida-to-Atlanta *Pilgrimage March*, but this was the first time they heard me tell my full story. We met with members of the staff and some missionaries that were home on leave.

After lunch at the Mennonite office, we joined the rest of the *Journey* folk at the Tolson Center to once again plant a tree in memory of murder victims. It was a very touching ceremony.

In the evening, we made the lengthy march to the Elco Theater in Elkhart. We were a bit weary, but our spirits picked up when we saw the theater marquee: ***JOURNEY OF HOPE . . . from Violence to Healing.*** It was great to see that. The program featured music by a group called "*Road Less Traveled*," and music by the Canaan Baptist Church men's choir.

I was on the list of speakers, but I didn't really feel like speaking. I was tired, and didn't know what to say. I thought everyone had heard my story, and I was too tired to think of anything new. I went down into the basement of the theater and prayed to God for strength. When I came back upstairs, "*Road Less Traveled*" was singing the old folk song, "If I had a hammer, I'd hammer in the morning . . . if I had a bell to ring . . . if I had a song to sing . . . . etc."

When I was introduced I started by saying, I did have a hammer, I did have a bell, I did have a song to sing and I was singing it all over this land. I don't remember what all I said after that, but it was one of the most inspirational talks I'd ever given. Praise the Lord.

Back to the state park. Once again we had our late night group meeting and the bonfire for the really late nighters. Those bonfires helped us build warm and lasting bonds.

As we drove Thursday morning to West Lafayette, the home of *Purdue University*, an eleven-year-old girl by the name of Morgan LeSuer-Mandernack of Flora joined us. She told the ***Lafayette Journal and Courier*** that she didn't much care for the death penalty. "There's no reason to kill somebody. It just makes one extra person dead in this world. And that's ridiculous." Out of the mouth of babes.

The Thursday march ended at the Tippecanoe County

Courthouse. Mike Lawson talked about his brother's death. "We feel that we've had enough violence . . . . [The death penalty] doesn't ease our pain . . . . It does not bring us an ounce of relief."

Pajama Lady (Helen Pajama) spoke out, "It's racially applied and that appalls me. They can't give it out fairly."

Ken Coates, our senior citizen from California spoke up. "Society shouldn't descend to the level of its worst citizens . . . We should not be in the business of killing people . . . not if we're trying to teach our kids that killing is wrong." Ken is a retired minister.

On Friday, we all went to Fort Wayne, my favorite Indiana city. Their media had been wonderful to us in their advance coverage of what the *Journey of Hope* was all about.

Several weeks earlier, we had a press conference in which the religious leaders of the city outlined their beliefs about the death penalty and urged residents to support the *Journey* event. Rabbi Richard Saffron represented the *Jewish* community, Monsignor Bill Lester represented the *Roman Catholic* community, Rev. Vernon Graham, director of *Associated Churches*, represented the *Protestant* community, and Rev. Sylvester Hunter, associate pastor of Union Baptist Church represented the *African-American* community. At that meeting, I presented the philosophy of the *Journey* and told of Nana's story and of the Paula Cooper case.

In Fort Wayne we gathered at 10:00 A.M. at Lawton Park downtown. We marched to Freimann Square for a rally. In addition to the *Journey* speakers, the mayor spoke: he declared it ***Journey of Hope Day***. The day's events in Fort Wayne were held in conjunction with Black Expo Days.

In the evening, we went for a special service at St. John Missionary Baptist Church. The evening started with a wonderful meal of delicious fried chicken and all the trimmings. There was a citywide youth choir of one hundred teenagers who sang before George White and I spoke. George had stepped in a hole earlier in the day and twisted his ankle. He nearly had to be helped to walk on the stage to talk, but gave a wonderful presentation. It was the first time I'd heard him preach a sermon. It was a memorable night

Once again it was very late when we got back to the state park. And we had to leave very early in the morning to go to Chicago.

In Chicago we had some advance radio publicity, including a one-hour talk show with Catherine Johns on ***WLS*** a week before the *Journey*. ***WMAQ*** ran spot announcements all day Saturday while we were in Chicago.

We had a march and rally, where Jeanne Bishop and Jennifer Bishop Jones talked about their sister, Nancy Langert, and her husband who were murdered in their Winnetka, Illinois, home in 1990. "We are here to say: Don't kill in our name! We've suffered from killing, and violence, and we reject it," Jeanne said.

"The death penalty is not a proper punishment, it is in fact a crime," said Jennifer. "I want to live in a country where life without the possibility of parole is the worst punishment available for the crime of murder."

The Bishop Sisters, Jennifer and Jeanne,
speak about the death of their sister Nancy,
when the *Journey* visited Chicago

At the Chicago *Journey of Hope* rally, Charlie King sang. Sam Reese Sheppard spoke about his father's case. Sam said that if his father had been executed, he would have died along with him. "I was traumatized by the murder of my mother. Then I was traumatized five months later by the state that wanted to execute my father for a murder he did not commit."

While in Chicago, we saw an art exhibit of paintings and poems from death row inmates in Illinois. We went to a city park and did some street theater that included giant puppets. We drew a large crowd of onlookers.

Back at Indiana Tippecanoe State Park, we prepared for a move to McCormick Creek State Park in the southern part of the state the next day, Sunday. But first, we had a really big bonfire to celebrate our last night there.

Chapter 37

Welcome to the *Journey*

McCormick Creek State Park was a perfect location with plenty of space reserved just for us. A great variety of people were joining us as the *Journey* continued on.

For example, Marie Deans and Pat Bane came during the middle weekend and that gave us new voices. And when Teresa Mathis joined us, it meant that all five of the original founding board members of *Murder Victims' Families for Reconciliation* had come to the *Journey of Hope*. Marietta Jaeger was only able to be with us on the weekends, but was a very important voice when she was there. Marietta was *MVFR*'s newest board member along with Pat Clark, both joining the board shortly after the *National Coalition to Abolish the Death Penalty* conference in Chicago.

Then Sue Norton, from Arkansas City, Kansas, joined us. I had first read about Sue in a publication of ***OVM*** (*Offender Victims Ministries, Inc.*) and contacted her about the *Journey*. Sue told how she and her brother had received a painful phone call on January 9, 1990, to tell her that her daddy and stepmother had been shot to death in their Oklahoma farmhouse.

Sue asked the question many *MVFR* members have. "Why did it have to be my family, why?" They were killed for $61 and an old truck!

Robert Wesley Knighton was arrested for their murder. He

had already been in jail for thirty of his forty-eight years and had just recently been sent to a halfway house to prepare for his parole.

Sue said that the first time she saw him was in the courtroom, wearing jail clothes and his hands and feet were shackled to a leather belt. She said what she remembered most was his eyes. His eyes didn't waiver when he stared at her. She later learned his eyes were wild from drugs.

At the end of the preliminary hearing, Sue said she was numb with hurt and very sad. She couldn't understand the mindset of a person who seemed so determined to destroy anything that got in his way.

Sue spent all summer getting ready for the October 1990 trial, and still found it hard to believe that her daddy and Virginia were dead. The trial lasted three weeks. The last two days of the trial, her heart ached and tears rolled down her cheeks.

As she listened to the evidence, she found discrepancies. She began to fear that BK (Knighton's nickname) might be innocent. She began looking at him a lot as the trial progressed. Their eyes locked often as the trial drew to an end.

BK was found guilty on two counts of murder. On November 7 the DA said the jury would give their recommendation of a sentence by the next day. Sue's eyes were red and her body shook from sheer nerves. She couldn't eat.

Sue said she thought about statements that people made to her about BK: "They should have shot him the first time around . . . killing him is too good for him . . . they should not waste taxpayers' money on him . . . . An eye for an eye . . . ."

Sue thought about how society expected her to hate BK and she couldn't stop the tears from flowing as she began to pray. "God forgive me for my sins. Forgive me for being so distant from you. God, my heart is breaking. Daddy is dead, Lord! Now another man's life is at stake. God, what is wrong with me? What am I supposed to be feeling? Lord, I am so scared!"

Sue fell asleep praying but woke up in the middle of the night with a remedy to her heartache. *"I do not have to hate BK!"* As a former Sunday school teacher, she knew that God forgives. She felt if God could forgive BK, she should, too. She forgave BK that night.

Sue went to visit him the next day in prison. She gave him the gift of love and forgiveness. BK told her, "Nobody has ever done anything nice for me. I'll be better off dead. Then I can't hurt anyone else. I want to die!"

A short time later, the jury came back with the sentence—death by lethal injection. BK is now on death row in Oklahoma and Sue has visited with him many times.

Sue says his life is changed. She said he is no longer mean and his anger is dying. Sue says, "Forgiving has been the powerful medicine that has made me strong in this very difficult period of my life!"

Sue said, "People think I have lost my mind, but I have found it. I have the peace that comes from doing God's will. If I ever have a question about the right thing to do, I think about what Jesus would have done. I know he would have forgiven and reached out and wrapped his arms around BK."

"If I don't speak out against the death penalty, I'll feel as if I have BK's blood on my hands, just like the blood I have cleaned from my parents' home," she said.

Welcome to the *Journey*, Sue Norton.

Aba Gayle also joined the *Journey*. Aba Gayle came from Santa Barbara, California to tell how she had come to forgive the killer of her daughter, Catherine Blount, who was nineteen years old when she was killed. Aba Gayle suffered for several years in grief, anger and rage.

In 1992, Aba Gayle says she was directed by a loud, clear voice to forgive the man who killed her daughter. She wrote him a letter and offered forgiveness and sent him a blessing from the "Christ in her to the Christ in him." When she wrote the letter, there was instant release from the deep anger and rage, she says. In the place of anger, she was filled with love, joy and peace. She was healed and knew immediately that it didn't take the government murdering someone to have the completion she needed.

Aba Gayle now begs the government not to murder in her

name. She does not want to tarnish the memory of her beautiful child with another senseless killing.

Welcome to the *Journey,* Aba Gayle.

Of course not everyone who joined the *Journey* was a victim's family member. Many were there just because they strongly supported victim's families or wanted the death penalty abolished.

People like Grant Verbeck. Grant, a neighbor of Bob Gross, was one of the most pleasant surprises of the *Journey.* He took over the job of logistics and transportation, and made sure the vehicles were always ready to go. He made sure that the drivers had directions to where the speakers were going. Grant was very dependable and filled an important role. I hadn't even thought about a vehicle coordinator and who would handle it, but Bob knew of Grant's abilities and it worked out great.

Other newcomers included Bill and Lora Shain from New Hope House in Georgia. They came for this second week of the *Journey.* They traded places with Ed and Mary Ruth Weir who were there for the first week. Bill was retired from the U.S. Air Force.

The growing *Journey* group included Elizabeth Arnett from Sweden. She was involved with *Amnesty International* there. Kim Donnelly, her daughter Foveae, and her mother Karol Copeland came for the full two weeks from Coventry, England. Our foreign friends made it an international event. Leigh Dingerson, the executive director of the *NCADP* joined the second week; as did Rev. Joe Ingle. Magdaleno Rose-Avila, my good friend from *Amnesty*, also joined us. Mike Heath, whom I had met on the Texas *TASK March*, came up for the *Journey.* And Jana Lee Huffman, the author of *No Flowers for Their Graves*, from Las Vegas joined us.

Ron Carlson and his wife came up from Texas for a few days. Ron preached a sermon on Sunday, the first time he ever preached in a church. He praised the Lord. He talked about forgiveness. He told how it took away the hate and anger he had for Karla Faye Tucker who had killed his sister.

Welcome to the *Journey,* Ron.

Sally Peck joined us from Michigan. She heard about the *Journey of Hope* from Marietta. Sally's mother, Bernice O'Connor, was eighty-two years old when she was raped and killed. Killing her killer would desecrate her mother's memory, she believes. Sally said her mother raised her to believe in forgiveness. Sally was glad to see that there were men on the *Journey* who were also able to forgive.

Welcome to the *Journey*, Sally.

A few days into the *Journey of Hope*, I called Randall Dale Adams. When Randall answered the phone, I asked how he was. I told him we missed him in Michigan City at the opening rally. He responded by saying that the *Journey* didn't start until June. I told him it was the 8th of June already. He seemed stunned for a second and then began to apologize. He said that after twelve years in prison, he really wasn't used to looking at a calendar much. After asking me to forgive him several times, he said he would join us as soon as he could, and sure enough, a few days later he came. What a wonderful addition Randall was to the *Journey*.

Randall was from Columbus, Ohio, and was just sort of drifting through Texas at the time of his arrest. He was arrested, convicted and sentenced to death for the murder of a Dallas policeman. A death warrant was signed and Randall was given a date to die. He came within seventy-two hours of being executed when he received an indefinite stay.

Through a documentary on his case, ***The Thin Blue Line***, Randall's story became well known. The documentary gave compelling evidence of his innocence including a statement from David Harris, the real killer, who admitted that Randall was innocent. Harris is now on death row in Texas for an unrelated murder.

When Randall speaks, it is with great authority. He has been there. He often says, "People, make no mistake about it. If you have a death penalty in your state, sooner or later you will execute an innocent person." He says, "That cost is too high."

Some people look at Randall and say that because he was not

executed, it is proof that the system works. Randall will tell you that he is alive and a free man today, not because of the system, but in spite of the system. Welcome to the *Journey*, Randall.

Don and Kathy Norgard joined us from Arizona. Their son was on death row. He is guilty of the crime for which he was convicted, but Don and Kathy are trying to do what they can to save his life.

Shirley Dicks became ill on the *Journey*. Her blood pressure went up pretty high, and so after some treatment, she had to leave. Her daughter Marie was able to stay. Marie had become good friends with my step-kids and didn't want to leave yet. Shirley had adopted Marie. Marie's father, Jeff, who was on death row in Tennessee, was Shirley's son. Shirley was her grandmother, but Shirley adopted her as her own daughter.

What the death penalty does to the families is what I call cruel and unusual punishment.

On Monday, the *Journey of Hope* went to Bloomington, the home of *Indiana University*, where Micki Dickoff and Sunny Jacobs joined us. Micki was a film producer doing a documentary about Sunny. Sunny had been on death row in Florida and Micki had helped prove her innocence. Micki wanted to record as many of the *Journey* events as possible. I am such a firm believer in the power of the media that I was willing to do whatever I could for her. The camera crew from the Mennonite Church had left after the first weekend and would not be returning until the *Journey* reached Indianapolis, so I made my van available to Micki, Sunny and their cameraman Chris.

I was so happy that Micki joined us that I spent a lot of time talking with her and didn't really get much of a chance to talk to Sunny. In the *Indiana University* classroom, when I heard Sunny tell her story, I was in for a shock. Sunny and her husband were arrested, convicted and sentenced to death for the murder of two Florida highway patrolmen. Her husband was executed in 1990. In 1992, Micki Dickoff was able to prove that both were innocent. Sunny had been out of jail only a short time when they joined the *Journey*. Her case sounded familiar.

Then it hit me! Her husband was Jesse Tafero, the man who was electrocuted back in May of 1990, the day the Florida-to-Atlanta *Pilgrimage* began! Chills started up my back. It was that botched execution! Sunny was the other half of the "Bonnie and Clyde" team! Bonnie and Clyde were the names the media used for their sensational reporting of that case. Now we were finding out that they were innocent. Micki had proven it. Sunny had spent seventeen years in prison for a crime she didn't commit!

Christy Webb, Micki Dickoff and Sunny Jacobs

Sunny talked about how the death penalty affected her children. Tina, her daughter, was less than a year old when Sunny was arrested. When Jesse was executed, Tina, then a teenager, tried to kill herself.

I felt very close to Sunny, because I knew about Jesse's death and had met his mother Kaye, Tina's grandmother. Sunny and Micki both spoke to several classes at *Indiana University*. Altogether, our group spoke to ten classes at *IU* that Monday.

Then it began raining like I have never seen before. There was a small creek running in front of the school. We had parked our vehicles down in a little gully. Suddenly, the little stream was like a roaring river. We tried to get our cars out of the lot where we had parked them. It was already flooding. We got the first three out okay but the fourth one got caught in the rising water. We were able to get it out, but not before it had slid into a tree, doing some body damage to the van. No one was hurt, but Bob Gross looked like a drowned rat by the time the vehicle was brought to safety.

After several hours, the rains subsided and we marched through downtown Bloomington. What a day!

Chapter 38

Journey's End

We left the state of Indiana for the second time, on Tuesday, driving to Dayton, Ohio. Originally we were not going to go to Ohio, but an amazing young lady, Jana Schroeder, the criminal justice program director for the *American Friends Service Committee (AFSC)*, was insistent that the *Journey* should come to Dayton.

After a city-hall rally in Richmond, Indiana, we headed into Ohio to meet up with the rest of the group who had gone to the *University of Dayton.*

Jana Schroeder had lined up no fewer than eighteen churches for us to speak at that night! We sent two or three Journeyers to each church. Each church had a carry-in dinner by its members so everyone was once again well fed. I could not believe Jana had lined up so many churches. She evidently had no fear of rejection. Don't tell her it can't be done. By the way, Jana is blind.

During a Dayton interview, Sam Reese Sheppard told how most of his life he had run away from his famous father's case. He told the ***Dayton Daily News*** that only in recent years had he been able to translate his tragedy into activism. He said he was now finally able to face the memory of the mother that he lost at age seven.

"For years, I couldn't bring myself to display her picture. But now I have this incredible photograph of her at eighteen, with a smile on her face. And I've been able to live with that," Sam said.

Sam also told the ***Pall-Item News***, "We want to create platforms for reconciliation. Violence is out of control."

Marie Deans had to leave and go back to Virginia because they were getting ready to execute someone with whom she had been working. She also had been involved with the man's family. We all hated to see her go, but we understood.

It was a three-hour drive back to the Indiana State Park, including stopping to fuel up at a *McDonald's*. We got to bed very late and had to get up early again to go to Evansville and Terre Haute.

While in Terre Haute on Wednesday morning, we had a chance to do a small segment for ***ABC**'s **Good Morning America.*** In Evansville, after the noon rally at the Federal Building downtown, there was a tree planting, which drew about eight people who were protesting what we were doing. The evening covered-dish meal at the Nazarene Baptist Church was followed by a "prayer of hope" service with the public invited. There, Ken Coates, the retired minister from Claremont, California, said, "The *Journey of Hope* is opposed, as a group, to personal or state violence. That's why we are here."

Wayne and I missed the Evansville events because we went to Louisville, Kentucky to do some advance contact work. That night, Wayne and I got a hotel room and watched the Chicago Bulls play. They were going for their third consecutive championship. Wayne had never followed basketball much, so I had fun, turning down the sound and narrating the game for him. Of course, anytime you have a Scottie Pippen and a Michael Jordan playing, it's exciting. And, of course, the Bulls won.

On Thursday, George and Marietta Jaeger spoke at a rally in downtown Louisville at the Jefferson Square Park. George said he understood the desire for revenge. "If I could have gotten my hands on the murderer that night, I would have killed him. It's a natural reaction. Every surviving family member that I've come across understands what that need for vengeance is . . . . Members of the *Journey of Hope* have realized that an execution will not bring back their loved ones."

George continued, "Killing another human being isn't going to heal our pain, it's just going to make it, in some way, part of what we hate. We're giving in to this lynch-mob mentality. This death penalty stuff is about retribution. Let's call it what it is. It's about perpetuating the hate."

Marietta spoke at both the rally and at the Cathedral of the Assumption. Marietta said, "I see that those who retain a vindictive mindset have really given the offender another victim. The quality of their lives is diminished. They're bitter; they're unhappy and they don't have peace. However justified they feel, they're not healed."

Marietta talked about her wrestling match with God. She said, "I had to remind myself that however I felt about this man, in God's eyes, he was just as precious as Susie. Jesus died for him, too."

Marietta talked about revenge being a natural first reaction. "You're hurting so much that, somehow, it just seems like if you can hurt somebody else, it will make you hurt less. You just want to lash out. There is no way that you're going to bring that person back."

While we were in Louisville, the ***Record*** ran an article discussing the *Roman Catholic Church*'s stand on the death penalty, which was not a hot issue in Kentucky. The electric chair had not been used since 1962, although there were now thirty people on Kentucky's death row.

Father Patrick Delahanty, an archdiocesan priest active in the *Kentucky Coalition against the Death Penalty* said he didn't know why more priests don't talk about capital punishment. He said:

> Not many people care about whether or not there's a death penalty. There are a few of us that do. It seems worthwhile that somebody keeps reminding people that this punishment is immoral.
>
> A call to abolish the death penalty by victims' families is especially poignant. I think it's valuable for people to know that you can suffer extremely tragic events in your

> life and overcome so-called natural responses because of grace. It's a sign that grace is that powerful.

Another great day on the *Journey*, but Thursday wasn't over yet. We went back to the state park a little earlier than usual. Because we knew it would be the last opportunity for us to meet among ourselves, we had a special group session with all *Journey* participants. Everyone sat in a large circle and had a chance to share. It is amazing; the bonding that takes place in this sort of event.

There was a consensus that we should do another "*journey.*" Pat Bane suggested maybe Virginia in two years.

Tom White spoke up and said that he was a bit apprehensive when he came with his dad to the *Journey* because he didn't know what to expect. He said he was glad he came because he saw more love on the Indiana *Journey* than ever before in his life.

George and Sam had taken a side trip to Columbus, Ohio, to do an interview, so George told how he stood there looking at the old state penitentiary where Sam's father had been incarcerated. He could imagine Sam as a seven-year-old boy whose mother had been killed and his father taken away and convicted. He said he saw and understood Sam in a new light.

As we went around the circle, my wife Judy was videotaping what everyone said. So was Micki Dickoff's crew. Micki's crew was in the center of the circle; Judy was taping from her spot as part of the circle. Then people wanted Judy to say something. She stepped out from behind the camera and said, "When Bill and Wayne came back from the *TASK March* two years ago and started talking about doing this event in Indiana, I thought, 'Oh, no, here they go again.'" Then she looked down at where I was and gave me a "thumbs up" and said, "It's been great."

It meant a lot to me for her to say that. Judy had wavered on her stance about the death penalty after being on the *Pilgrimage March* three years earlier. A heinous murder of a nineteen-year-old girl working at an all-night convenience store happened a short distance from where she worked. Judy felt that one of the people arrested in the case, Stephen Miller, deserved the death penalty. When he was found guilty and sentenced to death, Judy did not want me to get involved in his case.

As we were working on plans for the *Journey*, guess who showed up at my house wanting to help us organize? It was Steven Miller's wife, Beverly, and his daughter Sherrie. As Judy learned more about the case, she realized that perhaps the man might be innocent—but she was still not ready to withdraw her support for the death penalty in some cases.

Judy had been a tremendous help to me while preparing for the Indiana *Journey*. She not only helped with the mailings but also put up with all the time I spent on organizing efforts at home and away. Every other steering committee meeting was held at our house and she helped cook and feed those who showed up. She had been a real trooper. She took off work for all seventeen days of the *Journey*.

Judy came to a new realization during this *Journey*. Not only did she fall in love with Marie, Marietta, SueZann, Sam, George and the others, but she also began to see the death penalty in a different light. Tina, in particular, changed her perspective.

Tina Schnebelt's brother, Timothy Bunch, was executed by the state of Virginia on December 10, 1992. Tina told of the pain and suffering she went through when he was executed.

"It hurt me so bad when I saw my brother that last day. If my brother had been murdered, I wouldn't want the killer's family to go through what my family has gone through." Tina is having counseling; her father suffered a nervous breakdown; her mother is "totally beside herself."

Tina told what the electric chair did to Timothy. She had a copy of the autopsy report and pictures taken after he was executed. Timothy had asked her to do this so she could let people know what the electric chair does.

Judy was able to relate to Tina more than any other speaker on the *Journey*. Judy thought about her three brothers whom she loved dearly and realized that one of them could possibly get into trouble someday and end up on death row. She couldn't stand the thought of one of her brothers being executed. Right then and there she knew she could no longer condone the death penalty. I never tried to force her to be against the death penalty. I gave her the reasons why I was, but it took Tina's story to win her over completely, once and for all. Thank God for Tina.

When the meeting was over, Sam and George were the first to hug each other. Judy and I were the second. There were lots of group hugs at this last group meeting. We lit the bonfire and got ready for our final two days in Indianapolis.

On Friday morning, we spread out over the city. George White and I went to a radio station and did a call in talk show together. Following the radio program, we went to the *Christian Theological Seminary* for a special program on forgiveness. The guest speaker was Robin Casarjian, an author from Massachusetts. Robin had written an article about forgiveness for our second issue of ***THE VOICE.*** Mrs. Brown, the wife of a local pastor, whose son had been killed, spoke. After Marietta and I spoke, Robin followed with a workshop on forgiveness.

In the evening, there was a large gathering at *Martin University* in downtown Indianapolis. The university president welcomed us and special music was provided. Randall Dale Adams and Marietta were the keynote speakers. Afterward, we went back to the campground for another late bonfire.

Early Saturday morning, we left the state park for the *Indiana Women's Prison* in Indianapolis, where the four girls who killed Nana were incarcerated. It is also where the women on Indiana's death row are kept.

We gathered at the prison gates for a rally. I held the Bible in my hand that I had bought for Paula Cooper. I told those at the rally that someday I would be able to visit with Paula and give her the Bible. I told them that most people wanted out of this prison, but that I wanted in.

Magdaleno Rose-Avila brought a letter from Joan Baez. Joan requested that I be the one to read it on the last day of the *Journey*. She wrote:

Dear friends:

Two weeks ago many of you began this march, this Journey of Hope, to publicly show your opposition to the most severe form of punishment carried out by our justice system, the death penalty. Many of you are also family and friends of murder victims, survivors of violent crimes. And by being here and taking part in this historic event, you are stating clearly that the systematic execution of a human being is not the way to put an end to the violence in our society. It will not make our streets safer; it will not make our consciences clearer.

I feel a special affiliation with the abolitionists in Indiana because while on tour in Italy in 1988, I was fortunate enough to join in an impressive and moving march protesting the scheduled execution of Paula Cooper. I will continue to speak out against this policy, which places the United States in a category that includes countries with abysmal human rights records such as China, Iran and Iraq. We must work at being more creative, more loving and more caring in order to be a nation that civilized people of the world do not look upon with confusion and distaste. You have taken a courageous step toward this. I thank you for being here and for the work you are doing.

Carry it on.

Joan Baez

Then we began our march to the state capitol building, one hundred strong.

We stopped half way to the capitol for a short rally. Magdaleno, Randall Dale and several others spoke. Then we marched on to the capitol for our final rally of the Indiana *Journey of Hope*.

Paula Sites of the Public Defenders Office in Indianapolis told the crowd that during the two weeks the *Journey* was in Indiana, there were three capital trials taking place. She informed us that all three juries came back with non-death verdicts, which she attributed to the fact the *Journey* was in the state. She said that the press the *Journey* had been getting was fantastic.

We reserved the United Auto Workers hall for a closing party and concert. There was dancing and a good time was had by all. We passed out awards to people who had done so much work. Bob Gross especially had done one fantastic job. No one could have done it better. Thank God for Bob Gross.

Kim Donnelly, our friend from England, told the ***Indianapolis Star,*** "I'm really glad we came. It has been really moving." Kim said she felt called from afar to take part. "I don't think we should just sit back and accept it, even if we are in another country."

Achebe Lateef of Indianapolis told the ***Star***, "I was turned against the death penalty after a speech on forgiveness by Bill Pelke. I was really moved by the fact he felt like he did about Paula Cooper. This was a voice of reconciliation, man; it was powerful."

One last bonfire, Sunday morning church services, and the 1993 Indiana *Journey of Hope* was over. People headed for home.

On the two-and-a-half-hour drive home, I was able to listen to the Chicago Bulls play basketball. It was the finals. One hour from home, John Paxton made a three-point basket and the Bulls won their third straight NBA championship. God is good.

It was great to look back on the incredible seventeen days of the *Journey of Hope* . . . . Fifteen major cities . . . four states . . . . over eight thousand people heard *MVFR* speakers in groups large and small . . . four mayors made formal declarations in favor of the *Journey* and *MVFR* . . . over thirty murder victims' family members took part . . . over three hundred people participated in the *Journey* itself, including the forty who started and the seventy-five who ended . . . seven international visitors took part . . . over a million people heard about the *Journey* on TV, radio, or newspaper. We even ended "in the black," with revenue exceeding expenses.

I can never thank Bob, Laura, Toni, Maureen, Wayne and all the others enough for making the Indiana *Journey of Hope* happen. We kept our pledge to Marie Deans to put *Murder Victims' Families for Reconciliation* on the map. The abolition community was now aware of *MVFR*. We were adding a powerful voice to the abolition movement.

You can believe I said many, many prayers of thanks to God.

CHAPTER 39

It Never Stops

The Indiana *Journey* was over; time for a break. Wrong.

It wasn't long before I received a call from Ed Weir of New Hope House in Georgia. When Ed and his wife got back from Indiana, they began talking to their friends how impressed they were by what they witnessed. They asked the *Journey* to come to Georgia!

Ed said they would do all the work and all the *Journey* would have to do is come. He said that they would raise the money, do the organizing, the whole ball of wax. It was a great offer. I told Ed that since the *Journey* was an *MVFR* project, he should send the board a written proposal.

When our *MVFR* board met in Montgomery, Alabama, in early fall, we agreed to go to Georgia for a *Journey* the following year, 1994. The board let me call Ed right then and there to tell him we were coming.

The *MVFR* board made a decision about ***THE VOICE.*** Several people felt there was "too much Christian stuff" in it. Someone else volunteered to edit it and my job as editor was history. Although I felt I had been fired, being editor had been such a tremendous amount of work I was a bit relieved and also glad to see others in the organization take on responsibilities.

Rick Halperin invited Carrie Kennedy, Marietta and me to be on a panel discussion at *Southern Methodist University* (*SMU).*

After the session, Rick met with Marietta and me to discuss his thoughts about some sort civil disobedience to protest the death penalty. That meeting was the seeds to the beginning of the *Abolitionist Action Committee (ACC).*

November West and others joined us in planning our first action. We decided against civil disobedience for the time being and settled for a fast and vigil at the U.S. Supreme Court in Washington D.C. We chose the dates of June 29, when the *Furman vs. Georgia* decision by that court brought a moratorium to the death penalty in 1972, and July 2, which was the date of the *Gregg vs. Georgia* decision that brought the death penalty back in 1976. We chose to do a four-day fast June 29 to July 2, 1994.

Cofounders of the *Abolitionist Action Committee (AAC)* Rick Halperin, Marietta Jaeger and Bill at the annual Fast and Vigil in front of the U.S. Supreme Court

In the summer of 1994, the United States Supreme Court was scheduled to make decisions dealing with the issue of the death penalty. We set about doing the work to get the necessary permits to do a fast and vigil in front of the Court.

When Rick, Marietta, and I met in Washington, D.C. on June 28, 1994, we anticipated that at least twenty people would be part of the fast and vigil. As the three of us sat in front of the Supreme Court building a few hours before the fast was to begin, Kathy Ford joined us from California. The following day, others from around the country came: Phyllis Pautrat from Philadelphia, November West from New York, Mike Penzato from Iowa, and others.

We had permission to use the *ACLU (Americans Civil Liberties Union)* office across the street from the Court, giving us a place to sleep and shower. In my van I had brought a table and chairs from home. We "set up shop" in front of the Court with anti-death penalty literature from various abolitionist organizations, and offered petitions for people to sign to show they were opposed to the death penalty. Representatives from several organizations—including the *NCADP, Amnesty International, MVFR,* and others—joined us. Sheldon and his documentary crew showed up for some interviews.

The four-day Supreme Court fast and vigil was a great success and we decided to make it an annual event, but I missed Judy greatly. When I saw people walking their dogs near the Court, I thought that Judy would have enjoyed bringing our Great Dane, Trixie, and being with all these wonderful people. When I got home and told Judy we could bring Trixie, she said she'd come to the Supreme Court event next year.

When the time came for the Georgia *Journey of Hope*, Judy and I arrived in Atlanta on the 30th of September, the day before it began. Many of the "regulars" were there, including Marietta, SueZann, Sam Reese Sheppard, George White, Sally Peck, Sue Norton and Aba Gayle.

The most interesting part to me, was hearing the personal stories of the new participants. For example, Dale Williams came from Brunswick, Georgia, and told us how his mother, Elizabeth, was killed in 1980. She was running for county tax commissioner, and her opponent was accused of hiring someone to kill her.

After four trials, the man was acquitted. But James Castell, the gunman, was given the death penalty, and Michael Jones, who drove the getaway car, was sentenced to life. Castell committed suicide while in prison.

Dale said, "Since the murder of my mother, my family has never been the same. My mothers' parents were alive at the time. They've since died brokenhearted that nothing was ever done to the person we think was truly responsible."

When interviewed, Dale told the ***Macon Telegraph***, "I've just had my feelings on hold, but in the last year or so I've tried to get to the point to see where I was, to see how I could make something good come out of it."

Dale said that for a period of time he carried around a pistol with him, just hoping to run into one of the people involved so he could kill them. And he thought how much he would enjoy pushing the button on the electric chair.

"For me, even at times today, I have the anger that wants to do something about it. I don't think it's in any of our nature to turn the other cheek." However, Dale knew that is what he needed to do.

People told him he would feel better if one of the people involved in his mother's death got the death penalty. When one did, he didn't. He was still angry; he still felt empty. "The way I felt about wanting to kill one of them was no less of a complete disregard for life than what they felt when they killed my mother. Their behavior was consumed by hate and anger. I couldn't live feeling that way. I had to find something else," Dale said.

Dale found forgiveness. He stopped feeling angry about his mother's death and forgave the men charged with her murder. "I can live better forgiving them than I can being angry with them. There's not a day that goes by that I don't replay all of it in my mind, but I've let the anger end in me."

Dale told the ***Macon Telegraph*** that he was traveling with the

Journey through Georgia because our purpose was to educate the public about the experience of losing a loved one to murder and the eventual recognition that forgiveness is better than hate.

"I'm for forgiveness. I couldn't say that two years ago but I can now. I'm not saying I'm right because I feel this way and everyone else is wrong. I'm just saying this is right for me. It is a complete whole life. Forgiveness is the way for me."

Welcome to the *Journey,* Dale Williams.

While riding on the *Jubilee Partners'* bus, I met Ann Coleman and Barbara Lewis. They told me they were best friends from Delaware. Both had a story to tell.

Anne Coleman's daughter, Francis, was shot and killed while driving her car through Los Angeles, California, in September of 1985. No one was ever arrested for the murder.

When Anne and her youngest son, Daniel, picked up the car from the police compound, they found that the car had not even been cleaned after Francis's death. There was a horrific odor. Daniel was never able to get over his sister's death. He was very depressed and died of cardiac arrest two years after the murder as a result of taking antidepressant medications.

Anne felt the killer had killed two victims with the same bullet. Anne realized that vengeance belongs to God alone and that our duty was to "love our neighbor as we love ourselves."

Anne was shocked when she moved from New York, a non-death penalty state at the time, to Delaware, which was getting ready to execute a man. Ann went to protest the execution, but found herself alone.

She soon met Barbara Lewis, who also spent a lot of time alone. Barbara represented the other side of the death penalty debate. Barbara was a member of the forgotten victims' family members. Her son, Robert, was on death row for the murder of his girlfriend. Barbara told us that she also was a murder victim's family member with three relatives suffering death by homicide.

Anne and Barbara became best friends. Anne is white, Barbara is black. They travel together and speak a lot. They introduce themselves by saying they are twin sisters. They started an organization called ***BLAC*** *(Because Love Allows Compassion.)* It is also their initials.

They heard about the *Journey* and they came to Georgia. Welcome, Anne and Barb.

October first, the first day of the Georgia *Journey*, was the sixth wedding anniversary for Judy and me. That night, the *Journey* participants helped us celebrate. We had our Great Dane, Trixie, with us. It was Trixie's first *Journey*.

While in Savanna, Georgia, Judy took a picture of Trixie and me looking out at the river. We were standing in front of what looked like an old pirate's boat, and a bridge spanning the river in the background. We had it made into a 2' x 3' poster. I called it, "An Old Man and His Dog."

We were surprised to find out that Henry Heller, the executive director of *Virginians for Alternatives to the Death Penalty (VADP)* who joined us for the Georgia *Journey* also qualified as a *MVFR* member. Henry's grandparents, along with some aunts and uncles, were killed during the Holocaust.

The *MVFR* Board had decided the *Journey* would go to Virginia in 1996 and I was happy to get to know that someone as dedicated as Henry was already working for a *Journey*, two years away.

When Bob and Rachael Gross joined us, it was also their anniversary. We had a special cake and sharing time with them, too. Charlie King, the *Journey* troubadour, was with us, plus dozens of friends old and new.

Troy Reimer had done a fantastic job of helping Ed Weir organize the Georgia event. Participants in this *Journey* spoke at over 150 events, to over nine thousand people. Of the seventy-one travelers in the *Journey*, twenty-six were victims' family members. We spoke in thirteen major cities; through the media we reached millions. It was a great *Journey*, and a lot less work for me than Indiana!

CHAPTER 40

The *Discovery* Channel

Sheldon Himelfarb came back on the scene because the ***Discovery Channel***, as promised, came up with money in their 1994 budget for a documentary on forgiveness. Sheldon chose to do the program based on the lives of three people who had forgiven. He chose SueZann Bosler, Marietta Jaeger, and me.

For the program they chose the name, ***From Fury to Forgiveness,*** a phrase that Marietta used quite often when telling her story. Sheldon and his crew worked for ***Yorkshire Television*** in Great Britain, but they were doing the program for the ***Discovery Channel***. Sheldon made it clear the program was about forgiveness and not about the death penalty, but it would definitely touch on the death penalty in each case.

From Fury to Forgiveness aired on the ***Discovery Channel*** four times during October 1994. Susan Sarandon narrated the program, which was done in three segments: Marietta's part was first, followed by mine and then SueZann's, each lasting about fifteen minutes.

The first segment started with parts of a talk that Marietta had given in Fairfax, Virginia, to a group of people who had lost a loved one to murder. Most of the people at the meeting were still very much in pain, but listened closely as Marietta talked about the healing power of forgiveness.

From the Virginia meeting, Marietta's story went to the state of Montana, showing were the family had been camping when Susie was kidnapped. Sheldon managed to get television news footage from when the kidnapping took place twenty years earlier. A segment showed Marietta and her husband being interviewed, and there was a clip that showed the tent with a large cut.

Pete Dunbar, a Montana law enforcement official who had been in charge of the original investigation, was interviewed. Then part of the tape was played of the telephone conversation that Marietta had with the kidnapper on the first anniversary of little Susie's disappearance. It was amazing how Marietta had the presence of mind to turn on the recorder when the phone rang in the middle of the night and then carry on a remarkable dialog with him.

When the kidnapper called, he said, "Is this Susie's mother?" Marietta replied, "Yes, it is."

The kidnapper came back with, "Well I'm the guy who took her from you a year ago . . . ."

Marietta asked him, "Can we have her back?"

As the conversation continued, Marietta asked him, "Why did you take her?" At this point, the kidnapper began to break up as he responded with, "I always wanted a little girl of my own." Marietta kept the conversation going with the man in hopes the FBI could trace the call.

Marietta asked him, "What can we do to help you?"

The kidnapper responded with, "I wish I knew the answer to that."

Each year, Marietta goes to Montana to commemorate Susie's disappearance. For the first time ever, because of the film crew's help, Marietta was able to visit the farmhouse where Susie was kept hostage.

The story told how David was arrested and committed suicide while in jail. It showed Marietta meeting with David's mother at his burial site. Marietta brought flowers for the grave.

The segment ended with Marietta kneeling and praying at the farmhouse. As she rose to walk away, she made an anguished sound. Marietta told me later that she did not know they were taping her while she prayed.

Sheldon Himelfarb had done a beautiful job portraying Marietta's story, and I knew she would be happy with what he and his crew had done. Marietta's story is one of the most powerful stories on forgiveness I have ever heard.

Part two of the ***Discovery Channel*** program told of Nana's death. It began with an interview with one of the policeman who responded to the emergency call to Nana's house. It showed scenes of *Lew Wallace High School* and the urban decay of Gary.

Several times during this segment, they showed that beautiful picture of Nana.

The documentary crew had gone to Florida to interview my dad. I watched closely as he came on the screen. He said, "My wife and I went over to her house to talk about some repairs so she could sell the house."

Nana's response was, "I'll be *here*, till I go *there*." My dad raised his finger as she had and pointed to heaven. Then my dad said, "The next time I saw her, she was there." As my dad finished the last three words, he began to break up. When I saw this, I just wanted to give him a hug. He had been through so much, and now he was reliving it again. It was my fault. My activities over the years made him relive it again and again.

Later in the segment, my dad made the statement; "Ruth Pelke would have wanted the death penalty; that is how she felt." As I watched, I said, "No, dad, no!" He added, "Anybody who commits that sort of crime should be required to pay the full penalty of the law."

We definitely disagree as to how Nana would have felt. One of the best things about the love we have for each other is that we have agreed that it is all right to disagree.

The film crew went to the *Indiana Women's Prison* and interviewed Paula. While the crew was at the prison, they talked with the warden, Dana Blank. She was asked off camera why I was not allowed to visit Paula. Dana responded to them that she was unaware that I was not allowed to visit. She told them that the next time Paula put my name on the visitors' list I would be permitted to visit.

The crew came to my house, Bethlehem Steel and the U.S. Supreme Court to do interviews for my part in the segment.

The third segment of the ***Discovery Channel*** documentary was SueZann's story. It began with the courtroom scene of James Bernard Campbell's re-sentencing hearing. A higher court had overturned his initial death sentence. Sheldon had his crew in the courtroom in Florida for the new sentencing. The presiding judge was Leonard Glick.

SueZann took the witness stand. She said that she was there for three reasons. First, she was there for herself as a means of healing. Second, she was there for her late father, a peaceful man. The third reason she felt was the most important. That was the pending decision as to whether James Bernard Campbell would now be sentenced to live or die.

She told the court that she forgave James Bernard Campbell and wanted him to live. She hoped that the court would have mercy on him. The documentary then moved to the parsonage where SueZann and her father had been attacked. As SueZann told her story, the camera panned the house showing the rooms where the fateful activities took place.

SueZann said she had been attempting to visit James Campbell but he always refused to see her. She was told that he was afraid of her.

The scene went back to the courtroom in Florida. The judge was about to make his decision for Campbell. SueZann was very nervous. She had asked the judge for mercy, but she wavered in her thoughts as to whether he would give it or not.

Judge Glick delivered his decision. He said that Campbell's act was unforgivable by society and re-sentenced him to death.

Sheldon managed to get an interview with the judge. He was questioned about his statement that the crime was unforgivable and yet SueZann said she had forgiven him. The judge responded with, "Well, maybe SueZann Bosler is a better person than the rest of us."

That made me mad! What a copout! That is one of the most important misunderstandings about forgiveness. It does not make the forgiver some sort of saint! It is a simple decision that helps one heal. And it can help society heal, too.

The final scene of the ***Discovery Channel*** documentary was Marietta at Susie's gravesite. Marietta said a short prayer to God and spoke to Susie. She rose from her knees and made another anguished sound, wiped a tear from her eye, and walked away. End of documentary.

I thought Sheldon and his crew did a fine job. I was just sorry they had not been able to document the Indiana *Journey of Hope* the previous year. There was no indication in the documentary that Marietta, SueZann and I knew each other, were great friends and even working together.

Chapter 41

The Visit with Paula

The warden of the *Indiana Women's Prison* kept her word about my being able to visit Paula Cooper. I found out in early November that permission had been granted for me to visit. It had taken eight years.

Marietta Jaeger was going to Iowa for Thanksgiving to visit her sister. Since my house in Portage, Indiana, was half way between Detroit and Iowa, Marietta was able to spend Wednesday evening with us. I fixed a Thanksgiving meal and my kids came over and joined us for dinner.

Judy was working the day shift; so Marietta and I had breakfast Thanksgiving morning at *McDuffies Restaurant* in Portage. It was always special when Marietta was in Portage, but on this particularly special Thanksgiving Day I was finally going to have a visit with Paula. After breakfast, Marietta would drive on to Iowa and I would head to the women's prison in Indianapolis. Marietta seemed almost more excited about my being able to visit Paula than I was. She was excited for me, because she knew how long I had wanted to visit with Paula.

We prayed after breakfast and took off for our destinations. My drive took three hours. I had visited prisons before, so I was used to the routine: fences with barbed wire, the giant gates with locks, and the personal search before the visit. My name was on Paula's list. I sighed with relief when they told me to go on in.

I remembered what Paula said on the ***From Fury to Forgiveness*** documentary about wanting to look me in the eye and know for sure that I had forgiven her. I was in the visitor's room when Paula came in. I stood up and she came over to me. At the other prisons I had visited, you were allowed to give a hug at the start and end of a visit. I asked Paula if it was okay if I gave her a hug. She said, "Yes." I gave a short hug, took a step back, looked her in the eyes and said, "I love you and have forgiven you."

Paula and I had exchanged dozens of letters over the years. Many of mine talked about forgiveness. Paula had read a lot of articles about me talking about forgiveness. But if she wanted to look me in the eyes to know for sure, it was fine with me.

We talked about a lot of things. We talked about people we knew in common, like Father Vito, Father Greganti, Monica Foster, William Touchette, Anna Guaita, her grandfather, and her sister. We talked about the traveling that I had been doing. We talked about *Murder Victims Families for Reconciliation*, last year's Indiana *Journey of Hope* and the just completed *Journey* in Georgia. We talked about the people on death row and she told me how glad she was that I had shifted my efforts from helping her to helping them.

We did not talk about Nana or her death. We did talk a little about God, the Bible, and prayer. Before I knew it, our one-hour visit was over. It was time to go. I gave her a good-bye hug and told her once again that I loved her.

As I drove home, I felt more like I was floating or flying than driving. One word kept going over and over in my mind, the word *wonderful.* Whenever I began to sum up the day in my mind, the word *wonderful* jumped out at me.

Why *wonderful?* I had just visited with someone who had done a terrible thing to somebody I deeply loved, someone who had hurt my entire family immensely, someone whom I would have had all the reasons in the world to hate and have the desire for revenge. Yet I had none of those feelings.

I had feelings of love, compassion, and forgiveness. It *was* wonderful. I praised God for those feelings as I drove home. It was truly a *wonderful* Thanksgiving Day.

Chapter 42

John Wayne Gacy

John Wayne Gacy was the "poster boy" for the pro-death penalty crowd. Several months before his scheduled execution, a local paper, the ***TIMES***, interviewed me. The headline said *Death penalty foe works to stop Gacy execution*, with a picture of me sitting in my office at home.

My co-workers and friends raised an eyebrow when learning about my efforts on Gacy's behalf. When people would say, "You're not going to get involved in his case, are you?'" My answer was, "Absolutely. When you apply a philosophy of love and compassion for all of humanity, it applies even to John Wayne Gacy."

I told the ***TIMES*** that "Life without the possibility of parole is a better alternative than the death sentence for Gacy. People are upset at what he did, and rightfully so. He's a sick man but shouldn't be killed. Vengeance is not the answer."

I had little support. At the time, President Clinton supported the death penalty and polls indicated that the vast majority of the American public did, too.

However, a week before the Gacy execution, U.S. Supreme Court Justice Harry Blackmun announced that he would no longer "tinker with the machinery of death."

Al Manning, spokesman for the Illinois Attorney General Roland Burris, said, "The people of Illinois have decided that they want the death penalty, and this execution will establish more confidence in the criminal justice system. Gacy is a convicted murderer and deserves the death penalty . . . . This will remove one of the most heinous criminals from society. The families of the victims will have some sense of relief."

David Keefe, Gacy's attorney said, "I don't ask you to be in favor of the guy. He's not a very popular character. The thing is, if the death penalty is wrong, it's wrong for our basest, baddest citizens, and that's where we have to stick to our morals most."

Keefe also said, "We think it's bad for society to be in the business of killing people. When you cut away all the smoke, you really see that it's just satisfying blood lust. Is that the way for society to mature?"

A reporter from a Chicagoland cable TV news station informed me that she would be at the prison the night of the Gacy execution to host a live call-in talk show. The talk show would start at midnight, the time the execution was to take place. She said she knew a lot of "crazies" would be calling in and she told me she felt it was very important for someone with my philosophy to be there with her for these sorts of calls. I agreed.

Early on the night of the execution, May 10, I left my home for the seventy-five-minute drive to Joliet, Illinois, and the nearby Statesville prison death house. I knew several people from the *Illinois Coalition* would be showing up at around 9:00 or 10:00 in the evening. But I wanted to get there several hours early to meet with the cable reporter. I brought my suit to wear later.

As I was driving, I felt like everyone was looking at me. It seemed that every truck driver that drove past was looking at me and talking on their CB. The top news story for the day was the Gacy execution and here I was in my van with a bunch of anti-death penalty bumper stickers. I felt a bit paranoid.

I arrived at the prison at 7:30 P.M. I parked my van and was instructed to walk several blocks. No doubt this was going to be a media circus. An area was all lit up where the media satellite units were parked. Press and TV outlets from around the world were covering the execution.

At the entrance to the vigil area, I was put through a thorough search for alcohol, weapons and signs. There was a hallway of fences to follow that led to a larger holding area.

Then I realized that those *for* and *against* the death penalty were all going to be corralled in the same fenced-in area! That was different from the vigil I had been to in Idaho when Keith Wells was executed. In Idaho, the *for* and *against* were kept in separate sections. At Gacy's vigil, there was a large fenced field with a group of about fifty people already lined up against one side of the fence a hundred feet away. There were a lot of media folks on the other side of that fence.

I was wearing my red t-shirt from the *TASK March* in Texas, which made it very clear that I was opposed to the death penalty. I didn't plan on wearing it all evening because I had brought my suit. I didn't go up to where the group was standing but went further down the fence looking for the reporter I had talked with earlier.

A young lady came up on the media side of the fence and asked if I was Bill. She said she was an assistant to the reporter I was looking for. She told me that things had not worked out for me to go on the press side because they couldn't get me a pass. She told me they would do a live feed with me standing by the fence when the time came for the midnight execution.

Other members of the press who had been with the larger group began drifting my way. They started asking questions about Gacy. Soon there were eight or ten members of the media in front of me on the other side of the fence.

Then one of the blessed souls asked the question, "How would you feel if someone in *your* family was killed?" The "press conference" was on! I began to talk about Nana, Paula Cooper, love and compassion, forgiveness, Jesus, and the death penalty. When a reporter would get his question answered, he would leave to report to his studio. Whenever one would leave, another would take his place. At one point there were over a dozen media folks on the other side of the fence and just me on my side.

I found out one of the reasons for such interest was that the other fifty people across the corral who had showed up early were all for the death penalty. I was the first to arrive who opposed it. I was fresh meat for the media sharks. I loved it.

I had prayed a lot on my drive to the prison. I wanted God to give me the right words to say. Now God, it seemed, had allowed me a worldwide press conference for forty-five minutes, talking to the media of the world.

I had this corner of the big corral staked out for the abolitionists. Around 10:00 P.M. they began to show up. It was my guess that by the midnight execution time, there were two thousand for the execution and about one hundred and fifty opposed. The abolitionists formed a circle and lit candles. The death penalty supporters would come over and blow out candles and continually break up our circle.

I feared there would be a riot. The assistant from the cable news told me that the lighting was not very good where I stood. She pointed clear over to the other side of the corral and asked if I could go over there by the fence. I left our group and headed for the other side.

It took at least five minutes to work my way through the crowd. I was able to get to only within fifteen feet of where the reporter was waiting at the new site. She saw my plight and began calling to people to let me through. The people opened up a little aisle for me to move up. Each time someone got out of my way, I thanked them and then I could hear them say as I passed, "Hey, he is opposed to the execution." I still had on my *TASK* t-shirt.

I made it to the fence. It was about twenty-five minutes before midnight. The crowd was working itself into a frenzy. There had been a parade in Chicago that day hosted by one of the local DJ's who called it the Gacy Day Parade. The parade drew about three hundred participants. They had banners that said things like "Ground the Clown," a reference to the fact that Gacy had been a clown for special occasions before his arrest.

No one was allowed to take signs into the vigil area. But suddenly, the DJ who had hosted the Gacy Day Parade appeared on the media side of the fence. He displayed a large banner, about twenty feet long. It showed needles with poison shooting out and a picture of a clown. The crowd went wild. Everyone in this section supported the execution.

There were people sitting on people's shoulders, chanting and yelling. They were pushing the people ahead of them in a sort of rhythm. I could feel the pressure from behind. I kept one hand on the snow fence stake and the other on the fence. At any time, the fence was liable to collapse.

After several minutes, the Illinois state police went up to the DJ and made him put his banner away as it was about to incite a riot. Slowly he folded it up and put it away. State police were all over the place. On the media side of the fence, police were standing about ten feet back and were lined up six feet apart. I knew if there was any problem the assistant from the cable news would let the police know I had done nothing wrong and deserved their help. I was never so glad in my life to see so many policemen.

Midnight came and the reporter told me to hang on. A short time later, it was announced that Gacy was dead. The reporter again told me to hang on. As people began to leave, the reporter yet again told me to hang on, that it would only be a few minutes and I would be on. The state police began clearing the area out. They asked me to go, but I told them I needed to hang on for a few more minutes. The reporter said, "Two minutes and you'll be on."

The reporter came back in five minutes and said I had been pre-empted for something else. It was time for me to go home.

At work, during the days before the execution, only a few asked me if or how I would be involved with Gacy's execution. Mostly my co-workers would ask Wayne, "Hey, is your buddy going to hold a candle for Gacy?"

When I went to work the morning after the execution, there were no questions. I think I had been quoted on every Chicago TV channel, and in every daily newspaper in Chicago and Northwest Indiana.

The amazing thing was that each station and each paper had a different quote. Thank you, Jesus. Channel 7 (***ABC*** in Chicago) made the statement that Bill Pelke of Portage, Indiana, was the only one at Statesville that was opposed to the execution. It seems almost everyone from work watched ***ABC*** that night and said, "Yeah, that's Pelke, the only one opposed." The ***ABC*** reporter must have made that statement early, after that initial "press conference" and before the other 150 who were opposed showed up.

What an experience. I think standing by the fence shortly before midnight was as close as I had ever come to being intimidated. But I knew God was with me and I felt I was on a mission for Him that night.

CHAPTER 43

Wisconsin, D.C., California

Marietta and I were invited to come to the *University of Wisconsin* in Madison to speak at the first *National Conference on Forgiveness* in the spring of 1995. Bob Enright, a professor at the university, was hosting the conference. Someone had seen ***From Fury to Forgiveness*** and told Bob about it. On Thursday, the keynote speaker was Father Lawrence Jenco, the hostage who forgave his kidnappers. Marietta and I were the keynote speakers on Friday night. They showed the video before we spoke.

The result of the conference was the forming of *The Forgiveness Institute*. Bob Enright was appointed the director.

In the meantime, Marietta and I kept in constant touch about the coming California *Journey*, our major event for 1995. We would talk on the phone sometimes three or four times a day. We planned brochures, fundraising and other strategies for the event. Bob Gross was available for advice, but this one was up to us.

We got Charlie King lined up to come and sing for us and Sister Helen agreed to come to the Bay area and speak for us. There was a lot of excitement about Sister Helen. Her book, ***Dead Man Walking***, was being made into a Hollywood movie. Tim Robbins was the producer and Susan Sarandon was going to play Sister Helen.

My wife Judy came to the second annual midsummer fast and vigil at the Supreme Court in Washington, D.C. Judy told me that she would come but didn't think she would fast. She said she would try to fast the first day and see how it went.

Once again the fast and vigil was an outstanding event. One evening, as we were sitting in front of the Supreme Court building, a car pulled up and a man jumped out. He asked if he could have some of our literature. We said, "Sure, and would you like to sign our petition?" He did. I walked over and introduced myself. Several others did the same. He told us his name was Jesse Jackson, Jr.

He told us he was helping his father write a book about the death penalty and it was almost completed. He gave us his card; he was a congressman from Illinois. What a treat for us.

As our fast drew to a close at midnight on July 2, Mike Penzato's parents, who were visiting from Illinois, brought several loaves of wonderful bread to break the fast.

Judy enjoyed the Supreme Court fast and vigil. She met a lot of new people and fasted the entire four days. Trixie, our Great Dane, was with us. When Judy went back to work and people asked her where she had been, they were shocked to hear she had been fasting and sleeping on the sidewalk in front of the U.S. Supreme Court to protest the death penalty. She told them she had a great time, that it was "a real blast."

Judy had never told people at work how she felt about the death penalty. When the topic came up over the years because of my involvement, she always told them, "It's Bill's thing."

It didn't seem like long before we flew to California in October for another *Journey*. We arrived in Los Angeles and went directly to the Amnesty Regional office where Mike Penzato had been doing the on-site California organizing for us. Judy and I spent a lot of time with Mike on the Indiana and Georgia *Journeys* and it was Judy who came up with the idea of asking Mike to help organize California.

It was unusual for me to leave my van behind. It seemed like I drove my van everywhere I went and I felt almost naked without it. Not to fear, we rented four vans shortly after arriving in LA. I drove down to San Diego that night for the start of the *Journey.*

The opening night keynote speaker was Anne Coleman. It

was the tenth anniversary of the death of her daughter, Francis. She gave a powerful talk. We stayed overnight at a mission of sorts run by a very popular priest. Unfortunately, he was in favor of the death penalty, and when he found we were opposed to it he was sorry he had let us stay there. Oh, well . . . .

The first full day started at the Mexican-U.S. border. Half of our group went into Mexico and met us on the other side of the fence. We formed a circle holding hands with those on the other side.

Ricardo Villalobos, a *Murder Victims' Families for Reconciliation* member and a staff member of the *National Coalition to Abolish the Death Penalty*, led us in the ceremony.

In Los Angeles, we had a major rally. Tina Tafero, the daughter of Jesse Tafero and Sunny Jacobs, spoke to the crowd. It was the first time Tina had ever talked publicly about the death penalty. She told the audience what it was like to go from being a baby to a teenager with parents on death row and to go through her father's execution. She spoke for the children of those on death row.

We had a special treat for those attending the rally. Mike Farrell, the president of Death Penalty Focus of California, spoke to us. Mike, who played BJ Hunnicutt on ***M.A.S.H.,*** has worked for years for the abolition of the death penalty. Shelley Fabares, who is Mike's wife, and their daughter, were also there.

Judy asked Mike, "Was it cool being BJ?" Mike said yes it was "cool."

I always liked ***M.A.S.H.***, but ***Coach*** was one of my TV favorites and Shelley was the coach's girlfriend, Christine. I was really impressed with Shelly. I detected that she was touched by the rally that had taken place and by the hearing victims' families speaking out against the death penalty. Shelley has worked hard for years against the death penalty and for other human rights causes.

When we got to the Bay Area, it couldn't have been better. Claudia King and the *Bay Area Action Team* outdid themselves. Claudia not only organized this great second week but she was responsible for raising about $20,000. We stayed at youth hostels while in the Bay area. They were former lighthouses, located right on the ocean.

There was one problem that took me a little while to fix. During the Georgia *Journey,* there were a few times that the vegetarians in the group weren't happy with some of the meals. Mike, who is a vegetarian, made sure this didn't happen in California. It fact, he went to an extreme. In each city we went to, the people responsible for meals thought we were all vegetarians. It seemed like all we saw for the first week and a half was vegetarian food.

Several of us were serious meat eaters. We had some free time on Wednesday afternoon of the second week, so George White and I went to the store and bought steaks, ribs, hamburgers, chicken and some garden burgers. We had a gigantic barbecue. Everyone thoroughly enjoyed it. Even the veggies were happy.

Sister Helen had to cancel her California date with us. At first I was crushed, but she did give us several months notice so we were able to work around it, even though all of our printed literature said she was coming. Oh, well.

The rest of the California *Journey* went great, and because of Claudia, we didn't go broke. In fact, after all bills were paid and reimbursements made, I was able to write out a check to repay *MVFR* the initial seed money of $6,000 plus a few extra dollars.

One night, when we arrived at a new lighthouse hostel, Grant Verbeck, from the Indiana *Journey* was driving a van and I was riding in the front passenger seat. Anne Coleman and several others were in the back. Grant and I got out of the van, high on a mountaintop overlooking the ocean. As Grant and I walked away from the vehicle, it began to roll toward the edge of the cliff. Grant had not put the van in park. I was able to jump in through the open passenger door and use my hand to apply the brake and stop the van a short distance from the edge.

Anne has loved me ever since. Well, most of the time ever since.

Once again, Judy and I celebrated our wedding anniversary on a *Journey*. Celebrating with these friends is the best; in fact, on

Journeys, we all become like family. As George White says, "We are family. We are related. We are related not by birth or by marriage, but by the blood of our loved ones." California was indeed a special blessing.

CHAPTER 44

Oprah and Judy

On December 29, 1995, Gramercy Pictures released the movie ***Dead Man Walking.***

Marietta called me and said that she had been asked to be on ***The Oprah Winfrey Show*** as a guest with Sister Helen, Tim Robbins and Susan Sarandon. The reason for inviting Susan, Tim and Sister Helen was obvious, but it was not obvious to see why Marietta was going to be on the program.

Sarandon had worked on human rights issues for a long time, and had spoken on numerous occasions against the death penalty. But there was one question always thrown back at Susan that she didn't really know how to handle. It is the classic question that many pro-death penalty advocates bring up as a last resort argument: "What if someone killed your little girl, how would you feel about the death penalty then?"

Susan never quite had the answer for that until she narrated ***From Fury to Forgiveness***. After hearing Marietta's story, Susan knew that if—God forbid—anything like that would happen to her daughter, she would want to have the attitude of a Marietta Jaeger.

When it came time for ***The Oprah Show***, Susan asked that Marietta join her, Tim and Sister Helen.

Oprah arranged to take several busloads of audience guests, at her expense, for a private showing of ***Dead Man Walking.***

Since we lived close to Chicago, Marietta made sure that Judy and I could be part of the studio audience and see the movie.

When we drove to Chicago, it was a difficult drive because there was a tremendous amount of snow falling.

When we got to the studio, they put us on buses and drove us to a theater to watch ***Dead Man Walking***. I had read the book several times. The movie was quite different, but I felt Tim Robbins did a fantastic job in putting it together. Susan Sarandon was superb in playing the role of Sister Helen and Sean Penn was excellent playing Matthew Poncelet.

I also found it quite interesting that Sister Helen played a cameo role as a protester at an execution vigil. Abe Bonowitz and Magdaleno Rose-Avila were also in the movie as protesters.

Oprah made sure we were all fed, but the planned program did not take place because the snowstorm was so bad that the guests, Tim, Susan, Sister Helen and Marietta couldn't land in Chicago. The program had to be rescheduled for a few days later.

Judy and I drove back to Chicago for the program on January 14, Judy's birthday. We got to the studio a little later than we wanted. They were already passing out numbers for seats, and we knew we were too late to sit anywhere up front.

When it was almost time to let the audience in, they called for Bill and Judy Pelke. When we responded, an usher said, "Come with me." We were led to two seats in the very front row marked *reserved*. Marietta had told them we were coming and they kindly saved the seats for us.

First on stage were Tim Robbins and Susan Sarandon.

Oprah talked about one of Tim's other movies, ***Shawshank Redemption*** and how it should have won an Oscar. Oprah then talked about ***Dead Man Walking***, and said it should win an Oscar.

Tim and Susan were funny and likeable. The audience loved them, and when Oprah talked to Susan about playing the role of a nun, she admitted it was different because of hairstyle and lack of makeup.

Then Sister Helen came on. She was funny as she talked about how she didn't know much about Tim and Susan and how she had "checked them out" before agreeing to do the movie with them. She said they weren't the normal Hollywood types and knew she could trust them.

Marietta Jaeger came out last. Oprah first told Marietta's story in a very shortened version, then asked Marietta about forgiveness. When they took a commercial break, Marietta looked over at us, smiled at Judy, and mouthed the words, "Happy Birthday." We found out later when the program aired, the camera was still on Marietta and the whole world saw Marietta tell Judy happy birthday.

The last segment was very short as Oprah summed things up. She mentioned that Marietta was an extraordinary person because she had forgiven the killer of her loved one. When Marietta had one last chance to say something, she said that she was *not* an extraordinary person, but an *ordinary* person doing *extraordinary* things. She then said, "There are a lot of people in *Murder Victims' Families for Reconciliation,* like Bill Pelke who is here today (she pointed to me) who also travel around the world and talk about forgiveness." With that, the program ended.

Ever since it was announced that ***Dead Man Walking*** was going to be made into a movie, I wanted to meet Tim and Susan. As soon as the program was over, I walked up to the stage and gave Marietta a hug and kiss, then Sister Helen. I looked over to where Tim and Susan had been standing, but they were being led out of the auditorium. Too late. Well, maybe some other time.

The movie was excellent. ***The Oprah Show*** was excellent. Happy Birthday, Judy!

When I was asked to go to Monterey, California, to be on a panel about victims' families and how attorneys should approach them, for the annual Appellate Conference, we worked it out so Judy could go, too. It was over Valentines Day; it was a wonderful weekend. Judy was beginning to like abolition work more and more.

In June, Judy talked her friend Leah into coming with us to the annual fast and vigil at the Supreme Court building in Washington, D.C. Leah asked a lot of questions and it didn't take long before she would walk up to people going by the Court, hand them literature about the death penalty, and strike up a conversation with them and get them to sign our petitions.

We had always talked about bringing someone else with you the next year to the fast and vigil. I had first brought Judy, and now she was bringing Leah.

Judy had the ability to get along with everyone. Even though abolition of the death penalty was not her main focus in life, she was easily able to love those who had that for a goal.

That spring, Judy and I had gone for some counseling. On the third session, we were to bring a written list of the things we really wanted out of life. Judy's list included things like happiness and material things like money. At the top of her list was a *Harley-Davidson* motorcycle.

My list was rather different. At the top of my list was world peace. Abolition of the death penalty was next. At the end of that session, the counselor told us we didn't need to meet anymore unless a problem came up.

When I found out a Harley meant so much to Judy, we began to talk about it. Two of her brothers, Mike and Marty, had Harleys and so did her ex-husband. She told me she always wanted a Harley. She said she wanted to buy a "basket case" (where the bike is almost all in parts that needed to be put back together). She said it would cost around $5,000. She said she didn't know anything about how to put one together, but said she could find out. A friend of mine at work was selling her 1994 Harley Low Rider for $14,000. It was a red beauty, with lots of leather and chrome. I parked it in the garage while Judy was out shopping. When she saw it in her parking spot, she knew it was hers. I have never seen anyone happier in my life.

Neither of us knew how to operate a motorcycle. A Harley is no toy! We decided to take *ABATE (American Bikers Aiming Toward Education)* classes on how to safely and properly ride a motorcycle. We took a twenty-hour course in Indianapolis. Both passed. Judy scored even higher than I did.

Every time Judy would go for a ride, she would come back and tell me how much she loved me. She would wake up in the middle of the night and tell me how much she loved me. If I had known how happy a Harley would make her, I would have bought it years earlier.

Things were going well for Judy at work, too. She had transferred to the wellborn nursery. She liked it much better than the cancer floor, the cardiac floor and the others she had been on.

When the Virginia *Journey of Hope* came in October, we once again found ourselves celebrating a wedding anniversary on a *Journey*. It was our third in a row.

CHAPTER 45

Virginia Memories

The first day of the 1996 Virginia *Journey of Hope* involved a march to a *Roman Catholic* cathedral, which would seat about a thousand people. The keynote speaker, Sister Helen Prejean, was now a very popular person, not only in the abolition movement, but also throughout the world. ***Dead Man Walking*** had been nominated for four Oscars: Best Picture, Best Actor, Best Actress and Best Song. Susan Sarandon won the Oscar for her portrayal of Sister Helen. We were all delighted because it meant a lot for the abolition movement. With Sister Helen's newfound popularity, this first night of the *Journey,* fifteen hundred people came to the cathedral to hear her speak. People were sitting in the aisles, on the stage, standing against the walls, and listening in overflow rooms. What a great start for the Virginia *Journey*.

The headquarters for *MVFR* was now in Atlantic City, Virginia, where Pat Bane now resided. Marie Deans, the founder of *MVFR* also lived in Virginia so it made it a lot easier for the two of them to help with the organizing.

As Judy and I had been driving eastward to Virginia for the *Journey*, I began to think about the number of times I would be speaking. Forgiveness was always the key to my talks. I usually mentioned about not only forgiving Paula, but also how I had realized there were people at work that I needed to forgive.

Bill with Sister Helen Prejean and Marie Deans,
founder of *MVFR*

I began to realize that there were some people in the abolition movement that had been getting on my nerves—and the list was beginning to grow. I knew some of those people were going to be on this Virginia *Journey*!

Well, I knew I would have to take care of that. I couldn't be speaking about forgiveness while holding grudges. I started praying as we drove to Virginia asking God to help me forgive these people on the list; I asked God to give me compassion for them.

By the time we arrived in Virginia, I had the peace that all were forgiven. Anne Coleman's name had been on my list. On the California *Journey*, it seemed to me that Anne was always complaining about something, and, as the person in charge, I took all the complaints very personally. But I made up my mind that I was just going to love Anne no matter what.

I had the best time with Anne and really came to love her. One of the best parts of the Virginia *Journey* for me was that we got along so well.

As usual, the most interesting part was meeting new *MVFR* members and hearing them share their stories. For example, we met Sadie Bankston and her sister Florida Cyrus who drove from Nebraska. Sadie's son, nineteen-year-old Wendell Grixby, was murdered in 1989 while trying to protect a fourteen-year-old boy during an altercation.

Sadie said, "I am a mother who lost her son to violence, yet I bear no vengeance. Never once did I want the killer of my son to die for his death. We, as concerned human beings, need to band together in this fierce fight to abolish the death penalty. Always remember: 'God giveth and God taketh away.' The Creator doesn't need any help."

The killer of Sadie's son was sixteen years old. Sadie publicly forgave him. The community ostracized her for that. Many of her friends and family were also upset. Sadie said the importance of the trip far outweighed the inconveniences of traveling two thousand miles by car. Sadie said their travels only confirmed their opposition to the death penalty. "God calls us to forgive," Sadie says.

Kathy Dillon also came to the Virginia *Journey*. Her father, Emerson J. Dillon, was shot and killed in the line of duty as a New York State trooper. In 1974, he pulled over a speeding car. He didn't know it, but the occupants had been involved in a robbery. They shot him and pulled away, leaving him to die on the side of the roadway.

Ten years later, Kathy's boyfriend, David Paul, was shot and also left on the side of the road to die. Kathy says that she believes the death penalty, and the violence it brings, only undermines the efforts of those who seek a more peaceful world.

"All the negative feelings associated with the murder of a loved one could be frozen in time forever at the moment of execution. By allowing the passage of time, forgiveness is more likely to occur. What am I supposed to learn from these two murders? The answer, at least in part, has to be *forgiveness*."

Nancy Gowen, a resident of Richmond, Virginia, joined us. Nancy had been involved with Marie Deans and *MVFR* for a long time. Nancy's mother, Mary Weems Gowen, was murdered in 1979. Her mother's murder and the killing of about fifteen others were attributed to a group of three brothers and a juvenile companion. The state of Virginia executed one of the brothers, Lynwood Briley, in 1984.

Nancy had gone to an ecumenical prayer service before that scheduled execution. She wasn't sure if she was going to attend the execution, and if she did, she was not sure on which side of the street she would stand on. She did not know if she supported the execution or not.

After that prayer service, she picked up a poster that was against the death penalty. Then she stood with other abolitionists outside the prison gate. "It took me many years, but my journey has led me to know that all life matters, and that violence in any form is unacceptable," Nancy says.

"Killing is wrong. Taking lives does not send the message that it's wrong to kill. After my mother was murdered, the impending execution of one of the men responsible for her death only added to my pain. The execution would only feed the culture of violence in this country—a country that has already taken so many lives."

Ron Gillihan also joined us. Ron's twenty-eight-year-old son was killed in 1990. His body was found in a shallow grave five days later. Five months later, the killer turned himself in. During Ron's grieving period, his faith clearly showed him that the only way for him to find peace was through forgiveness.

Three years after Ron's son was killed, he was able to meet with the murderer and offer him forgiveness. Ron says that forgiveness is an act of Christian love. The knowledge that God was walking with Ron in this time gave him a total sense of closure over the craziness of his son's murder. Ron now travels to prisons, schools and other forums to deliver his message on the power of forgiveness and his opposition to the death penalty.

Rachel King, the Director of *Alaskans Against the Death Penalty* was on the Virginia *Journey* with the specific mission of taking pictures of the *Murder Victims' Families for Reconciliation* members, then doing interviews with them. Her plan was for the Alaskan group to make a booklet containing quotes and information of *MVFR* members who opposed the death penalty. She felt these statements would be important to various state legislators who were considering the death penalty for the state of Alaska.

Virginia *Journey* organizer Henry Heller
with Sister Helen

The most touching point of the Virginia *Journey* was George White speaking at a Charlie King concert. George's son Tom and his daughter Christie were in the audience. Tom and his dad had spoken together on various occasions, but daughter Christie had never heard her father speak. For the first time, she heard her father speak publicly about the death of her mother, and how he had been arrested and convicted of the murder.

George told several stories that night that involved Christie.

One was a visit to the prison when Christie told him it was okay to cry. She reminded him that Jesus wept.

At the end of George's talk, he asked everyone to close their eyes for a moment. When he said it was okay to open them, Tom and Christie were standing beside him and they had their arms around each other. Most of the people there did not even know that Tom and Christie were present.

The three of them gave the audience their summation of the death penalty, "Not in our names, our hearts have bled enough. Bless your heart."

There was not a dry eye there.

A film crew from Japan followed the Virginia *Journey* the entire two weeks. They mostly focused on George, Barbara, Anne and Aba Gayle.

A disturbing note came when we were informed that a group from New Orleans had contacted *Murder Victims' Families for Reconciliation* and asked that we not use the name *Journey of Hope* any longer because they had the name registered. Even though we had used the name *Journey of Hope* first, our director told them that after the Virginia *Journey*, *MVFR* would no longer use the name *Journey of Hope*.

That bothered a number of us because for so many years, we had worked very hard to get that name out into the public. The *Journey of Hope* had become my life. I had a large *Journey of Hope* logo on both sides of my van. Most of the t-shirts I wore were *Journey of Hope* shirts. Everywhere I went, I talked about the *Journey*. If we gave up the name, I felt like I was losing my identity.

MVFR also made it clear that the future direction they were going to pursue was in the lines of legislative work and state chapters. They decided there would be no *Journey* in 1997 and that a decision would be made later to see if and when another two-week event would ever be held. A lot of people were hoping for the *Journey* to go to Texas next.

The last night of the Virginia *Journey*, George and I treated the Journeyers by barbecuing dinner. Steaks, ribs, chicken, burgers, corn on the cob, we had it all. It was a meat lover's delight.

We also had some garden burgers for the non-meat eaters.

We had a special service that night that lasted almost five hours. It was just for the Journeyers and organizers. We have a tradition of an awards night the last night of a *Journey*, with special gifts to most everyone.

Bill wearing one of his few non-Journey t-shirt
on the Virginia *Journey*

At the end of that night, Judy and I were given the most special gift of all. It was a total surprise. Abe Bonowitz, Henry Heller and several others had collected a number of *Journey of Hope* t-shirts from the past years, and had a quilt made for our king-size waterbed. The quilts were in green and black squares, each with the *Journey* logo. The middle squares were from the backs of the shirts, which showed the states, dates, and cities, that each *Journey* had gone to.

This was surely a special treasure.

Chapter 46

A Bus and a Family Tragedy

Judy worked straight midnight shifts after she transferred to the nursery. I would work from 7:00 P.M. to 7:00 A.M. one week, and 7:00 A.M. to 7:00 P.M. the next week. When I would get off at 7:00 A.M., I would usually fire up the Harley and head in the direction that Judy would be coming, meet her, turn around, and come home. I had to go on Indiana Highway 149. One morning, I noticed a bus with a for sale sign on it sitting in a yard. I did a double take. It reminded me of the *Jubilee Partners*' bus. I knew I would like to have something like that for *Journey* events. The third time I rode by and saw it, I mentioned it to Judy. She said she had seen it, too, and thought about me every time she saw it.

Finally, I drove my van over to where it was parked. I wrote down the number that was on the sign, put the paper on my dresser, and forgot about it for several weeks. Then one day, I called. The man who answered the phone told me the bus belonged to the church he attended. He was a church trustee and had been empowered to sell it.

He told me it was a 1965 *GMC. Eastern Trailways* had owned it for twenty-two years and then sold it to their church about ten years ago. His church decided that vans were now the way to go and wanted to sell the bus.

He told me they were asking $7,500. I couldn't believe my ears. I thought that it would be at least $25,000. I knew I couldn't afford $25,000 but $7,500 was another story. I could borrow that much from the credit union. He went on to tell me how the motor had just been overhauled and a bunch of other details, but I just kept thinking $7,500, $7,500, $7,500.

When I talked to Judy, I told her, "I've found the motor home we had talked about getting some day!" When she looked up, I said I had called about the bus on the side of the road. I told her $7,500 was the asking price and I thought I wanted to get it.

She responded, "No way, it's not the kind of motor home we had talked about. It doesn't even have any beds! And it costs too much!"

I said, "$7,500 is a good price." She said, "$7,500? I thought you said $75,000." She then said, "If it is only $7,500 then you have got to get it."

Boy, was that good to hear. I was really glad I had bought her that Harley.

I called Wayne and told him I wanted to look at the bus and asked if he would come with me. He agreed and we went to look at it. The trustee took us for a ride. We went on the expressway. It rode real smooth.

Wayne and I talked about it for several days. I really wanted it, so I subtracted 10 percent and offered the deacon $6,750. He accepted and brought the bus over to my house. It came with several pallets of parts. It seems this was one of the last busses (model 4806) to be produced and these parts had been following the bus all these years.

I immediately called George White and Abe Bonowitz and told them I had bought a bus. A few days later, George called and asked if I would do him a favor. He said he wanted to name the bus. I was a bit taken aback at first, thinking, it was my bus, I should name it, but I asked George what he had in mind.

"*Abolition Movin'*," George responded. I said, "George, that's perfect. We will call her *Abolition Movin.*"

The next night, on November 10, 1996, we had a *Murder Victims' Families for Reconciliation* board meeting by way of telephone. It was also the thirtieth anniversary of the day I was hired at Bethlehem Steel. I was now able to retire at any time. I told them I had bought *Abolition Movin'* to celebrate my anniversary and of my plan to have a journey-type event in Texas in 1998. I told them I wasn't ready to retire yet, but at least I was eligible. I personally thought I might retire in about a year and a half, just prior to the Texas event.

All the members of the *MVFR* Board gave me their blessings for the bus tour and my retirement. We didn't know yet if we would call the event in Texas a *Journey of Hope*, Bill's Bus Tour or what, but we knew that the journey-type events would continue in some form, just not under the auspices of *MVFR*. I remained on the *MVFR* Board.

Two Saturdays later, when I came home from work, Judy was gone. A few minutes later, I got a call from her son Jamie. He told me that his mom was at the police station and wanted me to come join her in Valparaiso right away. After questioning, I found out that Judy's sister, Carol, had been shot by her husband Ron, who then barricaded himself in the house. I went immediately to the Valparaiso station.

Carol and Ron had married fourteen months earlier, on my birthday. We knew that they were not getting along very well, but Ron had never been violent. Nick had seen his mother get shot before he ran out of the house to get help. Nick was only ten years old.

As we waited at the police station, Nick knew that his mother might not live. Nick looked at me and said, "I bet I have flashbacks about this."

Nick knew I traveled around speaking against the death penalty. He said, "If my mother dies, I hope Ron gets the death penalty." I nodded understandingly. About forty-five minutes later, he came over and said that the death penalty would just be another death and he didn't want Ron to die, too.

After spending five agonizing hours with Judy, her mom, her two brothers (Marty and Bill) and Carol's two children, we got the word that Carol was dead and her husband had killed himself. What a shock! Unbelievable!

I tried to play the role of comforter. It was difficult. Judy was beside herself, and her mother was worse. Parents are not supposed to have to bury their children. Carol was buried the day before Thanksgiving.

After the funeral we all went to Otter Creek, Wisconsin, to Mike's house. We spent the Thanksgiving weekend there together.

It was after this time at Mike's log cabin, as a family, that I realized how nice it would be for the *Journey of Hope . . . from Violence to Healing* to have a retreat center so that friends or families of our movement that had a tragedy occur would have a place to go. The retreat center would always have someone on hand who could help this family. It could also be a place for Journeyers to stay when they weren't on the road. People who had been through similar situations would be there. It was very important for Judy's family to get out of the area for a while and be among themselves. They didn't need phones ringing; they needed healing.

Carol had done most of her Christmas shopping already, and at Christmas, everyone had something from her. Of course Christmas was not the same. It was very sad. I knew from my own experience that life would never be the same for any of this family, especially for Judy, her mother, and Carol's two children.

I didn't know how to drive my newly acquired bus and winter was coming, so it just sat in the parking lot. I did find out that if I converted it to a recreational vehicle, I didn't have to have a special driver's license. As a recreational vehicle, there was a limit of fifteen passengers. That was okay with me. The bus sat and collected snow while Judy and I took off to the Florida Keys for the second New Year's Eve in a row. It was especially important to get away this year.

It was a long drive back to Indiana. Back to the mills and hospitals and the cold weather and all of life's realities.

Chapter 47

Arrested in Washington

The 20th anniversary of the Gary Gilmore execution was January 17, 1997. His was the first execution in this country after the U.S. Supreme Court's decision to restore the death penalty. The *Abolitionist Action Committee* decided on an act of civil disobedience at the Supreme Court on that anniversary day.

For civil disobedience, you not only need people willing to be arrested, but also need a support group of at least two people for each one that is going to be arrested. As I drove to Washington, D.C., I was not sure if I was going to be a support person or be arrested. I didn't really want to be arrested.

I finally decided that if Rick and Marietta were arrested and I was not, I would regret it for the rest of my life. I chose to be one of those arrested—eighteen of us made that choice. We met in D.C. the day before to discuss our plan of action.

We had acquired the services of two attorneys to help with legal issues. Somehow, the Supreme Court police found out we were planning an act of civil disobedience. This bothered many of us because we wanted to unfurl a banner and get a photo opportunity in the process. We were afraid that they would try to thwart that plan.

During our years at the annual summertime Supreme Court fast and vigil, there was one thing that always bothered Rick, Marietta, others and myself. We had the right to legally protest and demonstrate on the *sidewalk* in front of the Court, but whenever anyone in our group would inadvertently step up on the *steps* leading to the Court, a Supreme Court policeman would tell them to move to the sidewalk. We were told that freedom of speech stops at the first step of the U.S. Supreme Court. It irked us that the institution that is supposed to defend our rights to freedom of speech would not allow someone to step up on the first step.

Marietta had always thought that someday, we should do something like wearing t-shirts with different letter on each shirt to spell some sort of slogan. We could go up onto the Supreme Court plaza individually and then suddenly come together, and spell out a phrase like *ABOLITION NOW.* We talked about taking a picture with the Supreme Court in the background and having posters and postcards made of it.

The photo idea was what led to the idea of unfurling a banner. We chose the words *STOP EXECUTIONS.* We wanted to unfurl it and take pictures. So we devised a plan to get around any previous knowledge the Court police had of our activity.

We planned a legal demonstration and rally in front of the Court at 10:00 A.M. on January 17. All of those who were supporting those getting arrested gathered for that activity in front of the steps to the Court. The Court police felt that civil disobedience would come from that group. George White was the emcee for the rally.

Those of us planning to be arrested waited inside the Methodist Building across the street from the side of the Court. During our annual summertime fast and vigil at the Supreme Court, we noticed that many tour groups visit the Court. We decided we would act as a tour group to get onto the mall area of the Court, then we could go on to the upper steps leading into the Supreme Court building.

John Steinbach was chosen to be our tour guide. John had a great knowledge of the history of the Court and also a loud booming voice. We waited at the Methodist Building until we got a call saying that George was about to speak. That was our signal to begin moving.

About ten minutes before the call came, I stepped outside to smoke a cigarette. I noticed that the Court police were lined up at the top of the steps where the rally was taking place. They were only ten feet away from those taking part in the rally. Some were wearing riot gear. It was obvious they didn't want anyone from that group going up the first flight of stairs and onto the mall area.

There was also a side entrance to the mall area. I noticed there were only a couple of police there. I went back inside and told the group if we went to the side entrance, there should be no problem.

It was a very cold day. We were all wearing green sweatshirts that said ***I OPPOSE THE DEATH PENALTY—Don't Kill For Me***. We wore our winter coats over these sweatshirts and headed to the Court when the call came. One of the ladies put the folded banner under her coat. She looked pregnant. We walked to the side entrance all huddled together in a group. The police paid little attention to us.

John's voice was booming out the history of the Court, telling us what the different pillars stood for, when the Court was built, and so on. I heard one of the officers tell another, "It's just a tour group." We walked across the mall area and on to the top flight of steps. No one said anything to us.

One policeman on top of the first set of steps had the sole duty of watching George as he led the rally down below. As George held the microphone in his hand he would walk back and forth when he talked to the crowd. Every time George went left, the policeman went left. When George went right, the policeman went right.

Suddenly our banner was produced, we opened it up and spread it out. It was forty feet long, and easy to read from a distance.

As soon as the banner was in place, George turned around and pointed at us. The policeman dogging George let out a few choice words and had a very sheepish look on his face when he saw what we had done. We had accomplished the first part of our mission.

Many people down below took pictures, including the media. Those of us holding the banner began to sing songs like, “We shall not be moved”, “We shall overcome some day” and others. We chanted some abolition chants. The police surrounded us and ordered us to disperse or we would be arrested. We had all decided to be arrested, so we just stayed. It was obvious that they did not want to arrest us. They gave us twenty minutes, but no one left. Finally, one by one, they led us away. Kurt Rosenberg was the first one arrested. Then Jon Holtshopple, Stephanie Gibson, Joseph Byrne, Tom Muther, Jr., Sally Peck, Lorig Charkoudian, Maury Mendenhall, Phyllis Pautrat, Bill Streit, Art Laffin, Jeremy Schill, John Steinbach, Thomas Dornbeck, Abe Bonowitz, Rick Halperin, Marietta Jaeger and I followed.

Arrest of the DC-18 at the U.S. Supreme Court

We were taken to the basement of the Court where we were processed. We had our hands cuffed behind our backs with plastic cords. We were told no talking but we could sing.

So there in the basement of the court, we sang our hearts out. Art Laffin led us with his wonderful voice. We know we touched some of the guards' hearts also. There was a point when one in our group asked Marietta a question and Marietta told her story. Everyone there, including the guards, listened, even though we weren't supposed to be talking.

After three hours or so, my shoulders began to really ache because of the way I was cuffed. Abe noticed that I was uncomfortable. He told one of the young officers, "That Viet Nam veteran needs to have his cuffs loosened." The officer apologized as he released me and prepared to put on new cuffs. He told me to go ahead and shake it off before he put the new ones on. After a couple of minutes, I told him I was ready. He told me to shake it off some more and gave me another five minutes. I really appreciated that. This time, he used three plastic ties instead of two, which gave me much more flexibility. I thank him and I thanked God.

Finally, we were taken to the D.C. district lockup. They weren't so kind there. They didn't like all the paperwork they were going to have to do and I don't think they liked our cause. It wasn't until they got a call from Ron Hampton, the executive director of the *National Black Police Association*, that things got better. Around 8:00 P.M. those of us that paid $10 for bail were released from jail. Four refused to pay and stayed in jail all night. Not me, I got out.

Jon Holtshopple arranged for us to go to a steak house and covered the cost for those that did not have the money for that sort of meal. The next morning, we all had to go back to court to be arraigned.

We were told to be at the court by 9:00 A.M. They made us sit all day, until we were the very last ones. Beginning at 3:30, four at a time went before the judge. Each of us was wearing either the green sweatshirt that said *I OPPOSE THE DEATH PENALTY—Don't Kill for Me*, or a blue sweatshirt that said the same thing. My group was one of the last ones called up and it really looked sharp watching each group go ahead of me.

We were really proud of the stand we had taken. Nothing like that had ever been done at the Supreme Court protesting the death penalty. I don't think anywhere else in the country eighteen people had ever been arrested protesting the death penalty. We dubbed ourselves "The DC-18."

We told our attorneys that we would all be back in the D.C. area for the annual Supreme Court fast and vigil at the end of June. Although the court originally gave a date in March, the judge allowed us all to come back for trial on the twenty-seventh of June. Since we had all planned to come back on the twenty-eighth for the vigil at the Court anyway, it saved us from making an extra trip.

I drove back home to Indiana in a hurry. I wanted to see Judy. It had been quite an experience. I had a few moments of anxiety in the paddy wagon and in the jail cell. I wanted to get home and be in Judy's arms.

Chapter 48

SueZann Did It!

The twelve-year anniversary of Nana's death—May 14, 1997—I chose as a symbolic date for my retirement.

By age forty-nine, I had thirty years in at Bethlehem Steel. I was still young enough to do other things, like be a full-time abolitionist. People at work were not as shocked as I thought they might be because they all knew I was retiring to continue my journey of hope. Even those who didn't agree with me on the issue wished me the best. I will long remember Larry Click, Dave Thomas, Tom Sullivan, Cool Chuck Brady, Richard Smith and many others. I was going to work for another year, but once I bought the bus, I knew I needed to get started with the *Journey* right away. May 14, 1997, sounded like a great day to do it.

Wayne Crawley and Dennis Eaton, fellow crane-operators, counted down the days with me. They were almost as amazed as me that I was retiring.

When I first talked about retirement, Judy said she didn't think we could afford it. I showed her how we could be out of debt except for the house payment. With my retirement check and her hospital paycheck, we'd be all right. Judy told me I would have to change my lifestyle and tear up the Visa card. I was used to buying whatever I wanted and then working overtime to pay for it. But I felt good about retiring. I loved Judy, and I wanted to show her I could succeed; that the faith she had put in me was well founded.

The day after I retired, I drove my van to Chicago to meet Sam Reese Sheppard. He had written a book called ***Mockery of Justice*** and was in Chicago on a book-signing tour. After he spent the day on book promotion interviews with TV, radio, and the print media, I brought him back to Portage with me.

The next day Sam and I headed to Florida. Our plan was to pick up George White, who was in Florida attending his daughter Christie's high school graduation, and then the three of us head to the Miami area, to meet with SueZann Bosler. While at SueZann's we talked about incorporating the *Journey of Hope . . . from Violence to Healing* into a non-profit organization.

James Bernard Campbell, the man who murdered SueZann's father, was coming up again for re-sentencing. George and I wanted to be with SueZann when the hearing began, but we had to leave for commitments in Texas.

This was the third sentencing hearing for James Bernard Campbell. The first two decisions, that sentenced James to death, were found to be in error. SueZann was determined that James not be sentenced to death again. The judge warned SueZann before she testified that she could not give her opinion of the death penalty to the jury. When SueZann began her testimony, the prosecutor asked SueZann three questions. First, he asked her what her name was. She replied, "SueZann Bosler." Then he asked her where she lived, and she responded with the city in which she now lived. Then he asked her what she did for a living and she responded with, "I have two jobs. I am a hairdresser and I travel around the country speaking for abolition of the death penalty." There was a hush in the court.

The judge called a time out in the proceedings and the jury was ushered out of the courtroom. The judge again threatened SueZann with jail time and a fine if she said any more about the death penalty. The television program ***48 Hours,*** covered the courtroom action and showed SueZann in tears. After a few more questions the attorneys decided that she didn't need to testify any further. SueZann had got her point across to the jury; the damage to the prosecution had been done.

When Campbell's attorney gave the final appeal, he pleaded for the jury not to sentence Campbell to death. As he spoke, SueZann set in the courtroom with both arms half raised and fingers crossed. The jury knew how much it meant to SueZann that James Bernard Campbell not be sentenced to death. When the defense attorney finished his summation to the jury, he walked back to the defense table. Before he sat down he looked at SueZann and said very clearly, "Thank you, SueZann."

After deliberation, the jury came back and cast their vote for life, not death. James Bernard Campbell would serve four consecutive life sentences and never get out of prison. This is what SueZann had worked so hard for over ten years to accomplish. SueZann Bosler did it—she saved James Bernard Campbell's life.

Chapter 49

Texas and Bus Troubles

When George and I left Florida, we drove to Texas to scout out the great state that would host next year's *Journey.*

George went back to Kansas and I drove my van back to Indiana to start working on *Abolition Movin'*. I didn't know anything about buses. My friend Randy Walker was a mechanic for U.S. Steel, so I asked him for help.

It was an old bus with some serious problems. *Abolition Movin'* required two big expensive batteries. I bought several, but they kept going dead. I replaced the voltage regulator. I did it wrong the first time and burned it right up. That was $150. The first one I bought was the only one the parts store had in stock, so I had to wait to get a second one on special order. The pressure was on. I had committed myself to bringing *Abolition Movin'* to Houston, Texas, in late June for the annual *National Coalition to Abolish the Death Penalty* conference. The plan was to take a group from that Texas conference to Washington, D.C. for the trials of the DC-18 and the annual Supreme Court fast and vigil. I had only three weeks to get *Abolition Movin'* ready, and I couldn't even keep it running long enough to check it properly.

At the *NCADP* conference, we would be presenting our plan of having a *Journey* in Texas the following year. It would be our first major event as a new, separate organization and this would be a great way to introduce and promote it. We wanted *Abolition*

Movin' there to help. The *National Coalition* newsletter ***Lifelines*** in its last issue before the conference had an article called "A Dream Come True," telling the story of *Abolition Movin'*. It told about *Abolition Movin'* coming to the conference, and the plan to take a group of abolitionists from Texas to the fourth annual fast and vigil in Washington, D.C. The article included a picture of *Abolition Movin'* wearing the *Journey* banner.

I felt like I had to get *Abolition Movin'* there or it would be another *Fulton's Folly*.

Abolition Movin' in Portage with George White, Bill, Sam Reese Sheppard and Abe Bonowitz

When Randy changed the starter for me, it didn't work right. The parts store had given us a left turn starter instead of a right turn. It was a hard job, and he had to do it all over again. It was the beginning of summer and Randy didn't want to spend it all working on my bus.

When I shut off the diesel engine on *Abolition Movin'*, it would not start up again until it cooled off. I was also having trouble getting it into reverse. Randy was mad that I didn't ask him to look at *Abolition Movin'* before I bought it. He said it was a hunk of junk.

I took *Abolition Movin'* out to my brother-in-law Marty's house, and did some work there. I took out all but sixteen of the seats. As long as there were not over fifteen passengers, I could drive the bus with my current driver's license, and didn't need to apply for a CDL (Commercial Drivers License). With Marty's help, we built four beds in the back of the bus where seats had been. Each bed had privacy. There was a toilet compartment and I built a desk and filing cabinet in the back seat area. I put in a CD player to go with the stereo tape player, all hooked into the loudspeaker system. Then I got *Abolition Movin'* titled and registered as a recreational vehicle.

I changed the oil, bought a new tire and made plans to drive to Texas even though all the problems weren't fixed yet. I didn't want to drive alone and was really happy when Judy decided to take a few days off of work and come with me. By the time we left, there were four of us, including Josie Roche, a Dutch lawyer, and Trixie, our Great Dane, who immediately claimed one of the four beds.

We had about a five-hundred-mile drive before we were supposed to meet George in Springfield, Missouri. The drive went well, but didn't dare shut the engine off. And I only pulled into places where I would not have to back up because it still wouldn't go into reverse.

A lot of pressure was lifted when we met up with George. He and I took turns driving, and by the grace of God we made it to Houston.

We decided, after consulting with an attorney, that if we added the " . . . from Violence to Healing" after the words "Journey of Hope," our name would be legal and not infringe on the rights of the other group with a similar name.

At the conference we announced that *Journey of Hope . . . from Violence to Healing* was now a new legal organization, walking hand in hand with *Murder Victims' Families for Reconciliation* and other abolitionist organizations. We told of plans for the Texas *Journey* the following year, including six days with Sister Helen. She planned to be with us for the final march to the Texas state capitol building in Austin.

The *NCADP* conference had an action scheduled for Friday in downtown Houston at the office of District Attorney Johnny Holmes. More people have been sentenced to death out of his office than anywhere else in America.

Several buses were rented for the downtown action, and *Abolition Movin'* went along, too. *Abolition Movin'* is as big as a *Greyhound* bus. Driving it in downtown Houston during rush hour and making some of the incredibly tight squeezes and turns helped me gain the confidence that I could be a bus driver. Up until then I was not sure I could really pull it off.

Everybody that rode *Abolition Movin'* that day enjoyed the ride. We sang along with Charlie King's freedom tape as we rode. Steve Hawkins, the executive director of the *NCADP* was one of those aboard. One by one they said thanks as they got off.

Marietta was honored at the *NCADP* conference as the 1997 *Abolitionist of the Year.* When I was invited to present the award, I said that doing so would be the greatest honor of my life. I really meant it. The truth is she is the Abolitionist of the Century. Marietta's story has touched more hearts and changed more minds about the death penalty than anyone else I know.

She continues to travel and talk and tell of her little daughter and the worst moments of her life in order to show others how one can heal. Marietta has been my source of earthly strength for years. Together we have been able to look to heaven, because we know our strength comes from there. Without Marietta Jaeger, there would be no *Journey of Hope . . . from Violence to Healing.*

When the conference ended, twelve of us were planning to ride *Abolition Movin'* from Texas to Washington, D.C. for the trial of the DC-18. That was to be followed immediately by the annual fast and vigil at the Supreme Court. Just as we were ready to leave, we found out that our friends on the *Jubilee Partners'* bus had a problem. Their bus was throwing oil and needed repairs. Some of their riders needed to get back to Atlanta to go to work. Atlanta was several hundred miles out of the way, but it was a chance to help *Jubilee Partners*, a great bunch of people.

With some all-night driving, we arrived at the Atlanta airport at 8:00 A.M. to drop off the Jubilee folks. Their rides were waiting for them. We took some more pictures and all said good-bye. Bill and Laura Shain from the Indiana and Georgia *Journeys* were part of the *Jubilee Partners* group. Others aboard had loved ones on death row.

We got back on the expressway and headed north to Washington D.C. It had been a long night and promised to be a long day. After only a few miles, we pulled off the expressway to have breakfast at *McDonald's*. I left *Abolition Movin'* running because it still did not want to start when the engine was hot.

After breakfast, we loaded up *Abolition Movin'*. I went to release the air brakes so we could begin rolling. The brakes would not release. I looked at the air pressure gauge and noticed there was not enough pressure to release the brakes. I knew something was seriously wrong. I let George and Abe know we had a problem.

Everyone had to get off the bus. It was too hot to sit in it if it wasn't moving. It was Becky's turn to sleep. She had just climbed into one of the beds because she had driven her van all night, following us and carrying some passengers so Abolition Movin' could remain legal. We immediately booked a room at a local motel so she could get some sleep. The room also offered a chance for others to take a shower and clean up.

We found a phone book and began a search for help. Under "truck repair" we found someone called "*The Diesel Doctor*." The *Diesel Doctor* made house calls and said he would meet us at *McDonald's* as soon as possible. Some of our riders went back into *McDonald's* where it was air-conditioned, and waited for *Abolition Movin'* to get moving. Others pulled out lawn chairs from the "basement" of the bus and sat under shade trees at the side of the parking lot.

The *Diesel Doctor* showed up an hour later. He looked at the signs on the back of our bus and shook his head in disbelief. One said: *I OPPOSE THE DEATH PENALTY . . . Don't Kill for Me.* The other said: *Execution is not the Solution.* They were posters that Abe had taped on the back window.

Still shaking his head, he said, "I don't agree with what you are all about, but my job is to get your bus running."

That was fine with me. I just wanted to get the bus running.

The *Diesel Doctor* told us we needed a new air compressor for $400 plus labor. He told us with luck and good traffic he would be back with one in about an hour. At his rate of $65 an hour we hoped it wouldn't take long.

Meanwhile, in *McDonald's* there was a man who took exception to the t-shirts that some of our crew was wearing. He became angrier as he talked. Ken and Lois Robison were two of the ones that he was giving a hard time. They responded to him with love and compassion, and his anger began to wane.

It turned out that his family was at *McDonald's* because he was having car trouble. His engine had overheated and they were waiting for it to cool down. When he found out that we were broken down, too, he was embarrassed for the way he had behaved and began to act more friendly. He came outside by *Abolition Movin'* and we talked about the bus.

When the *Diesel Doctor* came back with a new compressor, he took off the old one and put on the new one. It still did not work. The once angry *McDonald's* customer noted that a small gear was connected to the compressor. It was plastic, with half of the teeth missing. The man pointed out that we probably didn't even need a new compressor, just a new gear.

We told the *Diesel Doctor* that we would just go with a new gear. He had to go back across town, but we figured he didn't care how long it would take since he was getting $65 an hour for his time.

When the *Diesel Doctor* came back and started working on *Abolition Movin'* again, we began some serious dialogue. We told him what we were doing in Atlanta. He told us that those on death row should die. We told him about Ken and Lois Robison. We pointed to where Ken and Lois were sitting under a shade tree and told how the state of Texas wanted to kill their mentally ill son, Larry. We told him how Lois had tried to get him help. We told him how doctors said he needed long-term care, but unless he did something violent, there was nothing more the hospital or the state of Texas could do. We told him the first act of violence from Larry was to kill five people in a psychotic episode. We told the *Diesel Doctor* how the state of Texas then sentenced Larry to death.

When I told the *Diesel Doctor* that killing Lois's son would be cruel and barbaric, he nodded his head in agreement.

Eliza Hersh, an intern from the *NCADP*, joined our huddle. She asked the *Diesel Doctor* if he felt there were any innocent people on death row. He said that there were some who might be. He then changed the subject by saying that prisons were country clubs anyway.

I just pointed to George and said, "This man can talk about both of those points." The *Diesel Doctor* stopped his work to listen.

George told him he had spent two years and 103 days in a southern Alabama prison, and it was ***not*** a country club. When the *Diesel Doctor* asked him why he was in prison, George told him the story about being convicted of his wife's death. George told how the state of Alabama wanted him sentenced to death, but the all-white jury wouldn't sentence him to death because he was perceived to be a white male yuppie of some worth. George told him, "If I was black, I would have been sentenced to death."

George talked about seven years of hell from the time of Char's death until the proof of his innocence was brought forth, proof had been rotting in the prosecutor's office. George assured The *Diesel Doctor* that "for sure, an innocent man can be found guilty."

One of our group said, "Do you remember the Dr. Sam Sheppard case?" The *Diesel Doctor* said, "Yes, he's the one who was accused of killing his wife a long time ago." We said, "This is his son," and pointed to Sam. We told him how Dr. Sam was found not guilty at a retrial after spending ten years in jail wrongfully convicted. We told him how his son has walked all over this country in an effort to curb violence.

Abe talked to him about the Jewish views of forgiveness and

compassion. Then he talked about the pragmatics of the death penalty issue. George and I talked from the Christian perspective.

The air compressor was finally fixed. We figured, as long as we had the *Diesel Doctor* there, we would have him do a few other things. Since we had not been able to shut off *Abolition Movin'* and check the oil, we just added a gallon of oil every time we would stop to make sure it didn't get low. When the air compressor broke and we had to shut it off, we realized that we had put in too much oil. We found out that too much oil is as bad as not enough.

The *Diesel Doctor* helped us take out several gallons. After all was said and done, the doc told us he was not going to charge us at the $65 an hour rate, but would only charge $55, which is the truck rate. The bill came to $440. We gave him our Visa card but he said he could not take credit cards. Sam Sheppard agreed to go to an ATM machine and get some cash. George went with Sam and the doc waited in the parking lot with us. We continued to talk about the death penalty for another half hour.

When Sam came back with the money, we stood there as Sam counted it out. One, two, three, four hundred dollars were handed to the doc. When he was handed the last two twenties, he gave them back to us. He said, "You are a pretty good group of people. You are not just wasting time by drinking and stuff, but trying to do a good thing." He told us to take the forty dollars and buy the group dinner.

I gave the *Diesel Doctor* a book on forgiveness and one on the death penalty. Abe gave him some pins and bumper stickers. He looked at Abe and smiled as he said, "I want one of those shirts." Abe gave him an "I Oppose the Death Penalty" t-shirt. The *Diesel Doctor* was not the same man we had met seven hours earlier.

Chapter 50

Trial of the DC-18

After a good dinner, we began the all-night drive to Washington, D.C. George and I took turns driving. *Abolition Movin'* was beginning to give us a hard time shifting. We called Joan Betz first thing in the morning. Joan was to meet us in D.C., and we asked her to find a place in the area where we could take *Abolition Movin'* for repairs. In addition to the clutch, we needed work on the battery cables and help to shut off a valve that continued to give us unwanted heat in the bus. This was not the easiest of jobs we gave Joan, because many bus repair places don't want to work on a bus as old as *Abolition Movin'*

We arrived in D.C. in the afternoon. It was hot and the traffic was terrible as we took the belt line to a garage in Maryland that worked on old buses. As we came down the block to the garage, there was Joan Betz waving at us to show us where to go. God bless Joan Betz.

The trial for the DC-18 was to begin the next day. We stayed at the Community Center for Non-Violence, a homeless shelter in Washington. We knew the judge in the trial was actually against the death penalty. It was our belief that the prosecutors were also against the death penalty. However, the trial was not about the death penalty; it was about the right to unfurl the *STOP EXECUTIONS* banner on the steps of the Supreme Court.

The hearing took two days. We each got to tell why we did what we did. The prosecution played a video from the arrest scene. It showed us holding the banner and you could hear us singing. I agreed that we should have been arrested, not for unfurling the banner, but for our singing!

The prosecution unrolled our banner in front of the judge. It was really neat to see *STOP EXECUTIONS* in the courtroom. The judge ruled against us. Our lawyers said they would appeal on the basis of freedom of speech, granted by the first amendment.

We had planned our court trial to coincide with the fourth annual Supreme Court fast and vigil. When the trial ended, it was time for the vigil to begin.

This was my fourth year at the event. I was the only person who had been there every day since its inception, and had fasted every day. We always made it clear that fasting was not a requirement, but there was solidarity with those in attendance who did fast. Those who wanted to eat just left the area and went to a local restaurant and then came back, but didn't talk about what they had eaten.

An execution took place in Baltimore the second night. We loaded up a group on *Abolition Movin'* and headed to Maryland. It was the first time many in our group had ever been to an execution vigil. It was held across the street from where the execution took place. Stephanie Gibson of the *Maryland Coalition Against State Executions* organized the rally. She was greatly affected by what was taking place.

Judy, my wife, was also greatly affected. It was her first execution vigil. The sight of all the police lined up on the other side of the street and doing nothing while a human was being killed reminded her of how the police waited outside her sister's home and did nothing for hours the night her sister was killed.

The four day fast and vigil ended with folks from the *Catholic Workers House* bringing us a wonderful meal at midnight. It was served on tables on the sidewalk in front of the Supreme Court. Art Laffin, one of their members, organized the meal. Art was also a member of the DC-18. He was one who could sing.

Chapter 51

The *Bruderhof* Children

Claire Stubber, a member of the *Bruderhof Community* in Farmington, Pennsylvania, was one of the people I met in front of the Supreme Court. She worked for their publishing company, *The Plough*. Claire told me that the children of the *Bruderhof* were planning an August march for abolition of the death penalty; she felt the children would really like to see *Abolition Movin'*.

Claire asked if we could stop by Farmington on our way back to Indiana. It was only about thirty minutes off of the expressway. When we got to the *Bruderhof*, we pulled *Abolition Movin'* up by the dining hall. Someone rang a bell and suddenly a lot of children began to appear.

When we had a meeting with the kids, George and I told our stories. The children told us of their plans to do a march from Farmington to Pennsylvania's death row in August. It was called the *Children's Crusade*, and would take three days for them to march the forty miles.

They invited us to come and to bring *Abolition Movin'*. We said we would come back in August, and we did.

I have never seen anything so inspiring in my life as that *Children's Crusade* to death row. The *Bruderhof* are a group of Christian communities that live communally the way they feel the

New Testament teaches. There are five communities in this country and several in England. They also recently opened one in Australia.

The *New Meadow Run* and *Spring Valley* communities in Farmington, Pennsylvania, together have about seven hundred members. The children came up with the idea of a march and the adults supported them as they made plans. Children from *Bruderhof* communities in New York and Connecticut joined them for the *Children's Crusade*.

The first morning of the march featured about four hundred children, all wearing bright yellow shirts that had one word in green lettering on the back. It was the word ***LIFE***.

It was foggy when the children began their march, and I was a bit worried about their safety. I thought it would be dangerous to walk alongside the highway going up and down the mountain outside Farmington but soon realized the adults had taken every precaution.

As the march began, hundreds of children, along with the adults, began the walk with singing and enthusiasm. They soon stretched out along the highway for as far as one could see. After all of the children were on their way, I took *Abolition Movin'* and slowly passed by the marchers as they began walking up one of the steepest peaks in Pennsylvania, **The Summit**.

As *Abolition Movin'* passed by the marchers, I honked the horn continuously. The children would wave and yell as we drove by. To see them strung out, seemingly endlessly, was an inspiring sight. When we had driven past all of the marchers, we found a place to pull off of the road. We waited for the children to catch up, and stood by the road waving as they walked by.

Lunch was held at a large park along the route. Lots of reporters were covering the event and several of them were sent to me for interviews. As the day passed, we repeatedly drove past the marchers with *Abolition Movin'* honking the horn and then our stopping to wave as the children passed.

The first evening was spent at a church with a huge field in back. Many of the older children camped out, and the younger ones were taken back to Farmington. For the younger ones, the march was over.

During the evening, there were several speeches and a band played. The group had marched about fifteen miles. I had never seen anything like it.

The next day was the same, but the evening was entirely different. The first night had been for outside groups, but the second night was for the *Bruderhof* only.

This second night the music was provided by the children as they sang songs they had written for the march. Christoph Arnold, the senior elder of the *Bruderhof Community*, was the emcee. When I was asked to speak to the group, I told the children about Nana. I told them how she loved telling children Bible stories. I told them about how I had learned love and compassion from her.

The third morning, everyone was quite excited. It was still twelve miles to *SCI* (*State Correctional Institution*) *Greene*, where most of the death row inmates in Pennsylvania are housed. I have never seen such a large group so well organized in my life. The marchers left at the scheduled time. Once again, *Abolition Movin'* would repeatedly pass by the marchers honking, then pull over and wave as they walked by. Finally, we arrived at a gathering area only a few blocks from death row. Ironically, the road leading to death row is called Progress Drive. After a short rally before the final walk to death row, we all walked to the fence outside the prison.

A number of guards were standing in a line when we arrived. The young ladies of the *Bruderhof* took flowers and offered them to the guards. Most guards declined, so the girls laid the flowers at the guards' feet. After a few of the children made speeches, hundreds of balloons were released into the air. It was a spectacular sight, a spectacular event. I was greatly encouraged to see the young people so passionately involved in the anti-death penalty movement.

Trevor and Robin and their two babies, along with Ginny, Josie, Abe and I headed back towards Indiana. *Abolition Movin'* performed well. The *Bruderhof* liked our bus and the music we played. They especially liked the song that had the words "Get on board, children, children, get on board, children, children, get on board, children, children and work for human rights."

Chapter 52

Troubles Galore

My fiftieth birthday was in September, and Judy was planning a surprise birthday party. Problem was, I had been thinking about going to Texas to do some planning for next year's *Journey*. So, Judy had to tell me about the surprise plan to make sure I was in town.

I found out that she had talked to others at the Supreme Court fast and vigil about coming to Indiana for the Labor Day weekend for my birthday surprise. When Judy told me who was coming, I was impressed. I told her we could make it a bus painting party.

Friends came from all over the country. Rick Halperin and Joan Brett came from Texas. Henry Heller, Sunshine Richards and Joan Betz came from Virginia. Marietta came from Detroit and SueZann from Florida. Tim Spann and Abe Bonowitz came from California. Lynn came from Wisconsin. Trevor and Robin were there. Trevor had helped me prepare the bus for sanding before painting her with primer.

Local friends from Portage came, too, including Wayne, Dennis, Cuzzin Judi, Leah, her sister and others. My kids Chris and Bob also came and helped. It was a great weekend. I was thankful for so many friends. We got *Abolition Movin'* sanded, but didn't get to the primer.

Labor Day party in Portage with *Journey* members from around the country preparing *Abolition Movin'* for paint job

A few days after the party, Trevor and I took *Abolition Movin'* to Marty's house. Marty was a good brother-in-law. I liked him a lot. He said we could use his yard and equipment to spray the primer on the bus. Trevor had worked at a body shop, so spraying was right down his alley. Judy, Trevor, Robin and I spent several days just taping the windows, wheels, mirrors and other areas where we didn't want the primer.

Trevor did a fantastic job—*Abolition Movin'* was now a beautiful gray. It looked better than it did before, but we knew that when it was actually painted, it would look great. We had bought the finishing paint, but didn't have time to paint it yet.

Sam Reese Sheppard had asked George White and me to be with him when his father's body was exhumed for DNA testing. It was part of the plan to get the State of Ohio to declare Dr. Sam Sheppard innocent. It looked like we would be leaving on September 17, the day after my fiftieth birthday. We were going to take *Abolition Movin'* and the van to Columbus, Ohio, where his father was buried.

"Good Morning America" called Sam and wanted him to come to Columbus a day early to interview him. So we changed our plans. Sam flew into Chicago and we left the day *before* my birthday. I had really wanted to spend my fiftieth with Judy, but she said she understood I had to go. By staying for Sam's memorial walk from Cincinnati to Cleveland, I knew it would be about three weeks before I got back home.

The relationship between Judy and me had been bumpy the last week, and one more day together would have been good. But I had a commitment. I hoped Judy would understand.

We headed off to Ohio. George, Sam and Abe rode in the bus with me and Trevor, Robin and the kids rode in the van. We got to Columbus late in the evening and parked in front of Abe's parents' house. Sam got up early for his interview with "**Good Morning America**."

The next morning, we went to the gravesite of Dr. Sam Sheppard. Randall Dale Adams and his mother met us there. Randall's mom had tended to Dr. Sam's gravesite for many years.

The media were there in full force. The vault was lifted out of the ground and the coffin put in a hearse. The hearse followed *Abolition Movin'* to Cleveland because Sam wanted to make sure the hearse was never out of his sight. When we got to Cleveland, the autopsy was performed. The next day, a memorial ceremony was planned, so the body was cremated immediately following the autopsy. We spent the night at Sam's cousin's house.

Sam asked George and me to speak at the memorial service. George gave a wonderful talk; then I spoke about reconciliation. Sam's family had been torn apart by this tragedy over forty years earlier, but now there was some reconciliation beginning to take place. Dr. Sam's ashes were placed with Sam's mother's remains in the crypt at a Cleveland cemetery. You could see the peace on Sam's face. Sam was glad to get Dr. Sam out of Columbus, where he had been imprisoned for so many years.

The next morning at 7:00 A.M., Sam began his memorial walk to Cincinnati. George was walking with Sam. The rest of us took *Abolition Movin'*. Sam would not be speaking at the morning press conference because he had taken a vow of silence during the long walk ahead. The press conference was planned so that Sam would be walking by during the middle of it, with *Abolition Movin'* as the backdrop.

As we headed toward the designated spot, the rush hour traffic thickened and we began to wonder if we were going to make it on time. We pulled onto the exit ramp of the expressway at a snail's pace. When we finally got to the end of the ramp as next in line to get onto the exit road, *Abolition Movin'* coughed and died.

I tried to start it again but no luck. I looked through the rear view mirror and saw a lot of steam coming from the rear of the bus. I got out and looked. The water pump had gone out and was pouring radiator coolant all over the road. Traffic behind us was backed up. We were blocking the exit.

I went to a Shell station on the corner where I could see a tow truck, but the tow truck operator had not yet arrived for work. When he did come he said his tow truck was not big enough to move a bus.

Then the police arrived. I got off the bus to explain the situation. A policeman asked me if I was protesting. I said no—we were the support vehicle for Sam Reese Sheppard and had broken down. He informed me that their department had received several calls that a bus was blocking the exit as a protest about the death penalty. I assured him it was not a protest. He called for a tow truck that could move a bus.

Cars were able to pass us slowly, but they had to pull onto the grass and creep by. Several media vehicles had stopped when they saw us and did interviews as we sat there. Abe drove by with the van and saw our plight. He was late for the press conference, but so was everyone else because they had been held up by *Abolition Movin'*.

The tow was $300 plus the cost of a new water pump. We missed the press conference. We took the van and headed back to

Sam's cousin's house. When we pulled up in the driveway, she came outside and told us it was too bad about the bus. I asked her how she knew. She told us that the lead story on the noon news on the local TV station was how a Sam Reese Sheppard support vehicle had broken down and held up traffic by blocking the exit for three hours.

We had a lot of abolition signs on the bus. One of them that we used for marches said, "Abolition Stops Traffic." We all decided that it was a good thing I was not holding that sign when I got off the bus to greet the policeman when we broke down.

I had to leave the group in Ohio for a few days and fly to San Francisco to speak at a consistent ethics conference about the death penalty. When I arrived at the airport, I bought a paper to see if there was anything about Sam.

There was a picture of his father's raised casket and Sam bowing his head with his hands together in a sign of honor. George, Abe, Randall, and I were in the background.

During the San Francisco conference, I called Judy. The call did not go well and I knew I needed to get home to smooth things out. I flew back to Ohio the very next day, told everyone good-bye, and drove my van back to Indiana. Trevor and Robin came with me. I left *Abolition Movin'* in George's capable hands.

Judy and I were in real trouble. Before the week was over, she told me she was leaving. She said she needed to get away for a while to think things over. She said I had my dreams and goals, but they were not her dreams or goals. She needed to be alone, she said, to figure out what her dream was. She went to stay at Leah's mother's house.

The *Journey* had plans to do a seven-day event in Missouri the first week of October. I told Judy I would not go it; that I wanted to work things out. She told me to go. She said I needed to go. She told me that when I got back, she would have her stuff moved out.

I drove *Abolition Movin'* to Missouri in a daze. The first weekend in Missouri was a board meeting of *MVFR*. I told them of the problems Judy and I were having and asked them to pray for me. After the board meeting, George White and I drove *Abolition Movin'* throughout the state for our *Journey* events after picking up Sam, SueZann, Barb Lewis, Anne Coleman and Sally Peck at the airport.

The entire time I was in a daze. I could not believe what was happening. After the event was over and everyone headed home, I aimed the bus towards Indiana. I was always in a hurry to return home from events. There were times I would drive hours on end to get home before Judy would go to work just to be able to see her. This time it was different. Judy would not be there and I was in no hurry to go to an empty house. I pulled over at a truck stop half way home. I stayed there for hours, thinking, sleeping, and thinking some more, before I drove back to Indiana. When I got there, the house was empty. Judy was gone. I was like a zombie.

I cried, I prayed, I begged for sleep. The only thing that kept me going was the upcoming *Journey* in Texas. If nothing else, I had that to live for. It was still seven months away, but it was the only positive thing I could think of to keep me going. Otherwise I would just as soon have died.

Chapter 53

One High, More Lows

After George and I spoke at an *Amnesty International* regional conference in Philadelphia, George, Ann Coleman, Abe, Robin Dicks, and I took *Abolition Movin'* and headed to New York. I had made an appointment to see Christoph Arnold, senior elder of the *Bruderhof*, who lived at the *Woodcrest Community* in Rifton, New York. I had met Christoph at the *Children's Crusade* in August. I needed help and felt he might be able to give me some.

The closer we got to Rifton, the worse the bus ran. *Abolition Movin'* would hardly pick up any speed as we left the last few tollbooths.

At Rifton, I was expecting a personal, private meeting with Christoph, but he invited all of us to his place. He had a number of guests there from the community. About twenty were gathered in his dining room as he asked what they could do for us.

I began to pour my heart out. He knew about Judy from when her sister was killed. I told him about the situation with Judy and about how devastated I was. I told him about Texas *Journey* and how we needed help to organize it—interns, money, and many other things. I also told him about having problems with *Abolition Movin'*.

Christoph immediately said that his son-in-law was an expert diesel coach mechanic. He made a call and ten minutes later, his son-in-law, Robert, appeared. Christoph told him to go through our coach with a fine toothcomb and make it safe and roadworthy for our friends. He asked us how long we could leave it at *Woodcrest*. We told him three weeks.

When Abe and I went back three weeks later to pick up *Abolition Movin'* from the *Woodcrest Community*, our plan was to head to Washington, D.C. area, where the *Religious Organizing Project* was having its first annual conference. The conference was based around Sister Helen's book ***Dead Man Walking*** and her involvement in the movement. Marietta Jaeger and I had been asked to speak in a plenary session after a showing of ***From Fury to Forgiveness***.

When Abe and I got back to Woodcrest, we immediately found Robert, the mechanic. He showed us a long list of repairs that they had done. It was unbelievable. The repair that intrigued me the most was the plate that held the steering housing. Two of the four bolts were missing and the other two were loose. They had gone through the bus with a fine toothcomb all right and fixed many things. There was no charge.

Not only was *Abolition Movin'* now safe and roadworthy, but also it had a new look. Robert had taken the paint we had stored in the bus's "basement" and painted it. Boy, did she look beautiful—a shiny dark green body with a white roof, with the area around the windows painted black.

Abe had gotten decals from Tim Spann in California, and with the help of several teenage volunteers of the *Bruderhof*, put the *Journey of Hope . . . from Violence to Healing* logos on the sides. We had new decals for the back that said **I OPPOSE THE DEATH PENALTY . . . DON'T KILL FOR ME.** All of the lettering was white and looked sharp. I saw my dream come true.

While we ate lunch in the community-dining hall, I had a chance to thank everyone. *Abolition Movin'* was brought up to the door outside the dining hall and everyone was invited outside for pictures.

The *Bruderhof* surround the newly coated *Abolition Movin'* and sing a farewell song

When we were ready to leave I stood in the doorway of *Abolition Movin'* and waved goodbye. My eyes moistened as they sang a farewell song to us and I gave thanks to God. I could not have spoken if asked. It was one of the most touching moments of my life.

We headed to the conference with Abe and two of the *Bruderhof*, Martin and Burgel Johnson. They rode on *Abolition Movin'* and Abe drove the van. It was a great trip. *Abolition Movin'* ran and looked great. I was so happy; I could not stop thanking God for the kindness of the *Bruderhof*.

We parked the bus close to the entrance of the hotel that was hosting the *Religious Organizing Conference* in Chevy Chase, Maryland. Next day, *Abolition Movin'* got its picture on the front page of the daily paper put out by the conference.

We wanted to use *Abolition Movin'* for photo opportunities, and we asked Sister Helen to join us. When she came outside, Abe took a lot of pictures, including Sister Helen at the door of the bus and in the driver's seat wearing the bus driver's hat Joan Brett had given me for my birthday.

Sister Helen appears ready to take Bill
for a ride on *Abolition Movin'*

During the conference, Sister Helen talked about her visit with the Pope. She said the Pope had kissed her on the forehead and now a lot of people wanted to kiss the place where the Pope had kissed her. I asked her if I could kiss her on the "Pope spot" and she said okay. Abe got a great picture of that, too.

After the conference, I drove *Abolition Movin'* back to Portage, Indiana. I now had a beautiful bus sitting in my driveway, but still an empty home. I was still crying myself to sleep at night. I loved Judy so much and I couldn't understand why she was gone. The only bright spot was what the *Bruderhof* had done and looking ahead to the *Journey* in Texas.

When Thanksgiving came, Judy asked me to have dinner with her family. I thought maybe that meant there was some hope of getting back together, but she informed me not to get my hopes up. Christmas was coming and I was not looking forward to it either. I was still in a fog.

Several days before Christmas, in papers across the United States, the ***Associated Press*** carried an article about forgiveness. It told my story and several others. The article never mentioned the death penalty, but in the picture of me looking out of *Abolition Movin's* window, the words on the window were very clear, "Yes, there is an alternative to the death penalty." I was glad God was still using my story even though my personal life was in chaos.

At Christmas, I was once again invited by Judy to have dinner at her brother's, with her mom and the rest of the family. Judy gave me a lot of presents, mostly clothes. I had none for her. My finances were getting the best of me. I was spending more than my income to keep the bus running. Once again, Judy cautioned me to not raise my hopes of our getting back together.

New Years Eve and New Years Day were very lonely. At times I thought I should just end it all. Then I would think about the *Journey* in Texas, and that would keep me going.

In late January, SueZann Bosler, Ron Carlson, and I were invited to be part of the ***Sally Jesse Raphael Show*** for a program on the healing power of forgiveness. I was to leave for New York on a Monday. The Friday before, I found out Judy had been seeing someone else ever since we separated. It was a Harley motorcycle mechanic that worked with her brother. I knew him. I was angry. Judy had always told me that there was not someone else. I called her immediately to ask why she had been lying to me. Her response was that she had not wanted to hurt me.

I was mad, angry, and very upset.

In three days, I was to go on a national TV program to talk about forgiveness and now I find out Judy had been lying to me. I had to practice what I had been preaching. I always told people that forgiving Paula Cooper did more for me than it did for Paula. I knew if I was going to get over this anger and pain I would have to forgive Judy before the TV show or I would be a hypocrite. It was a struggle, but after many tears and prayers, by the wee hours of the morning I knew I had forgiven her.

Judy stopped by the house the next afternoon. We had a good talk, and she knew I had forgiven her even though she didn't understand why. Judy said it was too late for us to work things out. Too much had happened. When she left I knew that there was not much hope for the relationship, but at least I was not mad any more. And for the first time I was beginning to understand what had happened. That and the forgiveness helped me begin to heal.

Three days later, on the ***Sally Jesse Raphael Show***, I was able to speak very strongly about the healing power of forgiveness.

Then it was time to go back to Texas for a third visit with *Abolition Movin'* to do some more organizing. George and Abe were coming along. We were going to be there for a couple of weeks with a lot of work to do. We arrived in Austin, the state capitol, in time for a rally in support of clemency for Karla Faye Tucker. Texas had scheduled Karla to be executed two weeks later, February 3.

From Austin, we went to Houston, Dallas and San Antonio for meetings, then back to Houston. On the morning Karla Faye was to be executed, we took *Abolition Movin'* to the airport and picked up Rachel King and Stephanie Gibson. We arrived in Huntsville, where executions take place in Texas, around noon. There were media representatives from around the world. We spread out our banners outside the *Walls Unit*, where the death chamber is housed, in downtown Huntsville.

The execution was scheduled for 6:00 P.M. By 4:00 there were several hundred people there opposed to Karla's execution. I had not seen such a media circus since John Wayne Gacy was executed. But Karla's case was entirely different. In Gacy's case most people wanted him to die. In Karla's case most people wanted her to live.

Karla's early life had been a tragedy. Her mother, of all people, had turned Karla on to heroin at age ten. Karla became a prostitute at thirteen.

After a three-day binge with drugs, Karla got involved in a robbery of a man she knew. She wanted to get back at this man for tearing up the only picture she had of her mother, who was deceased. Karla and a friend broke into his house. They didn't think he was home and were surprised to find him there. They killed him. Then they found there was someone else in the home, a girl hiding under a blanket. Karla grabbed a pickaxe and put it through the girl's heart. That person was Ron Carlson's sister, Debra Thornton.

While in jail, Karla decided to go to a meeting offered by a local church group. Karla heard about God's love and left the meeting with a Bible. She took one of the Bibles that were stacked on a table, thinking she was stealing it; she didn't know they were there for anyone who wanted one. As she began to read the Bible, Karla began to really think for the first time about the terrible thing she had done. She didn't understand all she was reading but knew she needed help. She began to pray for help. Karla had a beautiful transformation to Christianity; she was born again.

Karla began a ministry within the walls of the prison, affecting thousands of lives. Letters came from all over the world to Texas governor George W. Bush's office asking for mercy. Several voices that spoke up in favor of Karla had otherwise been strong supporters of the death penalty. Rev. Jerry Falwell and Pat Robertson asked for clemency for Karla. Ron Carlson, brother of her murder victim, spoke out for Karla. The media listened to this man who did not want revenge for his sister's killer but instead offered forgiveness and mercy.

Karla's supporters were not asking that Karla be released from prison, only that the State of Texas not kill her. One of the requirements for an execution under Texas law is that the person being executed is a future threat to society. Obviously, Karla was no longer a threat to society. She was not the same person who had committed the terrible crime fourteen years earlier.

The church group that ministered to Karla came to Huntsville. They set up a giant video screen and microphone in an area right across the road from where we had our *Journey of Hope . . . from Violence to Healing* banner. They sang Christian songs and showed a video of Karla's giving her testimony. The media and gathering crowd were able to learn more of Karla's conversion story.

Ron Carlson visited with Karla a number of times, and through Christ, they became very good friends. Karla asked Ron to witness her execution. It was the first time ever that a victim's family member witnessed an execution at the executed person's request.

The crowd began to swell as the time grew near. Many of us still held a hope that some court would sent word down that a stay had been granted, or, even better yet, that Gov. George W. Bush would give a stay and direct his parole board to grant mercy to Karla.

During the last hour, several hundred more people arrived. Many of them supported the execution. Many of those came from *Sam Houston State University* in Huntsville; a few appeared to be under the influence of alcohol when they arrived. This group brought with them a number of signs calling for Karla's execution. "Lethal Injection is Too Good for Karla", "Pick Axe Her to Death", "You *Axe* for This", "Die Bitch Die", "Rot in Hell" were just a few.

By six o'clock, there were about five hundred people around the Walls Unit. More than half of the crowd was opposed to the execution of Karla, but the minority made the loudest noise. Many of us who wanted mercy for Karla gathered in small prayer groups. Sometimes the cameras from the media would come over and start to film one of our people praying or talking, but then rapidly pull away when one of the execution supporters would began to cheer or yell loudly. They seemed to always put their cameras on the loudest ones.

About half past 6:00, the announcement was made that Karla Faye Tucker had been pronounced dead. The group that supported her death began to loudly sing the song that a crowd will sing at a baseball game when the manager takes out the pitcher and brings in a new one: "Nah Nah Nah Nah . . . Nah Nah Nah Nah, hey heyaaa, GOODBYE." They repeated it several times.

How sad to see people cheer the death of another human being. How barbaric!

At the same time, the church group that was there for Karla's support began to sing praises that Karla was now in a better place. I waited for Ron to emerge from the prison. I knew his role of witnessing Karla's death would be hard on him and I wanted to give him a hug. Furthermore, other members of Ron's family turned their backs on him when he began to support clemency for Karla.

We watched as Ron did interviews with the media and told of Karla's last words. Ron said that Karla looked at him and whispered, "I love you." Karla then looked up towards heaven and said,

"Father, into thy hands I commend my spirit." Then Karla was with her creator.

I vowed that Karla Faye Tucker's death would not be in vain. It was a long quiet ride in *Abolition Movin'* back to Houston that night. To me, February 3, 1998, was a day of infamy.

Chapter 54

New Bumps in the Road

Our plan was to drive *Abolition Movin'* back to Indiana after Karla Faye's execution. But when we found out that Charlie King, the troubadour of the abolition movement, was going to be in Dallas for a concert in two days, we decided to stop by and surprise him.

We contacted a Dallas friend, Muneer Deeb. Muneer had been on death row in Texas and was one of the lucky ones able to prove his innocence. When Muneer got out of prison, he first got a job as a taxi driver. He saved his money and bought a limousine. He started a limousine service and eventually bought ten limos. Muneer met us at the Charlie King concert and offered to take our group of thirteen out afterwards in his newest limo for dinner.

When Charlie King walked into the Dallas concert hall, he was wearing a *Journey of Hope . . . from Violence to Healing* sweatshirt. He was quite surprised to see us. This was the first time Charlie saw *Abolition Movin'*. When Charlie joined us for dinner afterwards, Muneer picked up the tab.

After driving *Abolition Movin'* back to Indiana, I found out that my stepdaughter Taniya was having marriage problems, too. Judy asked me if Taniya and her kids, Angela and Bubby, could move in with me. I said sure. My stepson Jamie had recently moved in, as well as Abe and two young men from the *Bruderhof Community* who were helping Abe organize the upcoming Texas *Journey*. The house was becoming a bit overcrowded, but at least I was no longer coming home to an empty house.

Lois Robison had offered us the use of her home for Texas *Journey* organizing. After Taniya moved in, it wasn't long before Abe, Nick and Jake took the van and headed for Lois's home in Texas.

In March, six of us—SueZann, George, Ken and Lois Robison, Jane Davis and I—went on a *Journey* to the Philippines. While there, I got an e-mail delivered to me from Abe. He had returned to Indiana to drive *Abolition Movin'* to Texas, but had encountered problems in southern Illinois. He informed me he had rented a truck and left the bus "in good hands". "But don't worry," he added.

While in the Philippines we went to the death row for men and met eight of those condemned to death. We also visited the women's death row and met with all twelve women who were on the row, as well as the warden.

We were the guests of several groups including *FLAG* (*Free Legal Assistance Group*), *Amnesty International* and a Jesuit group. We spoke in schools, churches, colleges, on TV and radio programs and also met with a victims group and a group of family members with loved ones on death row.

Although the death penalty in the Philippines had been done away with when Marcos left the presidency, it had been brought back and there were now five hundred people on death row. It looked like Leo Echegary would be the first one executed and that it could take place any time. That is why they asked the *Journey* to come. We met with Leo's mother and tried to comfort her, as she was very distraught. Although Leo received a stay, he was executed a short time later.

We met with Archbishop Cardinal Jaime Sin who assured us he was going to continue to do all he could to stop executions in the Philippines.

Bill with George White, SueZann Bosler, Ken and Lois Robison and Jane Davis on the Philippine *Journey*, sitting with the mother of Leo Echegary 1998

After I came home from our tour in the Philippines, I called to check on *Abolition Movin'*. I found out that the motor was burned up and would cost $7800 to rebuild. It was time to re-evaluate the financial situation. The *Journey* had no money and neither did I, though I did have some credit. I had a decision to make.

Abolition Movin' had already been to Texas three times in preparation for the summer *Journey*. I sure wanted her there for the main event. Micki Dickoff, my filmmaker friend from California, had told me that she was going to professionally film the Texas *Journey* and was going to borrow $50,000 on her credit cards to do the project. She had told me the movie would center around *Abolition Movin'*

I felt that if Micki had enough faith to borrow that kind of money, then I needed to have that kind of faith, too. I borrowed the money from my credit union and told the bus mechanic in southern Illinois to rebuild the engine.

At the end of March, Tim Robbins, the producer of ***Dead Man Walking***, hosted a benefit concert for *MVFR* in Los Angeles. Many of the invited artists wrote and recorded songs for the ***Dead Man Walking*** soundtrack. Ed Vedder, Rahat Nusrat Fateh Ali Khan, Anni DiFranco, Lyle Lovett, Michelle Shocked, Steve Earle, David Robbins and Tom Wait all performed. Those of us who were *MVFR* members were invited on stage. Sister Helen was the special guest of honor.

Journey of Hope . . . from Violence to Healing cofounders at the *MVFR* concert, SueZann Bosler, Sam Reese Sheppard, George White, Marietta Jaeger and Bill

I had met Steve Earle on the *TASK March* and when I invited him to the Texas *Journey*, he said he might come. He said we should send him information on the event. All five of the *Journey* cofounders were in LA for the concert and we met Anni DeFranco in the hotel lobby the next morning. Anni was almost in tears because she was so overwhelmed by the stories of murder victims' family members who didn't want the death penalty for the perpetrators and at the opportunity to perform for their benefit.

Anni DeFranco is a beautiful person.

Shortly after the concert, Wayne Crawley drove me to southern Illinois to pick up *Abolition Movin'* with its newly rebuilt engine. We headed to Kansas to pick up George. From Kansas we drove to Burleson, Texas, where Abe had established the office at Ken and Lois's home. From Burleson we drove to Houston.

In the Houston area, awaiting the *Journey* start, we stayed at Jill Fratta's home. Her brother Bob is on death row in Texas. Jill helped us organize the Houston area. The neighbors were not real keen about *Abolition Movin'* being parked in their neighborhood. I slept in Jill's office. One of the books on her shelf was *Adams versus Texas,* by Randall Dale Adams. I had read it years earlier, a great book.

I asked Jill if she had ever met Randall. When she said no, I told her I would introduce her to him when the *Journey* started and she could get her book autographed.

Randall Adams never wanted to come to Texas again. Who could blame him? When I first talked with him about coming to Texas, he was very hesitant. But he especially liked Sister Helen, and wanted to see her when she joined the *Journey* in San Antonio and Austin.

Randall's mother did not want him to return to Texas. Randall had to do a lot of talking to her before he came. And then he came for the whole seventeen days. I thought it was of utmost importance for the people in the state of Texas to listen to an innocent man they had almost executed.

Chapter 55

Journey, Texas Style

Micki had come early with her camera crew so they could set up and not miss anything. To me the most exciting part of this *Journey* would be that Micki was going to get it on film for posterity. Sunny Jacobs had come with Micki from California and her daughter Tina Tafero would join us at the start. Tina and Sunny were going to be a big part of Micki's film.

Micki wanted us to start the film with all of us washing *Abolition Movin'*. *Abolition Movin'* got the washing of her life as we waited for Tina. When Tina arrived, we stopped washing *Abolition Movin'* to give her a big warm *Journey* welcome. The cameras were rolling as we welcomed her with warm, soapy hugs.

Tina's testimony would be very powerful, especially to young people. She was only a baby when she was taken from her mother and both of her parents put on death row by the state of Florida. She was fourteen when they executed her father, Jesse Tafero. She was a young lady by the time they were able to prove her parents' innocence and see her mom released from prison.

Soon, the familiar *Journey* faces appeared: Randall Dale Adams, SueZann Bosler, Sam Reese Sheppard, Sally Peck, Ken and Lois Robison, Joan Betz, Stephanie Gibson, Mike Kennedy and others. From Ireland came John, Trish, Liam and Magda. From Italy, Carlo and Sergio. England sent Peter, Piers and Rob. Altogether, six foreign countries were represented on the Texas *Journey of*

Hope—Texas, the state that executes more of its citizens than any other.

Surprisingly, the ***Houston Chronicle*** had given the *Journey* some favorable advance press coverage. Like many of our other abolition events, this one started at death row. On Saturday, our first full day, we planned to be in Huntsville, the home of the infamous *Ellis Unit One* where death row prisoners were housed and the *Walls Unit* where executions take place.

On Saturday morning, I fired up *Abolition Movin'* to move it from the parking lot to the front of the dormitory. It was going to be a very hot day and I worried about people like Ken and Lois getting too hot riding on the bus since we had no air conditioning. But I soon realized there was a bigger problem than the heat: *Abolition Movin*' was clean and shiny, but lopsided.

Abolition Movin' has air shocks which rise about six inches as the air pressure builds up. On this morning, only one side rose up. I called a local repair shop. They told me to bring it in on Monday morning. They said it probably needed an air pillow and would only take a day to get it done, but *Abolition Movin*' would miss the first big activity.

We crowded into the other vehicles to begin our seventy-mile drive to Huntsville. When the temperature soon climbed over one hundred degrees, I was kind of glad we didn't have *Abolition Movin'*. I became really glad when the traffic came to a complete stop forty miles down the expressway. If we had been in the bus, we really would have suffered because the only relief on a hot day is the breeze with the windows open.

The rally in Huntsville started three hours late because everyone had been stalled in the traffic jam that had been caused by an overturned fuel truck. It was powerful for Randall Dale Adams to be back in Huntsville. It wasn't very many years ago that the state of Texas came within seventy-two hours of killing him in that very *Walls Unit* building. We took pictures of Randall and Sunny, our two innocent death row survivors, with the *Walls Unit* in the background. Steve Earle sang "**Ellis Unit One,**" the song he wrote and sang for the ***Dead Man Walking*** soundtrack, for our rally.

On Sunday, we went to several churches in the Houston area. On Monday, ten of the Journeyers went an hour south of Houston to the church that sponsored *Straightway*, a group that travels around teaching drug prevention. It was the same church that had ministered to Karla Faye Tucker. We had a great service there; Barbara Lewis, George and I spoke. Pastor David Kirschke took a special love offering for us and his daughter Melody sang a song she had written for the *Journey*. It was a very inspirational night, and Micki got it all on film.

The mechanic called with some bad news on Tuesday morning. Instead of telling me to come and pick up *Abolition Movin'*, he told me it was not an air pillow causing problems. He told me, "The bus is suffering from a severe case of deterioration of the undercarriage." In other words, RUST. *Abolition Movin'* had probably logged several million miles on the highways since 1965. The body is made of aluminum and will not rust, but the undercarriage is another story. Most of those miles were in the snow belt of the Midwest when *Trailways* operated it.

The salt damage finally caught up with her and the right side of the undercarriage had caved in.

I was told it would take a week and $2,500 to get her on the road again. I gave them the okay. Stephanie Coward could see how upset I was. Stephanie is a wonderful singer and one of her songs; "**His Eye Is on the Sparrow**" is my favorite. She took me by the hand and led me across the street to one of the college buildings. She took me upstairs to a room with a piano. She sat down and began to sing. The song starts out, "*Why should I be discouraged*?" and the chorus of the song is "*His eye is on the sparrow and I know He watches me.*" It brought tears to my eyes. The song was just what I needed. As we got up to leave, we saw a security guard standing around the corner. He had been listening to Stephanie singing. His eyes glistened as he held back tears.

We had to go to Dallas without *Abolition Movin'*. We stayed at a second rate motel that had a courtyard and swimming pool in the center. All the Journeyers would gather in the courtyard at evening time after our events for the day were finished. Steve Earle had left the *Journey* while we were in Houston but he rejoined us in Dallas. He had rearranged his schedule so he could spend more time with us. Steve had his guitar and he sang some songs as we sat around the pool. Although Steve is a great talent and star in his own right, he was just one of us and we found out what a great guy he really is. He told us he had always been against the death penalty, but with us, he was learning something new about activism.

Darren Routier joined us in Dallas. Darren's wife Darlie was on death row, found guilty of killing two of their children. Many are convinced of her innocence. Guilt or innocence is not a factor in our opposition against the death penalty. Darren was a victims' family member because his two sons were killed and if his wife is executed, he will be victimized again.

We held a press conference with Darren outside a movie theater in Dallas where we were showing the documentary ***From Fury to Forgiveness***. Since the film was also about Marietta, we hoped she could join SueZann and me for the showing. Her schedule would not allow her to join us until we got to San Antonio.

A special showing of the ***Discovery Channel*** Film
"*From Fury to Forgiveness*" on the Texas *Journey*

One of the main events of the Texas *Journey* was the meeting at *SMU* where Professor Rick Halperin teaches. Randall Dale Adams was the keynote speaker. Tonia Cropper, whose brother was on death row in Louisiana, joined Randall, Rick and me on the panel. Rick talked about an execution he had just witnessed.

From Dallas we moved to San Antonio, a beautiful city, with fantastic people. We got to know people like Jim and Rosalyn Collier, who let us stay in their home on organizing trips. Rev. Ann Helmke was a tremendous help. Anne and Rosalyn helped organize a large luncheon at the Peace Center.

Everyone was excited about San Antonio because both Marietta Jaeger and Sister Helen were joining us there. Steve Earle was also coming back after leaving for a few days to do a concert in another state. Sister Helen led the march to the Alamo and gave a great talk at the Catholic Church to an overflowing crowd. The media loved her. San Antonio treated us well.

Abolition Movin' was ready to be picked up. Kathy Harris, an ex Texan who now lives in Alaska, George and I were able to ride to Houston with Tom Marshall, from Ohio, who had joined the *Journey* for several days, but now needed to drive his rental car back to Houston so he could fly home.

We picked up *Abolition Movin'* and headed for Austin to meet up with the rest of the gang for the conclusion of the Texas *Journey.* At least *Abolition Movin'* would be involved in the most important part on Saturday when we marched to the state capitol building.

It was evening rush hour by the time we got *Abolition Movin'* on the road. We drove from the south side of Houston through the heavy traffic. Suddenly there was a terrific loud wrenching noise from the front left wheel. I had to pull the bus off to the side of the road. The wheel was extremely hot. We called the bus garage we had left about an hour earlier. We needed to be towed back.

There is an air hole on each wheel that allows air to get to the grease seal. When *Abolition Movin'* was painted, evidently the air hole got covered with paint and the grease seal couldn't breathe. As a result, it got hot and cracked. The grease leaked out through the crack. While we were driving through Houston, the wheel got so hot that it basically welded the wheel and axle together.

The mechanic told us it would take another week and about $2000 to fix it. So much for *Abolition Movin'* being the star of Micki's movie about the Texas *Journey*. It could not be fixed until the *Journey* was over. We wanted *Abolition Movin'* to be a symbol of the movement. However, it was becoming symbolic of the movement: often broke down and seemingly going nowhere. Normally, I might have lost it, but Kathy Harris helped me keep my cool. We called Austin and asked one of the interns to come pick us up.

Excitement was building for the march to the capitol on Saturday. Throughout the Texas *Journey*, we passed out flyers talking about the finale with Sister Helen in Austin on Saturday, June 13, 1998.

The Saturday temperature was expected to soar over one hundred degrees. Hundreds of people from all over Texas showed up for the march. An anti-death penalty march this big was unheard of in the "killing state" of Texas.

The heat could have been a problem, but we had vehicles at every corner with water and a place to rest for those who needed it. We marched the three miles from Houston-Tillison College to the state capitol building. At one point, the march went up a little hill. As I looked back, I could see for three blocks where the marchers were still coming around the corner, four abreast. It was a great sight.

Sister Helen was in the front of the march helping to carry the *Journey of Hope . . . from Violence to Healing* twenty-four-foot banner. We sang, chanted and shouted all the way.

We gathered on the limestone steps of the capitol for our rally. Magdaleno Rose-Avila was the emcee and Sister Helen gave the keynote. Ron Carlson also spoke, along with Sam Jordan, Randall Dale Adams, Marietta Jaeger, and others. Stephanie Coward and Charlie King sang. I thanked everyone, especially Abe Bonowitz, for his many months of work to see that the Texas *Journey* was a success.

To me it was the greatest day in the history of grassroots abolition, and Micki got it all on tape. Micki got over ninety hours of film during the Texas *Journey*, including lengthy interviews with many participants. Through Micki, this great day could live forever.

But it was also a sad day. Judy's mom, Fern, was buried on that day. She had died suddenly from a heart attack. Fern loved me and I loved her. I was really glad she had come to Italy with Judy and me on our honeymoon. In coming to Italy, she was able to fulfill a lifelong dream of seeing the Pope. I was sorry I missed her funeral in Indiana. I knew she understood, because she knew what I was all about.

I offered to leave the *Journey* and come home if Judy needed me, but I was assured by her she didn't. I didn't think the sight of Judy's boyfriend comforting her would do me much good anyway.

The Texas *Journey of Hope . . . from Violence to Healing* was now history.

Randall Dale Adams and Jill Fratta met on the Texas *Journey* and were married a little over a year later. They are pictured in front of the *Walls Unit* where executions in Texas occur.

Chapter 56

Van Troubles, Too

It was good to have *Abolition Movin'* moving again. We picked her up as we left Texas and headed for Washington, D.C. for the fifth annual Supreme Court fast and vigil. We were going to *Journey* all along the way, with engagements in Louisiana, Alabama, Tennessee and Virginia. Our core group was now twelve people.

In Louisiana, after a few days at a Catholic retreat center, we headed for Baton Rouge. There I stayed at the home of Sister Helen's sister. Her sister's family was wonderful. They told me that I had slept in Sister Helen's bed. I don't guess there are a lot of men who have done that.

The state of Louisiana was scheduled to kill Dobbie Williams. Sister Helen was Dobbie's personal advisor and friend and was with him at the prison. We were at a carry-in church dinner on the night of the scheduled execution. The evening schedule called for some talks and for a time of prayer. About half of us were preparing to leave the church after dinner and go to the vigil site at Angola Prison, but as we were getting into the cars to leave the church, someone came out and told us that Dobbie had gotten a stay of execution. Prayers answered.

In New Orleans, we had a march and rally. As a special treat that evening, Jon and Barbara Oren, whose son was on death row, took us to Bourbon Street for seafood delights.

The next day, we drove to Alabama to visit Judy Cumbee. After speaking at her church, we split into two groups. Some went with Abe in the van to death row in Atmore. The others—George, Mike Kennedy, Stephanie Coward, Grace Singleton (a lady who joined us for several days, whose son had been executed a few years earlier) and I—took *Abolition Movin'* towards Enterprise, Alabama. That is where Charlene White is buried and George wanted to visit the gravesite.

Both groups got back together in Huntsville, Alabama, for a luncheon meeting attended by fifty people. We met the mother and father-in-law of our long time *Journey* friend, Rev. Joe Ingle who, we were told, was not in good health.

After lunch, we headed for Tennessee to see Sara Sharpe. For over a year, she had been talking about having a major *Journey of Hope* event in Tennessee. We talked with her and the board of *TCASK* (*Tennessee Coalition Against State Killing*).

Steve Earle lived in Nashville and when he heard that we were thinking about doing a major event in Tennessee, he told us that if we did come to his state, he would try to arrange a concert with Emily Lou Harris, Jackson Browne and maybe the Indigo Girls. If we needed any further incentive, that was it.

While in Nashville, we stayed at an apartment belonging to Steve Earle. Steve wasn't there but he gave us keys and even bought extra beds for us. We met with the Tennessee organizers and decided to bring the *Journey of Hope . . . from Violence to Healing* to Tennessee the following year as our major event of 1999.

The next night, we stopped at a retreat center near Knoxville called the "Highlander." As we drove up the steep driveway, *Abolition Movin'* decided it wasn't going to work that hard. We parked halfway up. It was fun in the morning backing down the treacherous driveway. Then we headed for our next stop, Troy Reimer's in Roanoke, Virginia.

Almost out of Tennessee, heading up a fairly steep mountain, *Abolition Movin'* quit. A mechanic came but could do nothing. We had to tow her in.

Abe rented a truck and we loaded what we needed for the

Supreme Court vigil. We left the bus for repairs. *Abolition Movin'* needed new fuel injectors. New ones should have been put in when the engine was overhauled in southern Illinois, but evidently, they put the old ones back in. We headed to Troy Reimer's and then to Washington, D.C. with the van and a rental truck.

Steve Earle joined us for a few days at the Supreme Court for our fifth annual event. On the last night, he did an open-air concert on the sidewalk in front of the Court. We always maintain an all-night vigil on our last night. Many of us bring sleeping bags and pillows, and sleep right on the sidewalk. Steve joined us for the all-nighter.

While staying awake all night, as I usually do, I was talking with Joan Brett about the future of the *Journey of Hope . . . from Violence to Healing*. We knew that we needed to restructure the board and add a few members. We both thought Steve Earle would be a great choice. When Steve woke up, we talked to him about the *Journey*. He said he would do whatever he could to help, so we asked if he would be on our board. He answered, "In a heartbeat!" What a coup to have someone like Steve Earle on our board! We also added Joan Betz and Stephanie Gibson.

Steve had a first class airline ticket back to Tennessee, but decided he would ride with George and me to get *Abolition Movin'*. We drove in the van to the Tennessee-Virginia border and picked her up. The bill came to $700, and Steve generously paid part of it. Then we headed for Nashville, with George driving the van and Steve riding aboard *Abolition Movin'*.

Steve found a place for us to park *Abolition Movin'* near Nashville, so we left her behind. We weren't going to need her for a while and didn't have enough money to even get her towed if there should be another breakdown. We spent the fourth of July at Steve's house where we were treated to a barbeque.

George was eager to get home. On July 5, the two of us headed toward Kansas, driving the van as far as North Little Rock, Arkansas, before a motel stop.

The next morning, after several miles on the highway, we noticed that the transmission was starting to slip. We pulled off to find a repair shop. Bad news. The transmission needed replacing.

We got another motel room when we were told it wouldn't be done until the next day. The next day, the shop manager pointed to two transmissions lying on the ground side by side and told us to compare the new one and the old one. The new one did not have a steel finger on the casing like the old one. He said the company had sent him the wrong rebuilt transmission. It would be still one more day. We got another room.

North Little Rock, Arkansas, is a boring little town especially if you don't have a car. In the afternoon, we took a walk looking for a place to get a drink and pass some time. We walked several miles before we found one. We played a few games of pool and walked back to the motel.

The next morning, we were told it would be yet another day before it was finished. We stayed one more night in the room and called again the next day. The van was finally ready, but he told us that he couldn't fix the air conditioner.

We paid the bill and got back on the highway. Thirty miles down the road, a stream of smoke began coming up through the front panel of the van. I looked out the side mirror and saw a cloud coming from the rear. We pulled off at the next exit to call the transmission shop we had left a short time earlier.

They sent a car hauler to where we were, loaded up the van, and headed back to North Little Rock. George and I could only look at each other and smile. Another night in North Little Rock!

The van was ready the next day and we left for Tulsa, Oklahoma, where Becky would meet George. In Tulsa we checked into a motel that had a pool. I thought George would spend the night and enjoy the pool and the air-conditioned room. But George had had enough of me, and wanted to get home. Becky arrived within the hour to take him. I left the van in Tulsa and flew to Chicago for a *Murder Victims' Families for Reconciliation* board meeting. George had decided he was not going to make this one. He was exhausted.

We had been on the road for over six weeks.

Chapter 57

Late in Rome, Then Back Home

After picking up my van in Tulsa, I headed to California to spend several weeks "house sitting" for Micki Dickoff while she and her friend Christie went to Holland, and then stayed for a while to help Micki sort through the Texas *Journey* film footage.

While catching up on paperwork and reading at Micki's house, I got a call from Carlo Santoro. Carlo was one of the Italians who joined us on the *Journey* in Texas; he was involved with a Catholic lay organization in Italy called the *Saint Egidio Community*.

Carlos said that *Saint Egidio* was planning a campaign to gather signatures for a moratorium of the death penalty for Sister Helen's organization, *Moratorium 2000*. Sister Helen was coming to Rome to kick off of their campaign. Carlo asked if George and I could join Sister Helen on behalf of the *Journey of Hope*, and then stay on two weeks in Europe to participate in speaking events after Sister Helen came back to the States.

My passport was back in Indiana, so I called Judy and asked her to send it to Los Angeles. When I opened the envelope, I saw she had sent both my passport and birth certificate. I was more concerned about seeing my birth certificate than I was the passport because I didn't really want my birth certificate in Los Angeles. George was leaving from Kansas so we just planned on meeting in Italy.

This would be my first trip back to Italy since Paula was taken off of death row and I wanted to thank the more than two million people who had signed petitions on her behalf.

Sunny Jacobs took me to the Los Angeles airport. I stepped up to the ticket window and gave the lady my passport and ticket. She looked at me and said, "You're not going anywhere. Your passport has expired."

I was almost in a state of shock. Judy had sent me the wrong passport and I hadn't noticed. I had gotten a new one before I went to the Philippines, but Judy overlooked it when she went to my desk and sent the old one. She had noticed that it was expired and that was why she had sent the birth certificate, but I hadn't realized it.

What a mess. Wayne Crawley sent me my valid passport on something called "next flight out." It cost $296. I was twenty-four hours late in getting to Rome and missed the first big engagement with Sister Helen. George took my place with an audience of three thousand, the largest group George had ever talked to. That's larger than any group I have ever spoken to. George likes to remind me that I missed out on the opportunity, bless his heart.

It was great being in Europe on behalf of *Saint Egidio*. In the beautiful city of Naples, George and I spoke at a special evening service. Steve Earle, who had joined us for several days, sang a couple of songs. Afterward, George and I were given a standing ovation and flocked with people asking autographs. It was a new experience for us and Steve just stood in the background and smiled. Steve is always being asked for autographs when he is on tour.

On to Germany, Belgium, and Spain. In each city George and I went to, the people of *Saint Egidio* welcomed us. They were very caring and kind. I enjoyed talking about love and compassion and applying it to the death penalty. When I talked about the moratorium petitions, I was able to tell each person that they could make a difference. I told them how I believed the people of Europe had saved Paula Cooper's life by signing petitions.

Bill and George in Belgium with *St. Egidio Community*

The day George and I left Belgium, the local paper did a story about us that included a large picture. The newspaper was passed out to all the people on the plane. It was funny to see people as they opened their papers, look at the picture, look back at us, and then look at the paper again. Invariably they would get the attention of the person next to them, point at the article and then have them look back at us.

We flew to Barcelona, Spain. On the third day in Barcelona, I was told we would be going to a city called Manresa. Manresa was where Saint Ignatius of Loyola had his spiritual conversion while living in the caves imbedded in the surrounding mountains. A group of six of us took the beautiful hour-long drive. George stayed in Barcelona with others to do events there.

Upon our arrival in Manresa, we went to City Hall. The mayor greeted us. He wanted some pictures with us and then he gave us some gifts. He warmly welcomed the people from *Saint Egidio*. They were invited to put a display of their materials about the moratorium effort in the main hallway.

The local university had a very famous culinary school. We were guests at the restaurant for the noon meal. The cooks are "chefs in training" for elegant hotels of the world. What a special meal we had! It was the full seven-course spread, each course served with an explanation of how it was prepared.

Each bite was fantastic. There were four glasses at each setting for different wines. A fifth glass was brought at the end of the meal for an after-dinner drink. It was very eloquent. George had really missed out and I told everyone I would rib him about it. They thought it was funny that I was going to tease *Big George*.

Then it was time to go speak to a group crowded into a standing-room-only auditorium. I usually don't eat until after I speak, and I was reminded why that day. Fortunately, there were several speakers and also an interpreter. We all sat at a table on stage when we talked. That was a blessing for me.

One of the things I liked about Spain was when we drove through Barcelona, on the coast; there is a giant statue of Christopher Columbus. His arm is outstretched and pointing to America. I would tell my hosts each time we drove by it that I felt comfortable seeing that because at least I knew the way home.

In Milan, I was at the airport gate with George, who was waiting for his flight to Chicago. George was wearing his black *Journey of Hope . . . from Violence to Healing* t-shirt. I was wearing one of Abe Bonowitz's *"I Oppose the Death Penalty—Don't Kill for Me"* t-shirts. A lady sitting next to me said, "I like your shirt. You don't see many of those."

We talked for a minute about the death penalty and then her husband spoke up. He asked me if I knew "that guy from Indiana," but he hesitated trying to remember a name. Then he said, "What's your name?" When I told him it was Bill Pelke, he smiled and said, "You are the one I was thinking of." It turned out we had met years earlier in Little Rock, Arkansas, at a *NCADP* conference. They were headed back to Chicago after vacationing in Italy.

After George left, I caught a flight to Los Angeles. After a few more weeks in LA, I headed back to Indiana. It was wonderful spending over three months working out of Los Angeles, but I felt November was the time to get home again. But when I got home to Indiana, I begin to wonder why I had been in such a hurry to get back. It was very depressing. Besides, it was over with Judy and me, and I really didn't want to be in Indiana.

However, I needed to be in the area because something important was happening in Chicago. There was an innocence conference that was to take place at *Northwestern University*, hosted by Larry Marshall. At that time, there were over seventy people in this country who had been sentenced to death by various states and later found innocent. Larry had invited me to participate in a plenary panel session with Mike Farrell and Robert Meeropol (son of Julius and Ethel Rosenberg).

The seventy freed persons had all been invited to the conference. About thirty of them came. Some I personally knew, such as Sunny Jacobs, Randall Dale Adams, Muneer Deeb, Delbert Tibbs, Darby Tillis, and others.

> One by one they entered the auditorium and said, "I am *so and so* . . . the state of *such and such* sentenced me to death for a crime I did not commit. If the state of *such and such* would have had their way, today I would be dead."

Afterward, each would take a seat in one of the chairs that were set up in three rows behind the podium. It was not long until the stage was full of people who were sentenced to death by our country. All were found later to be innocent. Thank God they were able to somehow prove it before they were killed. Proponents of the death penalty claim that it shows the system works, but we all knew that these people are alive in spite of the system. People left this conference with a renewed hope that the abolitionist movement was gaining ground.

At the conference, I had a talk with Lois Robison. We were

standing on the sidewalk in Chicago waiting for several others to join us for dinner. Lois was very concerned that the state of Texas might soon be setting an execution date for her son Larry.

She asked if I would come to Texas if and when they were to execute Larry. She began to cry. I had never seen Lois cry before. She is a very strong lady. I told Lois that of course I would be there. I didn't know what else to say or do but to put my arms around Lois and hold her as she cried. Several others told Lois that they would come to Texas in the event Larry received a date. I have never felt more helpless in my life than when I stood there on the side of the street on that cold Chicago night with my arms around "Mom."

Chapter 58

A *Vatican* Christmas

One cold December day, I received a call from an Italian group called *Hands Off Cain.* They had sent two representatives to the Texas *Journey*, Alberta and Sergio. *Hands Off Cain* was sponsoring a march on Christmas Day that would go to the *Vatican* where the Pope would be giving his annual address to the world. I was asked to come as a representative of *Journey of Hope . . . from Violence to Healing* and bring someone with me to help carry the *Journey* banner at the front of the march.

What an honor. Kathy Harris of Anchorage, Alaska would accompany me. Kathy was a well-versed abolitionist working not only as the Alaska state coordinator for *Amnesty International's* death penalty program, but she was the treasurer *for Alaskans Against the Death Penalty* and Treasurer for the *Journey*. She spent a lot of time putting together the paperwork needed for the *Journey* to get its 501(c)3 status with the IRS. We informed *Hands Off Cain* that the two *Journey* representatives would be Kathy and me.

They asked us to come a week before Christmas to do media work for the march. It was impressive to walk down the streets of Rome and see posters all over advertising the march to the *Vatican*.

It was quite an affair, beginning early Christmas morning. Thousands gathered at a square called *Da Campo Dei Fiori a San Peitro*. Giordano Bruno, a philosopher, was burned at the stake in 1600 as a heretic at this square. That is why it was chosen as the rally point to start the march.

Several people spoke there, and a ladies quartet sang. Kathy Harris took turns with Barbara Bacci, one of the organizers, to read names of one hundred and eighty men on Texas' death row who had written the Pope, asking to be remembered in prayers. I spoke about the death penalty and the importance of the international community in helping bring about worldwide abolition of it.

As the march toward the *Vatican* began, the twenty-four-foot *Journey of Hope . . . from Violence to Healing* banner led the march. Behind us were people carrying the flags of over one hundred cities. The mayor of Rome marched with us. According to the evening news, there were as many as seven thousand people on our march to the *Vatican*.

Bill helping carry the *Journey of Hope . . . from Violence to Healing* banner leading the march to the *Vatican* Christmas Day, 1998

When we arrived at the *Vatican*, there were already thirty thousand people gathered to hear the Pope's annual Christmas address. Pope John Paul II began to read his prepared speech. He suddenly stopped his reading, and made mention about those who had marched to the *Vatican* protesting the death penalty. He thanked the organizers of the march and those who participated in it.

The purpose of the march was to ask the Pope to make a statement about the death penalty and the Pope did just that. For the first time publicly, he called for worldwide abolition of the death penalty. He said that it was cruel and unnecessary. The crowd applauded his words.

After the Christmas address, we joined members of the *Saint Egidio Community* who, every year at Christmas, feed the poor with a feast at various churches throughout Rome. Members of *Saint Egidio* serve the food. Because his flight was delayed, Sam Reese Sheppard missed the morning *Vatican* march, but he was able to join us for the Christmas meal. The president of Italy was also at the feast. His ranch provided the meat for the meal. It was quite an occasion watching the underprivileged people enjoy this special meal.

In the evening, we went to the apartment of Sergio and Allesandra. Sergio fixed spaghetti for Kathy, Sam, Melodee, Paulo and several of their friends who had joined us. As we watched the evening news, the lead story was about the Pope's annual address and mention of what he said about the death penalty. The second story was about the march. The *Journey of Hope . . . from Violence to Healing* banner, being carried by the marchers, was very prominent. They interviewed Sergio and me about why we were marching. The third story was about *Saint Egidio* feeding the poor people of Rome and how the president had also come to the banquet. How exciting it was to be at the center of what was happening in one of the largest and oldest cities in the world on the most important Christian holiday of the year. I was very grateful for the opportunity to talk about love and compassion for all of humanity and know that my voice was heard. What a wonderful way to end the year 1998. Praise the Lord.

Chapter 59

At the Grand Ole Opry

Steve Earle was true to his word. The 1999 Tennessee *Journey of Hope . . . from Violence to Healing* was starting out with a concert in Nashville, Tennessee, held in the Ryman Auditorium, the original home of the Grand Ole Opry. The lineup included Emmylou Harris, Jackson Browne, the Indigo Girls and Steve Earle, who also served as emcee. Sister Helen Prejean was guest of honor. What a night, with a sellout crowd of three thousand people. It was the greatest night ever for the *Journey*. All of the performers donated their services and talents. The journey will forever be thankful to Steve Earle, Emmylou Harris, Jackson Browne and the Indigo Girls.

I had tried to get my daughter Becky to come down for this concert because I wanted to treat her to something special for her twenty-first birthday. But she couldn't come because of her classes at *Ball State University* in Indiana.

After the kick-off concert, the *Journey* moved around Tennessee to Knoxville, Chattanooga, Memphis and then back to Nashville. Steve Earle did a free concert in each city. We had the regulars of George, Marietta, Sam, SueZann, Sally Peck, Barbara Lewis, Anne Coleman, Ron Carlson and others, but some first timers also joined us. Renny Cushing, the new executive director of *Murder Victims' Families for Reconciliation,* attended his first *Journey*.

Renny took over as head of *MVFR* at the first of the year. His father had been killed a number of years earlier.

Also joining us was Bud Welch. I first heard about Bud when ***Parade Magazine*** did an article about forgiveness a year and a half earlier. Bud's daughter, Julie, was killed in the Oklahoma City bombing that destroyed the Alfred P. Murrah building. Bud was filled with anger when his daughter was killed. He began to drink and smoke like never before. He wanted the people responsible for the bombing dead. Then, Bud came to realize that it was revenge he sought and that it was wrong. He knew Julie would not approve of his actions of hate and the desire for revenge. He quit smoking and stopped his drinking sprees.

He began to speak out against the death penalty. Since the bombing was such a high-profile story, Bud's voice was heard worldwide through the media. I remembered seeing Bud on the news during the Terry McNichols trial.

Bud also met with Timothy McVeigh's family. He knew that the McVeigh family was also grieving. Bud pledged to speak out against Timothy being executed. Having Bud join the Tennessee *Journey* was a real blessing for us.

Lois Robison was on the Tennessee *Journey* for the whole two weeks. Ken couldn't come because he had to teach his college classes. It was the longest Lois had ever been away from her husband since they were married. She loves Ken dearly and tells everyone they are still on their honeymoon, but she knew the importance of telling her story and trying to get help for her son Larry on the Texas death row.

While in Nashville, several members of the group were able to go to Tennessee's death row. Rev. Joe Ingle was able to get us permission to visit eight of the death row inmates.

One sad note about the Tennessee *Journey*: *Abolition Movin'* was parked in a bus lot just outside Nashville, but did not make it for any *Journey* events. There were no particular repairs that it needed; we just didn't have enough money to get the license plates and insurance. And if she were to break down, we didn't have the money to get it towed, let alone fixed. Those riding in the van with me—Marietta, SueZann, George and Kathy—stopped on our way from Knoxville to Memphis, just to see it and take a few pictures. It was sad to me that we weren't able to use her.

Steve Earle suggested that we should just take the bus and leave it in front of the *Walls Unit* in Huntsville as a symbol against the death penalty. Of course Steve doesn't love *Abolition Movin'* as much as I do.

Chapter 60

Larry's Got a Stay!

A short time later the state of Texas set an execution date for Larry Robison, August 17, 1999. I went to Texas ten days ahead of that date to do whatever I could to help his parents, Ken and Lois. I wanted to be there because I knew it was going to be tough on everyone.

Larry's case got a lot of media attention. When I had been in Washington, D.C. for the annual Supreme Court fast and vigil in June, I got a call from the TV program ***48 Hours.*** The producer asked what was going on with the *Journey of Hope*. I told them about Larry's upcoming execution date and I told them about "Mom and Dad" Robison.

The producer, Shashanna Wolfson, called Lois; ***48 Hours*** decided to do a segment about the Robison's story. They began doing interviews with Ken and Lois, and made several trips to Texas. When other media found out ***48 Hours*** was interested in the case, they also became interested. Although exhausted by the thought of the upcoming execution, Lois did everything she could to get the word out that the state of Texas was getting ready to kill her mentally ill son. She knew that she might not be able to save Larry's life, but hoped her efforts might save the lives of others.

Rev. Melodee Smith, an attorney was doing work for Larry's case. She invited me to join her and Larry's other attorney, Bill Harris, for a meeting at Governor George Bush's office. We talked with Gov. Bush's counsel about the possibility of the governor granting a stay for Larry. They were touched by what we had to say about the case. Gov. Bush's counsel asked us who Larry's guardian was. It had never been determined by the courts whether Larry was mentally competent or not. They said they would see what the courts had to say before they made any decision about a stay.

I felt the best chance of Larry getting a stay was with the Board of Pardons and Paroles. Historically, they had not given relief to death row inmates, but Melodee had launched an excellent clemency campaign, including not only scores of legal papers, but also thousands of signatures from around the world requesting that the board consider granting Larry a stay. National associations for the mentally ill, human rights organizations like *Amnesty International*, and places like the Jimmy Carter Institute asked Gov. Bush and the parole board to spare the life of this mentally ill man, and beloved son of Lois and Ken.

While we were at the governor's office, word came that the Pardons and Parole Board had unanimously rejected Larry's request for clemency. The only hope left was to file an appeal dealing with the issue of mental competency, or for Gov. Bush to grant a stay. No one thought there was much of a chance of either. Dejected, we went back to Huntsville.

Family and friends of the Robison's were beginning to arrive in Huntsville. A number of people from the *Journey* came: George White, Abe Bonowitz, Stephanie Gibson, Jake Zumpa, Phyllis Pautrat, Steve Earle, Mike Kennedy, Sally Peck, Kathy Harris, Sara Sharpe. Micki Dickoff came with a camera crew. Rev. Jane Davis who was counseling Larry, Randall Dale Adams and his new wife Jill Fratta, Karen Sebung, Ron and Debbie Carlson, Dave and Peggy Atwood and others, were arriving.

A camera crew was following Steve Earle for a documentary they were doing about his activism against the death penalty.

On the morning of the seventeenth, Ken and Lois went with other family members to see Larry for the last time. The execution was scheduled for 6 P.M. Around noon, Ken and Lois had to say good-bye. The ***48 Hours*** camera crew filmed them as they drove away from the prison.

Steve Earle invited everyone to meet at a local steak house and said he would buy lunch. About forty of us went to the restaurant. It took a little while for them to seat us all in an isolated section. Ken and Lois had not yet arrived when the waitresses began taking orders. We asked the media to leave us alone while we ate, so they stayed in an adjacent dining room.

Suddenly, Melodee Smith, who was talking on a cell phone, shouted out, "Larry's got a stay! Larry's got a stay!" The attorney had just gotten word that the Texas Court of Appeals had voted 4-3 to stay Larry's execution until the state of Texas could give him a mental competency test. It is against the law to execute a mentally ill person and the courts had never examined Larry.

Hallelujah! There would be no killing of Larry Robison this day by the state of Texas.

Our section of the restaurant went wild with joyous shouting. I called out, "Where are Ken and Lois?" and I was told they should be arriving any moment. I headed for the front door. Ken and Lois were just getting out of their car. I waited for Melodee, who was right behind me, to tell them the great news. Lois let out a scream. I joined Melodee, George, Steve and others in hugging Lois and dancing in the parking lot with her.

Micki Dickoff just happened to have her camera crew outside the restaurant interviewing Jane Davis. When she heard the commotion, she had the cameras get "the moment" on film. She managed to get Lois's reaction and the parking lot celebration.

It was indeed a joyous day. Lois and Ken entered the restaurant, and when things settled down, I changed my order from a hamburger to a steak. There was a reason to celebrate.

One of the local TV stations, ***FOX TV***, had been very kind to Ken and Lois as execution day drew near. They had been inside the restaurant when Ken and Lois came. They missed filming "the moment". I heard them lamenting the fact that they missed it, and informed them that Micki had gotten it. Right away, they wanted to make Micki a deal. They agreed to trade her some film of an interview they had gotten of Larry in exchange for "the moment".

The ***FOX*** crew wanted the tape right away, but Micki was not about to let go of it. She didn't trust the film out of our sight. I took the film and went with the ***FOX*** crews to their TV truck, parked in the lot outside the *Walls Unit* where the execution was supposed to take place. I sat in their truck while they copied it. They gave it back to me and then I went back to the restaurant and gave it to Micki. My steak was gone, but I didn't care.

That evening, a memorial service had been planned. Since Larry was alive, we made it an "interfaith celebration of life" service instead. I was asked to say a few words and to pray. I said, "I have three things to say: Hallelujah . . . . Hallelujah . . . . Hallelujah!" Then I prayed, and ended the prayer with the words, "in Jesus's name."

Later, I was told I really offended several of the people there by ending the prayer that way. I didn't mean to offend anyone. I was just so happy that Lois's son was not executed. "In Jesus's name" is how I usually end my prayers.

And again I say, "Hallelujah . . . Hallelujah . . . Hallelujah."

Chapter 61

A Whirlwind Tour

Inspired by the stay of execution for Larry Robison, plans were made for the *Journey* to travel to Europe on behalf of Larry Robison and his family. We remembered how the petitions from Europe had played a role in sparing the life of Paula Cooper a decade before. We left with armloads of petitions for people to sign. We wanted to raise awareness not only of Larry's case, but also how the U.S. allows killing of the mentally ill, juveniles, plus the whole issue of the death penalty and moratorium efforts. Seven of us—Sally Peck, SueZann Bosler, Bud Welch, Ken and Los Robison, Melodee Smith, and I—left from Philadelphia for a whirlwind two-week European speaking tour.

We had been in Philadelphia for the annual *NCADP* conference where Bud was honored as *Abolitionist of the Year*.

Our first stop was Paris, where Linda Lucasey, an American living in France, greeted us. She was doing volunteer work for *Amnesty International*. She lined up several speaking events throughout Paris, including a large audience at the American University.

We rented two cars in France and when we headed to England, we went by way of the *Chunnel*. The *Chunnel* is a train that travels in a tunnel under the English Channel. In London, several of the Englishmen who had been on the Texas *Journey of Hope* met us at the *Amnesty International* office. They had arranged both speaking events and press interviews.

Melodee Smith, Bud Welch, SueZann, Lois, Sally Peck,
Ken and Bill in Paris

When it was time to leave England we drove to the White Cliffs of Dover. This time we crossed the English Channel on a *Hovercraft*. (*Hovercraft* is a large boat that moves across water, gliding on an air blanket that it creates) After the crossing, we drove to Switzerland to meet with several groups, including *Amnesty International* and a group called *Lifesparks*. On our last evening in Switzerland, our hosts treated us to the best cheese fondue I had ever eaten. Driving through mountains of Switzerland, I was treated to undoubtedly the most beautiful scenery in the world.

In Belgium, we were able to meet with members of the *Saint Egidio Community*. They lined up a wide variety of opportunities for us to speak in high schools, colleges, and churches. At a dinner, we met a lady from the Netherlands, Marianne Sormani, who urged the *Journey* to come to Holland someday. We said, "Sure."

While in Belgium, we went to the European Parliament and talked with some of its members, asking them to present a resolution to the main body calling on Governor George W. Bush of Texas to take Larry Robison off death row. They were very interested in both the issue of the death penalty and the execution of the mentally ill. They agreed to bring it up to the body of the Parliament.

In Germany, we again met with *Saint Egidio* friends, staying at a university as guests of the school's president. We split into groups to speak in different cities. SueZann took a train back to France where she caught a flight home to return to her job as a hairdresser. Everywhere SueZann spoke in Europe, people just loved her.

After I went to Nuremberg to speak to several high school groups, I rejoined the rest of our group before going to Munich, and then back to Italy. In Rome, we met with members of *Saint Egidio* and *Hands Off Cain.* As Larry's attorney and a close friend of Lois, Melodee worked very hard in organizing the European *Journey* in an effort to save Larry's life.

While in Rome, I called Judy. She informed me that our divorce was now final. How ironic—we had gone to Rome for our honeymoon, and now I was in Rome when our marriage ended.

Back to the good ol' USA; first Philadelphia and then Portage, Indiana. It was a few days before my father's eightieth birthday. When I called him, I told him I would call again on his birthday.

I flew to Florida without him knowing I was coming. As I approached his house, I called on my cell phone to wish him happy birthday. We talked for a few minutes and then I walked up to ring the doorbell. He told me to wait a second; he had to answer the door.

I told him over the phone, "Don't bother; I'll get it." He said, "What?" and then saw me standing at the door. It was a wonderful surprise.

My father still supports the death penalty. On this trip, I went to church with my mom and dad for Wednesday night prayer meeting. My dad requested prayer for his son who would be traveling north the next day. My parents love me and always pray that I will have safe travels. They just don't pray that I will have any success when I get to where I am going. I am satisfied with that.

Chapter 62

Texacutions

The state of Texas started the year 2000 with a number of scheduled executions, including Larry Robison. Larry had undergone mental competency evaluation tests and was deemed competent to be executed. In Texas, you are competent to be executed if you just know two things:

1. You must be aware of the crime you committed. Larry was aware of his crime. It didn't matter to the state of Texas that he heard voices from God telling him to commit the crimes. All that mattered was that Larry understood what he was being punished for. Larry admitted he had killed the five people in a psychotic episode.
2. You must be aware the state is going to kill you as punishment for your crime. Larry knew the state was going to execute him. Larry did tell his family and friends, though, that the state couldn't execute him because they had already killed him.

The state of Texas set January 21 as his new execution date. Larry asked that no more appeals be filed on his behalf. He was ready to die. Once again, I went to Texas to be with Ken and Lois.

Four executions were scheduled within one week. On Thursday, an execution was scheduled for a man who committed his crime under the age of eighteen. On Friday, Larry's execution was scheduled.

I went to the prison on Friday and was able to see Larry. I also met Billy Hughes who was on death row and scheduled to be executed the following Monday. Ken and Lois had gotten to know Billy well over the years when they visited Larry. It was a double dose of pain for Lois to bear. Billy had the reputation of being a clown. He was an artist and drew cartoons. He may even have been innocent. I also met Johnny Penry, a man on death row who had the mind of a child.

Larry had a number of people visiting him. I was surprised they let so many people in to see him at one time. They were going to kill him in a few hours, so I guess they figured it was okay to let everyone in.

The visitor's room on Texas' death row was unlike any I had ever seen before. It was a no-contact situation. There was a room inside a room. The prisoners were ushered through a door into a room that contained only guards and prisoners. Their room was surrounded by metal mesh on three sides. The fourth side was a wall with only a door for the guards and prisoners coming in and out. Visitors sat on the other side of the three metal mesh walls and looked through the little holes in the metal. The men could sit on a chair in front of you. Those that were considered to be problem prisoners were put into small cages in front of their visitor. Those with death dates were also put into the cages.

I got to say hi to Larry but we didn't talk much. I was technically visiting someone else and couldn't stay by Larry's window more than a minute or two. Before long, it was time for everyone to leave. Ken and Lois said their final good-bye to Larry a second time.

Lois was not sure where she wanted to be when the killing time of 6:00 P.M. rolled around. Larry did not want her to witness his execution. At first, she thought she might want to be far away from the death chamber. But as time drew near, she elected to be as close to Larry as she could. She also wanted to be with her friends and others that were gathering outside the *Walls Unit*. We prayed, we sang and then we stood in silence with Lois, who was about to lose her son. When we saw the witnesses to the execution leave the prison, we knew that it was all over.

The official announcement was made a few minutes later.

Lois was in tears, surrounded by friends, when someone began to sing *Amazing Grace*. With tears pouring down Lois's cheeks, she joined in the song. A reporter took a picture of Lois singing. Her tears were clearly visible and she was holding a poster with a life-size picture of Larry's face. That picture was on the front page of the Huntsville paper the next day.

That night, after a memorial service, a group of twenty-five of us went to a Mexican restaurant in Huntsville so that we could all be together. We sat together and talked and gave each other support. Everyone in the restaurant knew we were there because of the execution. Many of us were wearing abolitionist clothes. I was wearing a *Journey* shirt.

As we left the restaurant and slowly headed to our cars, still talking to one another, one of the customers came out of the restaurant and yelled at us, "They should have killed the son of a bitch a long time ago." We all ignored him.

He yelled again, spewing out more unkind remarks. I walked towards him and explained that this mother had just had her son die, and we would appreciate it if he wouldn't say those things. He yelled a few more obscenities and then talked about the Bible saying the death penalty was okay. He talked about "an eye for an eye."

I took several more steps towards him and responded with, "Do you know what Jesus had to say about an eye for an eye?" As I walked closer, it was obvious that he was drunk. He threatened me with calling the police if I took another step. I just shook my head and walked away. We got in our cars and went to our rooms. It was a very sad day. It was a sad day for Lois, a sad day for the state of Texas, and a sad day for humankind.

I stayed over to go to Billy Hughes's execution vigil on Monday night. Ken and Lois were going to be there, too. Lois made it very clear that just because Larry had been killed, she was not going to stop working for abolition of the death penalty. She said that no other moms should have to go through what she had experienced.

For the Billy Hughes's execution, a large pro-death crowd gathered. Billy was convicted of killing a policeman. When I talked to Billy a few days earlier, he said that if his execution took place, he wanted to be cremated. He said after his cremation, he wanted his ashes spread all over the Huntsville post office. I asked him why, and he told me so that whenever anyone in Huntsville would put a stamp on a letter they would lick his ___. Billy kept his sense of humor to the end.

As his six o'clock killing hour drew near, we gathered in a circle in front of the *Walls Unit* and began to have a moment of silence. Suddenly we heard a commotion. There was a band with cheerleaders marching towards us. I then noticed a football scoreboard light up across the street. For the teams, it had two names: George Bush and Jeb Bush. George had a score of something like 120. Jeb Bush had a score of 2.

As the marching band got closer, I could make out the chants. They went something like: "**George, George, he's our man; no one can kill them like Georgie can.**"

It was about who could kill the most, George or Jeb! I felt sick. I had seen the outrageous conduct of some of the *Sam Houston State University* students at Karla Faye Tucker's execution. My first thoughts were that they had moved their act to another level.

The death penalty supporters were cheering the band. A camera was filming what they were saying. People were agreeing on camera that the execution should be celebrated. Finally, the pro-death penalty group realized that these cheering marchers were getting out of hand and began to disavow their tactics. But it was too late. Many of their group had already made outrageous statements that were caught on film.

We learned later that Michael Moore, who does film satire, had hired the band and marchers. He was responsible for producing the well-known popular satire *Roger and Me*. He was filming this for a future program about the death penalty. We also found out that Billy Hughes knew this was going to take place and had given his blessing. What a clown Billy was. He left this world the best way he could, with a marching band and a parade.

Chapter 63

The Dutch Connection

Marijke Jongbloed, a Dutch director, produced a film called ***Beyond Reason***. It included interviews with SueZann and me that had been made by her production company the previous year.

Beyond Reason was about a woman from Holland, Gea Knol, who had befriended a man on death row in Florida. Gea had written the inmate, Bryan Jennings, for a number of years, and helped raise the money so Bryan could hire a lawyer from New Orleans, named Bart Stapert, who was an excellent attorney. Gea wrote a book that told her experiences of writing and visiting Bryan. It sold well in Holland, so Marijke decided to bring Gea to Florida and make a documentary.

The men on Florida's death row were well aware that SueZann had saved James Bernard Campbell's life. Marijke was aware of SueZann's reputation and called her to ask if she would agree to be interviewed for the documentary. After she said yes, SueZann mentioned that I was going to be in Florida at the time of the interview. Marijke and Gea asked SueZann to contact me to see if I would be willing to be interviewed, too. When the Florida interviews were being done, Gea and SueZann really hit it off. Gea was in tears because she was so touched by our stories.

After the film was finished, Marijke wanted us to come to the Netherlands for the premier showing. *Amnesty International* helped finance the trip. Our friend Marianne Sormani, whom we had met in Belgium, helped plan our journey. During the process of planning, Marianne met Gea and they became friends.

Gea had told SueZann and me that she was really interested in *Abolition Movin'*. I had told her that *Abolition Movin'* was parked in Tennessee because we were short of money. She told me that if she could raise money for a lawyer, she felt she could also raise money for a bus. She asked what it would cost to put *Abolition Movin'* back on the road. I told her offhand that I thought it would take about $25,000 to keep it on the road for a year, including repairs, fuel, insurance, license plates and other incidentals. She promised to do what she could.

Well, praise the Lord. Gea and Marianne raised 12,000 Dutch guilders; about $5,500 through an organization that Gea started called the *Ronnie Hoke Foundation*. Hallelujah, *Abolition Movin'* would be moving again.

We spoke from one end of Holland to the other, traveling by rail from Amsterdam to Maastricht. SueZann stayed for one week as we spoke at schools, churches, *Amnesty* groups and several media events. We attended a special showing of ***Beyond Reason,*** which was very well received.

I stayed on an extra week after SueZann left. During the second week, I spoke at a Dutch Reformed church just outside Amsterdam. They said it is rare for that preacher to let anyone else in his pulpit. Since he had a reputation as a very strong social activist, he let me speak. That was my first experience speaking in a Dutch Reformed church. It reminded me of the Dutch Reformed background of my high school, *Illiana Christian High* in Lansing, Illinois.

I went with Marianne to a prison where she was involved in a weekly ministry. There I spoke to six women, who were part of the ministry program and a group of twenty male prisoners. Afterward, all of the men came up, shook my hand, and thanked me for coming and for doing the work I do.

When it was time for me to leave Holland, Marianne came to my hotel to pick me up to go to the airport. It was a good thing. As we were getting into the cab, I pulled a muscle in my back and was not able to move for a few minutes. Marianne helped me the rest of the way, not only by carrying my bags, but also letting me use her arm to walk. I felt really foolish, but I am so thankful she was there.

My flight took me back to Florida, so I spent the day with SueZann. Then I rented a car and drove to see my parents again. Once more, they prayed for safe traveling mercies for me.

The ninth biennial *International Conference on Penal Abolition* (*ICOPA*) was being held in Canada. Ten years earlier, I had spoken at the fourth *ICOPA* conference, when it was held in Indiana in 1990. At that time, I met a wonderful lady named Ruth Morris, and had stayed in contact with her through the years. She was very familiar with the work Marietta and I were doing in the area of forgiveness. She invited me to the Canadian *ICOPA* event.

For my talk on Saturday, at the last plenary session, I was asked to speak on forgiveness. It just so happened that Saturday was May 13, one day before the anniversary of Nana's death. Sunday, it would be fifteen years to the day since she died. It also meant I had retired exactly three years ago.

I was inspired for that speech both by the anniversary date and by Ruth Morris. Canadian Scholars Press had just published her new book, *Stories of Transformative Justice*. In it, she had included the stories of Marietta, SueZann, and me.

It was this Canadian conference that gave me the word that best expressed what had happened to me in the steel mill crane on November 2, 1986. Previously, people had called the experience a *conversion*; people had called it an *epiphany*; I had called it a *mountaintop experience;* I had said that it felt like I had been *born again*. But I realized at this conference fifteen years later that I had been *transformed*.

After the conference, I received a beautiful letter from Ruth. She told me that she knew Nana would be very proud of what I was doing. Reading her words brought tears to my eyes.

A short time later, I got another letter from Ruth. She had a kidney removed several years earlier and she had just found out that a cancerous tumor had grown in its place. In the letter, Ruth said it was inoperable. Ruth then went on to talk about God's grace. I have never met a person with more dignity. God bless Ruth Morris.

Chapter 64

Getting *Abolition Movin'* Movin'

After the seventh annual fast and vigil at the U.S. Supreme Court, the next project was to get *Abolition Movin'* on the road in time for *Journey of Hope* events planned for Pennsylvania in August. We found a place in Lafayette, Tennessee, just outside of Nashville to get *Abolition Movin'* worked on. Most people don't like to work on old buses, but this mechanic, John Allen, would rather work on old ones than new ones. He was very familiar with 1965 GMC coaches.

A few days and a few thousand dollars later, *Abolition Movin'* was back on the road again, almost as good as new. John had done some work on the throttle and we now had more power than ever. George and I headed her towards Pennsylvania with ease. After a stop at the *Bruderhof Community* in Farmington, we drove on to Philadelphia. Led by Jeff Garis, the *Pennsylvania Abolitionists United Against the Death Penalty (PAUADP)* sponsored the *Journey,* our first ever in Pennsylvania.

A year earlier, when I had been at the *Bruderhof New Meadow Run Community* in Farmington, the children talked about wanting to do another death penalty event. They were looking for a big-name participant. I suggested Sister Helen. They were excited about the prospects of Sister Helen. I told them that to get Sister Helen, it would probably take a year's notice. They decided to do a gigantic event in 2000 when Sister Helen could come. We agreed that the

Journey of Hope . . . from Violence to Healing would be tied into the children's event. The *Bruderhof* would help the *Journey* and *PAUADP* with seven days of Journeying throughout the state to precede the *Children's Crusade* 2000. We would tell everyone about the big plans the children had and invite them to join Sister Helen and the *Journey* in Farmington to begin the *Children's Crusade*.

The *Journey* started off in Philadelphia on August 3. It was a hassle driving *Abolition Movin'* around downtown and finding a place to park. We ended up finding a spot right across the street from the *Liberty Bell* where we were holding our opening rally.

The Pennsylvania *Journey* included some of the usual participants: George, SueZann, Ken and Lois, Sally Peck, Abe Bonowitz, Kathy Harris, and Phyllis Pautrat. Others joined us, mostly from Pennsylvania. The *Bruderhof* sent some people. Magda Finnegan of Ireland joined us once again, as well as first timer Andrew Eager, from *Amnesty International* in Ireland.

Abolition Movin' ran like new as we traveled throughout Pennsylvania with stops in Bethlehem, Allentown, Scranton, Wilkes-Barre, Harrisburg, Erie and Pittsburgh.

Cuzzin' Judi and her friend Kathy McBrayer joined us in Pittsburgh. After two days of activities there, we headed for the *Bruderhof Community* in Farmington. It was 1:00 A.M. when we arrived, but our hosts greeted us in their great welcoming custom and led us to our designated homes for sleeping.

At the *New Meadow Run Community* we were joined by hundreds of children from around the world who came to be part of the *Children's' Crusade 2000* with Sister Helen. Rubin 'Hurricane' Carter and Pete Seeger joined with Sister Helen and the *Children's Crusade* on Saturday. The weekend was a great time of celebrating life and concluded with a march to *SCI Greene*, Pennsylvania's largest death row.

We left *Abolition Movin'* at the *Bruderhof Community* for safe keeping until our next event. In October, my friend Wayne Crawley and I drove to Pennsylvania to pick it up. We brought it back to Indiana and parked it at Tom and Sara Kramer's house because we wanted to get it in the area for the *National March to End Federal Executions*, scheduled for November.

The night before the Indiana march was to begin, I was in Anchorage, Alaska. I had moved to Anchorage eight months earlier and set up the *Journey of Hope . . . from Violence to Healing* office in the spacious home of Kathy Harris. Kathy and I met on the Texas *Journey* and when I moved to Alaska, we became partners. I spend a lot of time on the road traveling and speaking, but when I am home in Alaska I am able to enjoy our time together.

Bill and Kathy met on the Texas *Journey*

It wasn't long before I was elected to be the vice president of *Alaskans Against the Death Penalty. AADP* was having their annual awards banquet and Governor Tony Knowles was going to attend and accept the award for political leadership. We wanted to honor him for his position on the issue. I wanted to be there for that.

When the night of the banquet arrived, I dressed in my *Alaskan's Against the Death Penalty* shirt that says, ***FRY FISH—NOT PEOPLE***. I wanted to get a picture with Governor Knowles while wearing that shirt. Tony Knowles put his hand on my back and the words, "***FRY FISH—NOT PEOPLE*** came out very clear. I thought it was a great photo for the *AADP* web site.

Bill with Alaska Governor Tony Knowles

I left the banquet early to catch a red-eye flight. I arrived about ten minutes before the opening rally began in Indianapolis. *Abolition Movin'* was already in place because George and Abe had picked it up from the Kramer's the night before, and parked it at a sponsoring church close to the rally.

Abolition Movin' was the perfect vehicle for this march. We had a core group of twenty people and *Abolition Movin'* was able to carry supplies and walkers who needed a rest, as well as serve as a place for journalists to conduct interviews during the march from Indianapolis to Terre Haute.

National March to Stop Executions
November 10-14, 2000

We spoke in churches, schools, rallies, media events and colleges. In Terre Haute, we were joined by a large number of local residents for the three-mile march from downtown Terre Haute to the prison.

After a successful rally at the prison, *Abolition Movin'* began to transport walkers back to the starting point to get their vehicles. We had a potluck dinner at a church that evening and we were finished, except for a radio show that George and I were to do the next morning.

After the radio show, Abe, George and I took *Abolition Movin'* and headed for Bill Breeden's home near Bloomington, Indiana. We planned on leaving the bus there until the Missouri *Journey of Hope* in March 2001. The plan was to drop off *Abolition Movin'* at Bill's and then the three of us would catch a plane to San Francisco to participate in the ***Committing to Conscience Conference.***

Only fifteen miles from Bill Breeden's home, the clutch on *Abolition Movin'* gave out. We were on a two-lane state highway on an inclining curve. We could not pull off on the side of the road. We had to direct traffic as we waited for a tow truck to come pick her up. Time was running short for us, so Bill's neighbor took George, Abe and me to the Indianapolis airport just as *Abolition Movin'* was being hooked up to the tow truck.

Chapter 65

Committing to Conscience 2000

It was billed as the largest anti-death penalty conference ever: ***Committing to Conscience** . . . Building a unified strategy to end the death penalty.* The conference was scheduled November 16 through 19, 2000, at the Cathedral Hill Hotel in San Francisco.

The conference had been in the works for over a year. The object was for all major abolition organizations to come together for the first time ever and combine their yearly conferences into one gigantic event. The theme was "2000 in 2000." We felt that if we could draw a large number of people, it would get the attention of the media. We wanted to have the conference *after* the 2000 presidential elections because the media would not be so tied up with politics anymore. As it turned out the election was still in doubt when the conference began.

Each abolitionist organization was to talk with their respective boards and decide what responsibilities they would take on. The two major sponsors of the conference were the *National Coalition to Abolish the Death Penalty* and the *Death Penalty Focus of California*. Joining these conference sponsors were seven participating organizations, including the *American Civil Liberties Union, Amnesty International, Murder Victims' Families for Reconciliation, American Friends Service Committee,* the *Religious Organizing Project, Citizens United for Alternatives to the Death Penalty,* and *Journey of Hope . . . from Violence to Healing.* I knew the conference would be the greatest one in the history of the movement.

When we got to the hotel, about twenty-five different organizations had already set up tables in the lobby. The wealth of information included books, brochures, case studies, t-shirts and a variety of paraphernalia dealing with abolition of the death penalty.

Journey of Hope . . . from Violence to Healing had a table next to *Alaskans Against the Death Penalty* so we were able to work together and cover the tables as the conference progressed. Board members Joan Betz, Abe Bonowitz, George White, Marietta Jaeger-Lane, Sunny Jacobs, SueZann Bosler and I represented the *Journey*. Stephanie Gibson was the only board member who could not make it. Our two other officers, Phyllis Pautrat and Kathy Harris, were also there. It gave us plenty of people to help.

One of the key themes of the conference was the issue of innocence. George White and Sunny Jacobs joined William Nieves and Gary Gauger in telling how they had been convicted of murders they did not commit. William had been released from Pennsylvania's death row one week before the conference. Larry Marshall, the professor from *Northwestern University* in Chicago, who had hosted the *Innocence Conference* in Chicago in 1998, was moderator. At the time of the San Francisco conference, over ninety people whom had been sentenced to death since the resumption of the death penalty in 1976 had subsequently been proven innocent.

Fortunately, most people in this country do not want to see an innocent person executed. We do make mistakes and came very close to killing many of the now over one hundred people proven innocent and set free. Many people have concerns about the application of the death penalty.

Murder victims' family members were out in force for the conference. I have never seen more *MVFR* people together for one event. I knew many of them from past journeys, but many new *MVFR* members came. Renny Cushing has done a fantastic job as director moving *MVFR* in the right direction.

The conference included a variety of workshops, including fundraising, organizing, developing strategy, working with death row families, and working with murder victim's families.

Mario Marrazitti, from the *Saint Egidio Community* in Italy, gave a plenary presentation about collecting over two and a half million signatures for their moratorium campaign. Mario showed a video highlighting their work. It included my saying, "The answer is love and compassion for all of humanity."

Over one thousand people registered for the San Francisco conference, making it by far the largest gathering of abolitionists ever. The Saturday night awards banquet was the climax, with Mike Farrell as emcee.

The most dramatic part of the evening was Gov. George Ryan of Illinois being presented a special political achievement award. Governor Ryan had surprised and delighted the abolitionist community when he declared a moratorium of the death penalty in Illinois. Gov. Ryan, a conservative Republican who had been a strong supporter of the death penalty, began to realize that the machinery of the death penalty was not working. Illinois had released from death row thirteen people that were found to be innocent. Gov. Ryan stated that no innocent people were going to be executed on his watch and declared a moratorium on executions. He commissioned a panel to study the death penalty issue. He said until they could guarantee that no innocent life would be taken, no executions would take place in Illinois.

Governor Ryan's decision had ripple effects all around the country. Because a conservative Republican made this statement, others began to look at their system. Some people like Governor George W. Bush said that the system in Texas was not broken like Illinois, and that the 150 killed in Texas under his watch were all guilty. But other states did begin looking closely at their systems and the media began digging into other possible cases of innocence.

Many of us didn't think Gov. Ryan would come to the conference, but people like Abe Bonowitz insisted that we invite him and lo and behold, he came. What a great thing!

Bill with Mike Farrell and
Illinois Governor George Ryan

Wisconsin Senator Russ Feingold gave the keynote address. He told us he had presented a bill to the U.S. Senate to abolish the death penalty in the United States. It is people like Russ Feingold that give me confidence in our country's political future.

Pat Bane was awarded a Lifetime Achievement award for her work on behalf of *MVFR* and Hugo Bedau was recognized for his work in writing books and serving the *NCADP* for many years.

Ken and Lois Robison were a unanimous choice for the *Abolitionist of the Year* award. It was my honor a month earlier to call Ken and Lois to give them the good news. Before their award was presented at the banquet, there was a special surprise for Ken and Lois. Micki Dickoff had prepared a short film with scenes from our Texas *Journey* and from Larry's two execution dates in Huntsville. Tears flowed as Lois accepted the award and talked about how even though Larry had been killed, she would continue to work to see that this sort of tragedy didn't happen to more mothers.

Bill with three former *Abolitionists of the Year* award winners, Sister Helen, Marietta and Father Pat Delahanty

Everyone left the San Francisco conference feeling positive about the abolition movement. We were finally seeing progress.

Chapter 66

The *Journey* Continues, *Abolition Movin'* Stays Behind

In the spring of 2001, the *Journey* was involved with a moratorium tour sponsored by *Floridians for Alternatives to the Death Penalty*. Abe Bonowitz lined up the events. George White, Bud Welch, SueZann Bosler, Marisa Gwaltney and others joined *Abolition Movin'* as we traveled around the state on a speaking tour.

From Florida we took *Abolition Movin'* to Tennessee for an *Amnesty International* Conference. From Nashville, *Abolition Movin'* went to a ten-day *Journey* in Missouri, where we once again joined with Sister Helen. Then it was home to Indiana for some tender lovin' care. Wayne Crawley, recently retired from Bethlehem Steel, spent his free time putting in carpet, curtains and other niceties in preparation for *Abolition Movin's* East Coast tour.

MVFR had their first ever conference in Boston. *MVFR* members from around the country came. It was a fantastic event.

However, we witnessed some setbacks in the movement when we took *Abolition Movin'* to the vigils in Terre Haute, Indiana for the federal executions of Timothy McVeigh and then a short time later for Juan Garza. It was sad to see the federal government resume executions after a thirty-eight year moratorium.

September 11 postponed some of our *Journey* plans. Five days of events in New Jersey were cancelled because many of the churches we were to speak at in Northern New Jersey were conducting funerals and memorial services for those killed in the World Trade Center disaster. It is my hope that tragedies like that horrendous event will only give us more respect for life. It was sad to hear those who immediately called for retaliation.

George and I took *Abolition Movin'* to Delaware and spoke at some schools and churches with Anne Coleman and Barbara Lewis. We drove to New Jersey and met up with Lorry Post. Lorry's daughter had been killed years earlier and he was now organizing our speaking events in New Jersey. We spoke in central and southern New Jersey before taking *Abolition Movin'* to our main event in North Carolina.

Steve Dear and *People of Faith Against the Death Penalty* organized two weeks of action in North Carolina in early October. *Abolition Movin'* performed well as we went from the mountains of Ashville to the shores of the Outer Banks with our crew. On our last leg to Raleigh, the transmission case cracked and we had to haul *Abolition Movin'* off to the repair shop. She had done well but couldn't finish the last fifty miles.

Abolition Movin' no longer moving on her own

In May of 2002, I had the opportunity to do an eight-city tour in Northern Italy with the *Saint Egidio Community*. The organizers had well attended events wherever I spoke. It is easy to encourage the people there to sign petitions for a moratorium on the death penalty. I tell them they can make a difference. I remind them how the people from Italy saved Paula Cooper's life by signing petitions.

Bill speaking in Northern Italy for the
St. Egidio Community

The trip concluded with an opportunity for me to go to Rome on May 13-14 and represent the *Journey of Hope . . . from Violence to Healing* as a member of the steering committee for the founding of the *World Coalition Against the Death Penalty*. The death penalty needs to be abolished around the world and it will take all of us working together. Members from many countries and organizations including *Amnesty* and the *NCADP* were represented there.

Abolition Movin' isn't moving anymore. It has sat idle since the North Carolina *Journey* in need of some repairs. But, 2002 brought some advancement in the movement. *MVFR* and the *Journey* are working more closely together to get the message out that not all victims want the death penalty. October's *NCADP* conference in Chicago helped unite us even more.

Bill representing the *Journey of Hope . . .from Violence to Healing* at the formation of the *World Coalition to Abolish the Death Penalty in Rome*

Bill and Renny Cushing, Executive Director of *MVFR* carry their banner in Chicago for the *NCADP* Conference march

The Journey of Hope . . . from Violence to Healing was honored in Nashville, Tennessee, at the closing performance of ***Karla***, a play written by Steve Earle in March 2003. Sara Sharpe played the leading role in ***Karla*** and it was one fantastic performance. It is my hope this play will be performed around the country. Sara and Steve are another couple who met on the Texas *Journey* and they have been partners for the last several years.

Sara Sharpe, Steve Earle and the *Journey* Boys, Abe, George, Bill and Ken McGill on the closing night in Nashville of ***Karla***

There is hope. I just hope the abolition of the death penalty comes in my lifetime so I can witness it and celebrate. When Governor George Ryan cleared out death row in Illinois, it was a great occasion. How much greater will the celebration be when the death penalty is abolished and death rows around this nation and around the world are emptied?

Most people want the death penalty simply because of the desire for revenge. Revenge is never ever the answer. The answer is love and compassion for all of humanity. I firmly believe that if we have the kind of love and compassion our creator wants us to have for fellow human beings, it is impossible to want to see anyone put into the death chamber.

An eye for an eye makes the world blind.

The Three Amigos, Bill Pelke, Rick Halperin and Magdaleno Rose-Avila, wearing Abe Bonowitz's *Abolition Wear* t-shirt "An eye for an eye makes the world blind"

It is my hope that we all keep the spirit of *Abolition Movin'*, moving. I hope that we can be a nation where the worst possible punishment is life without the possibility of parole. Let's stop the killing. Let's celebrate life.

I hope each of us will aspire to be like SueZann Bosler and say, "Let there be peace on earth . . . and let it begin with **us**."

END

Afterword

May 14, 1985 was the start of a long journey for me. It has been a journey from violence to healing. November 2, 1986, I made God two promises. The first was that any success that came into my life as a result of forgiving Paula Cooper, I would give God the honor and glory. I knew then that the only reason I learned about the healing power of forgiveness was because of God's love touching my heart. The second promise was that I would go through any door that opened as a result of forgiving Paula. To this day I have kept those two promises.

I did not expect the open doors to be in the arena of death penalty abolition, but those were the doors opened most often. As a result, the movement to abolish the death penalty became the primary stage for what has become my ministry.

Paula Cooper and I have exchanged hundreds of letters over the years. It is important to note that Paula Cooper is not the same person today that committed that terrible crime in 1985. She is a different person. If they were to execute her today they would be killing a different person.

Not only has Paula earned her GED, but also in the spring of 2002 she received a degree from *Martin University* in Indianapolis by successfully completing college correspondence courses. Her goal is to help other young people who have been raised in abusive situations by pointing them to positive responses rather than the violence she chose at the age of fifteen.

Today, Paula has been in prison for eighteen years, over half of her life. She is working for a company outside of the prison and after initially beginning for minimum wage; she now earns $7.50 an hour. She is allowed to keep 10 percent or $.75 an hour. The rest of her earnings are dispersed in several ways. Some of the money goes to a victims restitution fund, some to a prison fund that helps to pay for her board and room (prison upkeep) and some of the money goes to paying taxes like you and me.

Paula has gone for many years without any disciplinary write-ups. She prays that God will continue to work in her life and make her a better person. That prayer is being answered.

The *Journey of Hope . . . From Violence to Healing* has made an impact in the abolition movement and we continue to make a difference.

The next major event of the *Journey* will be in Ohio, September 26—Oct 12, 2003. It is sponsored by *OTSE* (*Ohioans To Stop Executions*). Jana Schroeder is the lead organizer. A blind lady will be leading the *Journey* through Ohio and I know we will make a difference there.

The *Journey* board elected not to spend any more resources on *Abolition Movin'*. It is parked in a bus retirement home in North Carolina. The board has voted to begin a campaign to raise funds for a better bus, *Abolition Movin' II*. We are looking for a bus like Steve Earle tours in, only ten to fifteen years older.

It is our goal to have a group of six to twelve people on tour going from state to state with the message of moving from violence to healing. We need help to accomplish this, so if you or anyone you know can help, please contact us.

The Journey needs funds to help get people from their homes to speaking events, and to hire a full time office manager to take care of fundraising, communications and logistics for the speakers.

We need opportunities to bring our message to the public. State and local organizations working together can bring the *Journey* wherever it is needed. We will continue to make a difference.

Recently, I was asked by the *National Coalition to Abolish the Death Penalty* to travel to Delaware and speak at a press conference at the state capitol where they are planning to introduce legislation to raise the minimum execution age to eighteen. This year the *NCADP, MVFR, Amnesty International USA* and other organizations are putting their emphasis on eliminating juvenile executions in the U.S.

When the majority of states turn away from what has been law for many years, the U.S. Supreme Court considers that a change in the evolving standard of decency. It is my hope that someday soon the Supreme Court will outlaw the execution of juveniles based on this evolving standard of decency. Currently twenty-two of the fifty states allow the execution of those who commit capital crimes under the age of eighteen.

If Delaware rejects the death penalty for juveniles and several other states follow suit, juvenile executions in this country should come to an end.

At the press conference several people who work with juveniles spoke. I was the last speaker. I talked about Nana's death, and about Paula Cooper. I emphasized that she is a changed person. I concluded my talk by saying, "A lot of people want revenge, but that is never, ever the answer. The answer is love and compassion for all of humanity."

As I took my seat there was a standing ovation. As the meeting was brought to a close, a lady in the audience raised her hand to say something. The convener asked her to step to the podium. The lady, who was State Representative Pam Meier, R-Newark came to the microphone. She was obviously overwhelmed with what she had just heard. It took almost a minute to gain her composure. Weeping she said, "I initially had reservations about supporting the bill. I guess the love and compassion the speaker talked about overcame my objections.

She said, "I had to let you all know that I am now convinced that this is the right legislation, the right time and I hope I can convince my colleagues to pass it."

On this *Journey* we are helping the country move towards the abolition of the death penalty, while encouraging Americans to become a more compassionate and forgiving people.

Will you help us ***JOURNEY ON***?

APPENDIX A

ABOLITIONIST OF THE YEAR

1987 HENRY SCWARTZCHILD
1988 SCHARLETTE HOLDMAN
1989 HUGO BEDAU
1990 MARIE DEANS & JOE INGLE
1991 SOUTHERN CENTER FOR HUMAN RIGHTS
1992 SISTER HELEN PREJEAN
1993 MILLARD FARMER
1994 MAGDALENO ROSE-AVILA
1995 DIANA RUST-TIERNEY
1996 BIANCA JAGGER
1997 MARIETTA JAEGER-LANE
1998 FATHER PAT DELAHANTY
1999 BUD WELCH
2000 KEN & LOIS ROBISON
2001 AJAMU BARAKA
2002 JANE HENDERSON
2003 SALIMA SILER MARRIOT

Appendix B

National Organizations Working to Abolish the Death Penalty

Abolitionist Action Committee

PMB 298 177 U.S. Hwy #1 Tequesta, FL 33469 (800) 973-6548
http://www.abolition.org

ACLU Capital Punishment Project

1333 H. Street, NW Washington, D.C. 20005
http://www.aclu.org/DeathPenalty/DeathPenaltyMain.cfm

Amnesty International USA Program to Abolish the Death Penalty

600 Pennsylvania, Ave, SE Washington, D.C. 20003 (202) 544-0200
http://web.amnesty.org/pages/deathpenalty_index_eng

Catholic Worker House

36 East 1st Street New York, New York 10003 (212) 254-1640

Campaign to End the Death Penalty

P.O. Box 25730 Chicago, IL 60625 (773) 955-4842
http://www.nodeathpenalty.org

Clergy Coalition to End Executions

Suite 450 1320 So Dixie Hwy. Miami, FL 33146 (850) 445-8575
http://www.ClergyCoaltion.org

Citizens United for Alternatives to the Death Penalty

PMB 298 177 U.S. Hwy #1 Tequesta, FL 33469 (800) 973-6548
http://www.cuadp.org

Citizens United for the Rehabilitation of Errants

P.O. Box 2310 Washington, DC 20013 (202)789-2126
cure@curenational.org

Death Penalty Information Center

1320 Eighteenth Street, NW 5th Floor Washington, D.C. 20036 (202) 293-6970
http://www.deathpenaltyinfo.org

Death Row Support Project

P.O. Box 600 Liberty Mills, IN 46946 (219) 982-7480
rgross@hoosierlink.net

Engaged Zen Foundation

P.O. Box 700 Ramsey, NJ (201) 236-0335
http://www.engaged-zen.org

Equal Justice USA/ Quixote Center

P.O. Box 5206 Hyattsville, MD 0782 (301) 699-0042
http://www.quixote.org/ej

Fellowship of Reconciliation

P.O. Box 27 Nyack, NY 10960 (845) 358-4601
http://www.forusa.org

Friends Committee on National Legislation

245 Second Street, NE, Washington D.C. 20002-5795 (202) 547-6000
http://www.fcnl.org/issues/cri/deaindx.htm

Journey of Hope . . . From Violence to Healing

P.O. Box 210390 Anchorage, AK 99521-0390 (877) 924-4483
http://www.JourneyofHope.org

The Lamp of Hope Project

P.O. Box 305 League City, Texas 77574-0305
http://www.lampofhope.org

Murder Victims Families for Reconciliation

2161 Massachusetts Avenue Cambridge, MA 02140 (617) 868-0007
http://www.mvfr.org

National Coalition to Abolish the Death Penalty

920 Pennsylvania Ave., SE Washington, DC 20003 (202) 543-9577
http://www.ncadp.org

Mennonite Central Committee

110 Maryland Ave NE #502 Washington, DC 20002-5626 (202) 544-6564
http://www.mcc.org

The Moratorium Campaign

P.O. Box 13727 New Orleans, LA 70185-3727 (504) 864-1071
http://www.moratoriumCampaign.org

Pax Christi USA

532 W. 8th Street Erie, PA 16502 (814) 453-4955
http://www.paxchristiusa.org

People of Faith Against the Death Penalty

110 W. Main St., Suite 2-G Carrboro, NC 27510 (919) 933 7567
http://www.pfadp.org

Religious Organizing Against the Death Penalty Project

1501 Cherry Street Philadelphia, PA 19102 (215) 241-7130
http://www.deathpenaltyreligious.org

Restorative Justice Center

Suite 450 1320 So Dixie Hwy. Miami, FL 33146 (850) 445-8575
http://www.RestorativeJusticeCenter.org

Restorative Justice Ministries UMC

1008 19th Avenue South Nashville, TN 37212 (615) 329-2279
hwray@gbgm-umc.org

Rising Son Ministries, Inc

P.O. Box 50770 Henderson, NV 89106-0770 (702) 454-6430

Southern Christian Leadership Conference

334 Auburn Avenue NE Atlanta GA 30303 (404) 522-1420
http://sclcnational.org

Unitarian Universalists for Alternatives to the Death Penalty

Box 233 Chester, VA 23831-8445 (804) 748-3265
tim@uuadp.org

United States Catholic Conference

3211 4th Street, NE Washington DC 20017 (202) 541-3190
dmisleh@nccbuscc.org

Appendix C

Statements of Opposition to Capital Punishment from Faith Groups

American Baptist Churches in the USA
P.O. Box 851 Valley Forge, PA 19482 (610) 768-2000
http://www.deathpenaltyreligious.org/education/statements/baptist.html

American Ethical Union
2 West 64th Street New York, NY 10023 (212) 873-6500
http://www.deathpenaltyreligious.org/education/statements/ethicalunion.html

American Friends Service Committee
1501 Cherry Street Philadelphia, PA 19102 (215) 241-7130
http://www.deathpenaltyreligious.org/education/statements/afsc.html

The American Jewish Committee
165 E. 56th Street New York, NY 10022 (212) 879-4500
http://www.deathpenaltyreligious.org/education/statements/ajc.html

Amnesty International
322 8th Avenue New York, NY 10001 (212) 807-8400
http://www.deathpenaltyreligious.org/education/statements/aiusa.html

Woodcrest Bruderhof
Route 213 Rifton, NY 12471 (914) 658-8351
http://www.deathpenaltyreligious.org/education/statements/bruderhof.html

Central Conference of American Rabbis
355 Lexington Avenue New York, NY 10017 (212) 972-3636
http://www.deathpenaltyreligious.org/education/statements/ccar.html

Christian Church (Disciples of Christ)
130 E. Washington Street Indianapolis, IN 46206 (317) 635-3100
http://www.deathpenaltyreligious.org/education/statements/disciples.html

Church of the Brethren
1451 Dundee Avenue Elgin, IL 60120 (847) 742-5100
http://www.deathpenaltyreligious.org/education/statements/brethren.html

Church Women United
475 Riverside Drive, Suite 500 New York, NY 10115 (212) 870-2347
http://www.deathpenaltyreligious.org/education/statements/cwu.html

The Episcopal Church
815 Second Avenue New York, NY 10017-4594 (212) 867-8400
http://www.deathpenaltyreligious.org/education/statements/episcopal.html

Evangelical Lutheran Church in America

8765 West Higgins Road Chicago, IL 60631 (773) 380-2710

http://www.deathpenaltyreligious.org/education/statements/elca.html

Fellowship of Reconciliation

Box 271 Nyack, NY 10960 (914) 358-4601

http://www.deathpenaltyreligious.org/education/statements/for.html

Friends Committee on National Legislation

245 Second Street, NE Washington, D.C. 20002-5795 (202) 547-6000

http://www.deathpenaltyreligious.org/education/statements/fcnl.html

Friends United Meeting

101 Quaker Hill Drive Richmond, IN 47374 (765) 962-7573

http://www.deathpenaltyreligious.org/education/statements/fum.html

The General Association of General Baptists

100 Stinson Drive Poplar Bluff, MO 63901 (573) 785-7746

http://www.deathpenaltyreligious.org/education/statements/generalbaptist.html

General Conference Mennonite Church

722 Main Street Box 347 Newton, KS 67114-0347 (316) 283-5100

http://www.deathpenaltyreligious.org/education/statements/mennonite.html

The Mennonite Church

421 S. Second Street, Suite 600 Elkhart, IN 46516 (219) 294-7131

http://www.deathpenaltyreligious.org/education/statements/mennonitechurch.html

The Moravian Church In America Northern Province
1021 Center Street P.O. Box 1245 Bethlehem, PA 18016-1245 (610) 867-7566
http://www.deathpenaltyreligious.org/education/statements/moravian.html

National Board YWCA of the U.S.A.
726 Broadway New York, NY 10003 (212) 614-2700
http://www.deathpenaltyreligious.org/education/statements/ywca.html

National Council of Churches of Christ in the U.S.A.
475 Riverside Drive New York, NY 10115 (212) 870-2511
http://www.deathpenaltyreligious.org/education/statements/churchesofchrist.html

Orthodox Church in America
P.O. Box 675 Syosset, NY 11791 (516) 922-0550
http://www.deathpenaltyreligious.org/education/statements/orthodox.html

Presbyterian Church (U.S.A.)
100 Witherspoon Street Louisville, KY 40202 (502) 569-5803
http://www.deathpenaltyreligious.org/education/statements/presbyterian.html

The Rabbinical Assembly
3080 Broadway New York, NY 10027 (212) 280-6000
http://www.deathpenaltyreligious.org/education/statements/rabbinicalassembly.html

Reformed Church in America
475 Riverside Drive, 18th Floor New York, NY 10115 (212) 870-2841
http://www.deathpenaltyreligious.org/education/statements/reformed.html

Reformed Church of Jesus Christ of Latter Day Saints: World Headquarters
P.O. Box 1059 Independence, MO 64051 (816) 833-1000
http://www.deathpenaltyreligious.org/education/statements/latterdaysaints.html

Union of American Hebrew Congregations Commission on Social Action
633 3rd Ave., 7th floor New York, NY 10017 (212) 650-4160
http://www.deathpenaltyreligious.org/education/statements/hebrewcongregations.html

Unitarian Universalist Association
25 Beacon Street Boston, MA 02108 (617) 367-3237
http://www.deathpenaltyreligious.org/education/statements/uua.html

United Church of Christ
700 Prospect Avenue Cleveland, OH 44115 (216) 736-2100
http://www.deathpenaltyreligious.org/education/statements/ucc.html

The United Methodist Church General Board of Church and Society
100 Maryland Ave, NE Washington, DC 20002 (202) 488-5600
http://www.deathpenaltyreligious.org/education/statements/umc.html

United States Catholic Conference Committee on Social Development & World Peace
3211 4th Street NE Washington, DC 20017 (202) 541-3000
http://www.deathpenaltyreligious.org/education/statements/catholicconference.html

Appendix D

International Abolition Organizations

Hands Off Cain

http://www.handsoffcain.org

St. Egidio Community

http://www.santegidio.org/en/pdm/index.htm

World Coalition to Abolish the Death Penalty

http://www.worldcoalition.org

Amnesty International

http://www.amnesty.org

The Council of Europe

http://www.abolition-ecpm.org/en/ap1.htm

Appendix E

Executions of Juvenile Offenders January 1, 1973 Through May 1, 2003

NAME	DATE OF *EXECUTION*	ST	RACE-SEX-OFFENDER *RACE-SEX-VICTIM*	*TIME OF EX*	AGE AT
Charles Rumbaugh	**09-11-1986**	TX	WM/WM	17	28
J. Terry Roach	01-10-1986	SC	WM/WM,WF	17	25
Jay Pinkerton	05-15-1986	TX	WM/WF,WF	17	24
Dalton Prejean	05-18-1990	LA	BM/WM	17	30
Johnny Garrett	02-11-1992	TX	WM/WF	17	28
Curtis Harris	07-01-1993	TX	BM/WM	17	31
Frederick Lashley	07-28-1993	MO	BM/BF	17	29
Ruben Cantu	08-24-1993	TX	LM/LM	17	26
Chris Burger	12-07-1993	GA	WM/WM	17	38
Joseph John Cannon	04-22-1998	TX	WM/WF	17	38
Robert A. Carter	**05-18-1998**	TX	BM/LF	17	34
Dwight A. Wright	10-14-1998	VA	BM/BF	17	26
Sean R. Sellers	02-04-1999	OK	WM/WM,WM,WF	**16**	29
Christopher Thomas	01-10-2000	VA	WM/WF	17	26
Steve Roach	01-19-2000	VA	WM/WF	17	23
Glen C. McGinnis	01-25-2000	TX	BM/WF	17	27
Gary L. Graham	06-22-2000	TX	BM/WM	17	36
Gerald L Mitchell	10-22-2001	TX	BM/WM	17	33
Napoleon Beazley	05-28-2002	TX	BM/WM	17	25
T.J. Jones	08-28-2002	TX	BM/WM	17	25
Toronto Patterson	08-28-2002	TX	BM/BF	17	24
Scott A. Hain	04-03-2002	OK	WM/WM,WF	17	32

All but one of these executed juvenile offenders were age 17 at the time of their crimes, with only Sean Sellers (Oklahoma) being age 16.

Source: http://www.law.onu.edu/faculty/streib/juvdeath.htm

Appendix F

Minimum Death Penalty Ages by Jurisdiction as of May 1, 2003

Age eighteen	*Age Seventeen*	*Age Sixteen*
California*	Florida***	Alabama*
Colorado*	Georgia*	Arizona**
Connecticut*	New Hampshire*	Arkansas**
Illinois*	North Carolina*	Delaware**
Indiana*	Texas*	Idaho**
Kansas*		Kentucky*
Maryland*		Louisiana**
Montana*		Mississippi**
Nebraska*		Missouri*
New Jersey*		Nevada*
New Mexico*		Oklahoma**
New York*		Pennsylvania**
Ohio*		South Carolina**
Oregon*		South Dakota**
Tennessee*		Utah**
Washington*		Virginia*
Federal Civilian*		Wyoming*
Federal Military		
16 States and 2 Federal jurisdictions	5 States	17 States

* Express minimum age in statute

** Minimum age required by U.S. Constitution per U.S. Supreme Court in *Thompson v. Oklahoma*, 487 U.S. 815 (1988).

*** Minimum age required by Florida Constitution per Florida Supreme Court in *Brennan v. State*, 754 So.2d 1 (Fla. 1999).

Source: http://www.law.onu.edu/faculty/streib/juvdeath.htm

Appendix G

Execution Statistics Summary

State and Year (as of 06/05/03)

Executions by State

Texas	304
Virginia	88
Oklahoma	64
Missouri	60
Florida	56
Georgia	33
South Carolina	28
Louisiana	27
Alabama	27
Arkansas	24
North Carolina	23
Arizona	22
Delaware	13
Illinois	12
California	10
Indiana	10
Nevada	9
Ohio	7
Mississippi	6
Utah	6

Washington	4
Maryland	3
Nebraska	3
Pennsylvania	3
USA	3
Kentucky	2
Montana	2
Oregon	2
Colorado	1
Idaho	1
New Mexico	1
Tennessee	1
Wyoming	1
Total executions since 1976	**856**

Source: http://people.smu.edu/rhalperi/summary.html

Appendix H

Executions by Year

1976	0
1977	1
1978	0
1979	2
1980	0
1981	1
1982	2
1983	5
1984	21
1985	18
1986	18
1987	25
1988	11
1989	16
1990	23
1991	14
1992	31
1993	38
1994	31
1995	56
1996	45

1997	74
1998	68
1999	98
2000	85
2001	66
2002	71
2003	36

856 as of 06/05/03

Source: http://people.smu.edu/rhalperi/summary.html

APPENDIX I

Race of Death Row

Inmates Executed Since 1976

Race of Defendant	Number *Executed*	% of total *Executed*
Black	292	35%
Hispanic	57	7%
White	487	57%
Other (Native Amer., Asian, Iraqi)	20	2%

Persons Executed for Interracial Murders

White defendant/Black Victim—12
Black Defendant/White Victims—178

Race of Death Row Inmates

Black	1600	42%
Hispanic	350	10%
White	1662	46%
Other	80	2%

Race of Victim

White	81%
Black	14%
Hispanic	4%
Asian	2%

Source NAACP LDF death row 04/01/03

(Over 80% of completed capital cases involve white victims, even though nationally only 50% of murder victims are white.

Source: http://www.deathpenaltyinfo.org
Death Penalty Information Center

Appendix J

Exonerations 1973-May 6, 2003

108 People were sentenced to death for a crime they did not commit. Fortunately their innocence was proven before they could be executed. How many innocent have been executed that could not prove their innocence? One is too many.

Total 108

Florida	23	Indiana	2
Illinois	17	Massachusetts	2
Oklahoma	7	Missouri	2
Texas	7	Ohio	2
Georgia	6	Idaho	1
Arizona	6	Kentucky	1
Louisiana	6	Maryland	1
New Mexico	4	Mississippi	1
Pennsylvania	4	Nebraska	1
Alabama	3	Nevada	1
California	3	Washington	1
N. Carolina	3	Virginia	1
S. Carolina	3		

Exonerations by Race

Black	49
White	45
Latino	12
Native Amer.	1
Other	1
	108

Source: http://www.deathpenaltyinfo.org article.php?did=412&scid=6
Death Penalty Information Center

Photo Credits

1. Ruth Elizabeth Pelke "Nana" - Olin Mills Page 9
2. Nana and Granddad - Olin Mills Page 19
3. Gary ***Post Tribune*** May 16, 1985 - Kathy Harris Page 24
4. Gary ***Post Tribune*** July 12, 1986 - Kathy Harris Page 60
5. Basic Training at Fort Leonard Wood, Missouri 1967 - Pelke Family archives Page 74
6. Nana - Olin Mills Page 77
7. Gary ***Post Tribune*** May 9, 1987 - Kathy Harris Page 97
8. Gary ***Post Tribune*** May 12, 1987 - Kathy Harris Page 99
9. Bill and Raffaella Carra prepare for the *Domenica In* program in Rome May 1987 - *Journey* archives Page 102
10. Bill with Father Vito Bracone at the *Vatican - Journey* archives Page 103
11. Bill with Father Don Germano Greganti at *Vatican Radio - Journey* archives Page 105
12. Gary ***Post Tribune*** September 11, 1987 - Kathy Harris Page 115
13. Gary ***Post Tribune*** February 29, 1988 - Kathy Harris Page 123
14. Bill and Father Vito lead the *Amnesty International* march in Atlanta, Georgia 1988 - *Journey* archives Page 128
15. The Pelke Family 1983 - Olin Mills Page 135
16. Gary ***Post Tribune*** July 14, 1989 - Kathy Harris Page 142
17. Bill speaks in Macon, Georgia during the *Pilgrimage March* on Mothers Day, May 14, 1990, the fifth anniversary of Nana's death - *Journey* archives Page 156

18. Bill speaks from the pulpit of the late Dr. Martin Luther King, Jr. at the Ebenezer Baptist Church in Atlanta, during the *Pilgrimage March - Journey* archives Page 159
19. Bill announcing the upcoming Indiana *Journey* during a conference in Indianapolis 1991 - ***Indianapolis Star*** photo Page 174
20. *Journey* members present Rev. Bernice King an Indiana *Journey of Hope* t-shirt at St. Monica/St. Luke Church in Gary - *Journey* archives Page 198
21. Bill and Cuzzin' Judi Weyhe participate in a memorial tree planting service at *Lew Wallace High School* in Gary, where Paula and the other three girls attended - *Journey* archives Page 201
22. The Bishop Sisters, Jennifer and Jeanne, speak about the death of their sister Nancy, when the *Journey* visited Chicago - *Journey* archives Page 210
23. Christy Webb, Micki Dickoff and Sunny Jacobs - *Journey* archives Page 218
24. Cofounders of the *Abolitionist Action Committee* (*ACC*) Rick Halperin, Marietta Jaeger and Bill at the annual Fast and Vigil in front of the U.S. Supreme Court - *Journey* archives Page 230
25. Bill with Sister Helen Prejean and Marie Deans, founder of *MVFR - Journey archives* Page 260
26. Virginia *Journey* organizer Henry Heller with Sister Helen - *Journey* archives Page 263
27. Bill wearing one of his few non-Journey t-shirts on the Virginia *Journey* - Abe Bonowitz Page 265
28. Arrest of the DC-18 at the US Supreme Court - *CUADP* Page 273
29. *Abolition Movin'* in Portage with George White, Bill, Sam Reese Sheppard and Abe Bonowitz - *Journey* archives Page 280
30. Labor Day party in Portage with *Journey* members from around the country preparing *Abolition Movin'* for paint job - *Journey* archives Page 294

31. The *Bruderhof* surround the newly coated *Abolition Movin'* and sing a farewell song - *CUADP* Page 301
32. Sister Helen appears ready to take Bill for a ride on *Abolition Movin'* - Abe Bonowitz Page 302
33. Bill with George White, SueZann Bosler, Ken and Lois Robison and Jane Davis on the Philippine Journey in 1998 sitting with the mother of Leo Echegary 1998 - *Journey* archives Page 310
34. Journey of Hope...from Violence to Healing cofounders at the *MVFR* concert, SueZann Bosler, Sam Reese Sheppard, George White, Marietta Jaeger and Bill - *Journey* archives Page 311
35. A special showing of the ***Discovery Channel*** film "***From Fury to Forgiveness***" on the Texas *Journey* - Kathy Harris Page 316
36. Randall Dale Adams and Jill Fratta met on the Texas *Journey* and were married a little over a year later. They are standing in front of the Walls Unit where executions in Texas occur. - Kathy Harris Page 319
37. Bill and George in Belgium with *St. Egidio Community* - *Journey* archives Page 326
38. Bill helping carry the *Journey of Hope...From Violence to Healing* banner leading the march to the *Vatican* Christmas day, 1998 - Kathy Harris Page 331
39. Melodee Smith, Bud Welch, SueZann, Lois, Sally Peck, Ken and Bill in Paris - *Journey* archives Page 341
40. Bill and Kathy Harris met on the Texas *Journey* - *Journey* archives Page 354
41. Bill with Alaska Governor Tony Knowles - Kathy Harris Page 355
42. *National March to Stop Executions* - Scott Langley Productions Page 356
43. Bill with Mike Farrell and Illinois Governor George Ryan - Kathy Harris Page 361
44. Bill with three former *Abolitionist of the Year* award

winners, Sister Helen, Marietta and Father Pat Delahanty - Kathy Harris Page 362

45. *Abolition Movin'* no longer moving on her own - *CUADP* Page 364
46. Bill in Northern Italy with *St. Egidio Community* - *Journey* archives Page 365
47. Bill representing the *Journey of Hope...From Violence to Healing* at the formation of the *World Coalition to Abolish the Death Penalty* in Rome - *Journey* archives Page 366
48. Bill and Renny Cushing, Executive Director of *MVFR* carry their banner in Chicago for the *NCADP* Conference march - Kathy Harris Page 366
49. Sara Sharpe, Steve Earle and the *Journey* Boys. Abe, George, Bill and Ken McGill on the closing night in Nashville of ***Karla*** - Abe Bonowitz Page 367
50. The Three Amigos, Bill Pelke, Rick Halperin and Magdaleno Rose-Avila, wearing Abe Bonowitz's t-shirt "An eye for an eye makes the world blind" - *Journey* archives Page 368

Cover - *Abolition Movin'* with Bud Welch, Bill Pelke and George White - Abe Bonowitz

Cover - Sister Helen - Grant·Guerrero Photography

Hardback — Front inside flap — "Nana" — Olin Mills

Hardback — Back inside flap — "Bill Pelke" — Sven-Erik Hanson